THE SKYWARD TREND OF THOUGHT

# THE SKYWARD TREND OF THOUGHT

*The Metaphysics of the American Skyscraper*
*Thomas A.P. van Leeuwen*

The MIT Press
Cambridge, Massachusetts

**Library of Congress Cataloging-in-Publication Data**

Leeuwen, Thomas A. P. van.
    The skyward trend of thought.

    Bibliography: p.
    Includes index.
    1. Skyscrapers--United States.   2. Architecture,
Modern--20th century--United States.   I. Title.
NA9053.S4L44 1988        725′.2        88-870
ISBN 0-262-22034-5


First MIT Press edition, 1988

Printed and bound in the United States of America.

'idea, edifice, piece of architecture, building, structure, fabric, erection, pile, dome, tower, skyscraper.' – ROGET'S THESAURUS, 'CAUSATION'

'Why is there anything?' – VOLTAIRE

'How comes there a wish to perform an action not before performed?'
– HERBERT SPENCER [1]

'Nations and civilizations may rise and fall and historians of the far distant future may say that we were not many things that we now think we are, but one thing is certain: they will of a surety say that we are a nation of builders, great builders, the greatest that the world has ever seen.' – COLONEL W.A. STARRETT [2]

'Author's Advertisement'

'I BEG – I BEG – I beg the reader of the pages that follow not to imagine that their author is that ludicrous and offensive being, the superior European ... who patronizes American peoples and institutions as if they were children or the products of childish minds. He is, I assure you, this Author, so instinct with the sense of the equality of all human beings – that sense of their equality is to such an extent an instinct with him that he takes all humanity very seriously – and pleasantly, humbly even, if he does not happen to know them well.' – FORD MADOX FORD [3]

# PREFACE

1. Herbert Spencer, *The Principles of Biology*, London, 1864, Vol. I, p. 406.

2. Col. W.A. Starrett, *Skyscrapers and the Men Who Build Them*, New York/London, 1928, p. 2.

3. Ford Madox Ford, *New York Is Not America*, New York, 1927, p. VII.

The idea of investigating the mysterious dual character of the American skyscraper first emerged as far back as 1971 when I was travelling through North America to assist Philo Bregstein in making his monumental film on Otto Klemperer, which later in the 1984 prize-winning version became known as *Otto Klemperer's Long Journey Through His Times*.

A few years later Fons Asselbergs of the Stichting Architectuur Museum and Rudy Oxenaar of the Kröller-Müller Museum enabled me to set off again, this time concentrating on architecture rather than music. While researching for the *Americana* exhibition, as part of the 1975 architectural year, I seized the opportunity to study American culture at closer range. It was then that I decided to give some serious, albeit immature thought to the American skyscraper in particular.

In New York I got to know Rem Koolhaas and Madelon Vriesendorp, who, with their profound insight and vast creative imagination inspired me greatly and offered me ample opportunities to exchange ideas; while in Chicago it was Langdon Gilkey who, in his natural Socratic way of transferring knowledge, introduced me to the serious business of thinking and to the histories of religions and ideas. Professor Gilkey's teachings were indispensable to attempt the understanding of the American character and culture.

After a six-year interruption I decided to pick up the lead again and devote my attention to the study of the skyscraper, not so much as an architectural *thing* but as an *idea* made visible through various approaches all according to the specific attention required.

With the help of the Netherlands-America Commission for Educational Exchange, a leave of absence from Leyden University, and a generous grant from the American Council of Learned Societies I could enjoy the hospitality of Columbia University and its invaluable Avery Library, and of all those New Yorkers who assisted me in my observations of the skyscraper in its natural habitat. Special thanks go to Helen Jessup, Philip Jessup Jr., Christine Walewska, Adolf and Beverly Placzek and the late Alfreda Rushmore. From July 1980 until April 1981 research was conducted in the dynamic dialectic of studying, discussing and above all lecturing. I want to extend due thanks to all those who have taken the trouble to invite me over and to have me share my ideas with them and their students. Robert G. Bruegmann, Leonard K. Eaton, William H. Jordy, Alan K. Lathrop, Narciso G. Menocal and Helen Searing deserve special mention. Professor Searing has been a pivotal figure in our later intercontinental creative and educational traffic.

The idea that the reflections of a European scholar upon American subject matter could be of some value to European instead of American audiences was shared by Hubert Damisch, Maristella Casciato, Stanislaus von Moos and Dennis Sharp, who in unwavering optimism encouraged me in the formation of my ideas. Unusually relentless in his efforts to give me access to the various centres of excellence was Professor von Moos, whom I wish to thank most warmly.

For the thankless task of transforming my exotic use of the English language into presentable texts I will remain deeply indebted to Nicky Cutts, Helen Jessup, Helen Searing and Mary Wall. Superfluous to say that they bear no responsibility whatsoever for all the shortcomings adhering to the text; these are all mine.

Editing of the text was limited to the individual essays and therefore the present volume may lack stylistic homogeneity. As for the pictures used, they were all, unless otherwise stated, made by myself and it was thanks to the Photographic Department of the Kunsthistorisch Instituut/Prentenkabinet of Leyden University that they were upgraded to the necessary printable state.

Owing to the often interrupted preparation time and a progressively failing memory, many a name has escaped this list of debt, but among those who have unknowingly, probably even unwillingly, inspired this work I wish to mention John Craib-Cox, the late Theo Dobbelmann, Morton Golden, Thomas A. Heinz, Maya Moran, Thomas Gordon Smith, Brian Spencer, Robert C. Twombly.

I should not forget the enthusiasm of my publishers Eelco van der Waals and Saskia ter Kuile, who acted as an inspiring force. Thanks also go to Inge Angevaare for her diligent assistance, and to Henk de Lorm for the way he gave shape to this book.

Hans van Leeuwen and Catharina M. van Leeuwen-Hamers deserve most of my gratitude because of their reassuring and undemanding presence which they share with the always lovable and understanding H.. It is to them that this book is dedicated, of course.

# *CONTENTS*

# *INTRODUCTION*

*The Skyward Trend of Thought* is the analysis of a paradox. Its raw material has been taken from the period 1870–1935, which covered most of America's unprecedented increase of commerce, wealth and building. This 'Imperial Age' or 'Gilded Age' or these 'Golden Days', sometimes subdivided into smaller portions of 'Brown' or 'Mauve' Decades, showed the rich burgeoning of a civilization which, although spread out over more than half a century, was as sudden and powerful as a primeval blast.[4] Wealth, natural as well as acquired, commerce and competition provided the explosive mixture which sent off the enchanting fireworks that brought forth a variety of extraordinary arch-beings of which the skyscraper was the most imaginative. Therefore, quite appropriately, the period 1870–1935 was also called 'The Skyscraper Era'.[5]

'Skyscrapers' (not to be equated with their German and Dutch counterparts, which by the sheer substitution of 'cloud' for 'sky' – 'Wolkenkratzer', 'Wolkenkrabber' – aim at a significantly lower level of imagination), represent a building type which with wonderful exactness reflects the civilization that produced them. They are not only America's most characteristic representative in the domain of architecture, they are also miniatures of America itself. Whoever studies the skyscraper, studies America. Lewis Mumford once said that the skyscraper 'shows all our characteristic weaknesses', which is true indeed, but it also shows all of America's strength, its brutal force as well as its imaginative power.[6] This power of imagination, and here is meant not constructive inventivity but artistic and poetic creativity, is, at least in the architectural history of the American skyscraper, generally underrated and even suppressed. In some of the contemporary sources – Talbot Hamlin, Thomas E. Tallmadge, Lewis Mumford, Henry-Russell Hitchcock and to a certain extent also Montgomery Schuyler – as well as in some of the more recent critiques – James M. Fitch, Wayne Andrews and those who operated in the wake of Pevsner and Giedion, such as Carl W. Condit – the skyscraper's aesthetic and ideological values have been judged as neutral to moderately positive. However, on the whole the skyscraper has been treated as a 'mere busi-

4. The last two adjectives refer to Lewis Mumford, *The Brown Decades, A Study of the Arts in America, 1865–1895*, New York, 1931, and Thomas Beer, *The Mauve Decade, American Life at the End of the Nineteenth Century*, New York, 1926.

5. R. Fleming, 'A Half Century of the Skyscraper', *Civil Engineering*, IV, December 1934, p. 634, quoted in: Stanley P. Andersen, *American Ikon: Response to the Skyscraper, 1875–1934*, unpublished Ph.D. thesis, University of Minnesota, 1975, p. 1.

6. Lewis Mumford, *The Brown Decades, A Study of the Arts in America, 1865–1895*, New York, 1971 (1931[1]), p. 63.

7. Major sources for the skyscraper history from a builder's point of view are the four memoirs written by the Starrett brothers, Louis Horowitz and Earle Shultz (in chronological order): Col. W.A. Starrett, *Skyscrapers and the Men Who Built Them*, New York/London, 1928; Louis J. Horowitz and Boyden Sparkes, *The Towers of New York, The Memoirs of a Master Builder*, New York, 1937; Paul Starrett, *Changing the Skyline, An Autobiography*, with the collaboration of Webb Waldron, New York/London, 1938; Earle Shultz and Walter Simmons, *Offices in the Sky*, Indianapolis/New York, 1959. Art history, architectural history and architectural criticism have taken a similar, or at least, related standpoint. The influential critic Montgomery Schuyler opens the list with his three important early essays on the skyscraper: 'The "Sky-Scraper" Up To Date', *The Architectural Record*, Vol. VIII, Jan.-March 1899, no. 3, pp. 231–260; 'The Skyscraper Problem', *Scribner's Magazine*, Vol. 34, August 1903, pp. 253–256; 'The Evolution of the Skyscraper', *Scribner's Magazine*, Vol. 46, September 1909, pp. 257–271 (the last two articles were reproduced in full in: Montgomery Schuyler, *American Architecture and Other Writings*, William H. Jordy and Ralph Coe, eds., 2 Vols., Cambridge, Mass., 1961). He is followed by (in chronological order): Talbot Hamlin, *The American Spirit in Architecture*, New Haven, 1926; Thomas E. Tallmadge, *The Story of Architecture in America*, New York, 1927; S. Fiske Kimball, *American Architecture*, Indianapolis, 1928; Sigfried Giedion, *Space, Time and Architecture, The Growth of a New Tradition*, Cambridge, Mass., 1941; James M. Fitch, *American Building, I, The Historical Forces that Shape It; II, The Environmental Forces that Shaped It*, Boston, 1947; Carl W. Condit, *The Rise of the Skyscraper*, Chicago, 1952 (see below, note 19); Henry-Russell Hitchcock, *Architecture: Nineteenth and Twentieth Centuries*, Harmondsworth, 1958; James M. Fitch, *Architecture and the Esthetics of Plenty*, New York/London, 1961; John Burchard and Albert Bush-Brown, *The Architecture of America, A Social and Cultural History*, Boston/Toronto, 1961; Wayne Andrews, *Architecture, Ambition and Americans, A Social History of American Architecture*, New York, 1964; Vincent Scully, *American Architecture and Urbanism*, London, 1969; *The Rise of an American Architecture*, Edgar Kaufmann, Jr., ed., New York/Washington/London, 1970; Leland M. Roth, *A Concise History of American Architecture*, New York, 1979; Paul Goldberger, *The Skyscraper*, New York, 1981; G.H. Edgell, *The American Architecture of Today*, New York, 1928. G.H. Edgell, *The American Architecture of Today*, New York, 1928; Sheldon Cheney, *The New World Architecture*, New York, 1932; and Charles H. Whitaker, *The Story of Architecture from Rameses to Rockefeller*, New York, 1932, are somewhat dissident in their interpretation of the skyscraper. William H. Jordy, *American Buildings and their Architects*, III & IV, Garden City, New York, 1976, has kept a carefully balanced neutrality, whereas Rem Koolhaas, *Delirious New York*, New York, 1978, has been the first to question the validity of the traditional opinions.

ness proposition' realized by 'practical architects', driven by the sole desire to make 'an easy buck'.[7] It may well be that practical architects and prosaic businessmen were responsible for many tall commercial structures, but the creation of the skyscrapers that were held to be the rivals of the ancient wonders of the world certainly also required imaginative architects and a poetic businessman — and they were numerous as well as poetic! Nevertheless it has been the 'tall commercial structure' that has dominated the field of architectural history since the advent of modernistic historiography. The authority of Nikolaus Pevsner, Sigfried Giedion and Henry-Russell Hitchcock had remained virtually unchallenged in its selection of the Chicago School of Architecture as the lawful predecessor of the Modern Movement. In this selection the alleged anonymous design of the Chicago buildings was put forward as the opposite of the Old World-based design of the East Coast architecture.[8] The 1973 exhibition *100 Jahre Architektur in Chicago*, organized by *Die neue Sammlung* of the State Museum of Decorative Art at Munich, devoted its attention to Chicago for the specific reason that 'there is no other city in the whole world in which origin and development of the architecture of our times are so clearly visible and identifiable.'[9]

In those years indeed the names of Holabird & Roche, Adler & Sullivan, Burnham & Root were inscribed in the hall of fame of architecture and post-World War II taste was dominated by the skyscrapers of Mies, Skidmore, Owings & Merrill and Murphy & Associates. For most students of architecture S.O.M.'s Lever Building and Mies's Seagram Building epitomized the right kind of skyscraper. Mentioning Cass Gilbert's 1913 gothicizing Woolworth Tower, as I once did in 1975 in the company of skyscraper cognoscenti, was a sure way to earn a reputation for bad taste, and what was more, for a complete failure to understanding American culture.

Now taste has made some sharp turns and under the influence of post-modern concepts of design the revisionist attitude of those days has become the 'opinion chic' of today. Cass Gilbert, who a mere twenty years ago was considered to be unspeakably vulgar, is now to be regarded as a great master of his trade.

Naturally, this shift in appreciation is subject to the fluctuations of taste and one might assume that the evaluation of the skyscraper would be modified accordingly. Not so. Quite recently Paul Goldberger, in his *The Skyscraper* of 1981, was expected to appraise Gilbert's still existing West Street (see p. 127, Fig. 7) and Woolworth Buildings and pay them due respect retroactively. But he could only do so reluctantly within a for Gilbert unfavourable comparison with Louis Sullivan: 'And though Gilbert sought no expression of structure, as Sullivan had, he ended up with it anyway ...'; and Gilbert's '... imitations of Gothic structural elements bear a striking resemblance to Sullivan's own verticals, and the building lifts upward with genuine, if fussy, grace.'[10] Goldberger's insistence upon the moralistic criteria of expressing the construction of the steel frame in Sullivanesque, i.e. proper terms is the unchanged continuation of the Pevsner-Giedion concept of architectural purity and therefore, notwithstanding his admitted reappraisal of the East Coast style of architecture, Goldberger finds himself unable to detach himself from the traditional interpretations. Taste has changed, but the structure and nature of the historical construct in which the artistic pretenses were framed remains the same.

The charm of the skyscraper has been intrinsically affiliated with the appeal America exercised as the ideological reflection of anything inadmissible in 'ancien régime' Europe: America was free, it was unlimited in space, it abounded in natural resources and in money. It knew no tradition, it had no history and no serious art to speak of. Yes, it had produced things that were found aesthetically satisfying, but they were created in aesthetic innocence. That these same Americans, like their European fellow beings, fostered the same cultural ancestry (after all, Plato, Homer, Vitruvius, Palladio, Shakespeare and Bach are common heritage to both cultures) was a right denied to them. What was admired in American culture was not its culture, but the absence of it. That Europeans followed the precept of tradition was found bad enough, but that American artists dared to do the same was found not only unforgiveable, but inconceivable.

The predeliction for the no-nonsense skyscraper and the appreciation of the Chicago style of building was not entirely due to European modernism. American nationalism, patriotic feelings and the re-discovery of the mythological power of the Frontier contributed just as much. After all, the Frontier's denial of a historical past and its claims to self-reliance must have acted on the modernistic mind as the confrontation with its own atavistic roots. The elements of the myth were simple, clean-cut and irresistible in their rhetoric power. They are best represented by Col. W.A. Starrett, who, in 1928, as he stated himself, was the first to have written a history of the skyscraper. To begin with, there must be not a trace of doubt that, as Starrett wrote, 'the skyscraper, to be a skyscraper, must be constructed on a skeletal frame, now almost universally of steel, but with the signal characteristic of having columns in the outside walls, thus rendering the exterior we see simply a continuous curtain of masonry penetrated by windows; we call it curtain

8. By the term 'modern movement' is meant the partly mythographic, partly historiographic reconstruction of that specific part of the twentieth century as it was covered by Nikolaus Pevsner in his *Pioneers of the Modern Movement, from William Morris to Walter Gropius*, 1936, by Sigfried Giedion, *Space, Time and Architecture, The Growth of a New Tradition*, 1941, and by Henry-Russell Hitchcock, *Modern Architecture – Romanticism and Reintegration*, 1929. Pevsner himself sketched the rough outlines of the modern movement in a stylistic sense when he qualified it as 'a genuine and adequate style of our century' (1st ed., p. 41), or as 'the recognized accepted style of our age' (current, post-1974 editions, p. 179). The concept of the Chicago commercial style of building as forerunner of the architecture of the modern movement sprang from the conviction that the 'new style' should be a reflection of the 'creative energy of this world in which we live and work and which we want to master, a world of science and technique, of speed and danger, of hard struggles and no personal security ...' (Pevsner, op. cit., 1949, p. 207). That a city like Chicago was held to be the most likely to meet these requirements was generally recognized in the early parts of the twentieth century (see 'The Skyward Trend of Thought', p. 20ff.). Sigfried Giedion, in *Space, Time and Architecture*, op. cit., exploited the Chicago model to the fullest and Pevsner, in one of his most recent publications, *A History of Building Types*, London, 1976, stated with unchallenged ease that the first step to the 'Twentieth Century Style' ... had been taken some years earlier in Chicago ...' (p. 218).

9. Oswald W. Grube, Peter C. von Seidlein & Wend Fischer with a contribution by Carl W. Condit, *100 Jahre Architektur in Chicago, Kontinuität von Struktur und Form*, Die Neue Sammlung, Staatliches Museum für angewandte Kunst, München, 1973, p. 3.

10. Paul Goldberger, *The Skyscraper*, New York, 1981, p. 42.

11. Col. W.A. Starrett, op. cit., p. 4: 'I found that no book ever had been written on its [the skyscraper's] history.' Defining the skyscraper has proven to be a problem of almost inexhaustable fascination. A tragic circumstance, especially on this specific subject, is the evident inability of the definition to (a) describe the *thing* scientifically and (b) safeguard at the same time the impact of the *idea*. Concentrating too much on the material aspects led to some oddly reduced objects, in which the logic of defining had completely destroyed the skyscraper's intrinsic meanings. Winston Weisman, for example, in his 1953 article 'New York and the Problem of the First Skyscraper', *J.S.A.H.*, XII, March 1953, pp. 13–21, started off following the lead presented a half century before by Montgomery Schuyler in 'The "Skyscraper" Up To Date', *The Architectural Record*, VIII, January-March 1899, p. 232, who claimed that the first 'sky-scrapers' were the New York Tribune and Western Union Buildings, because they 'were the first business buildings in which the possibilities of the elevator were recognized' and because 'they were much more conspicuous and comment-provoking ... because they were alone and because lower New York then had a skyline, from which they alone, excepting the church spires, were raised and detached.' But in 1970 on the occasion of the Metropolitan Museum's centennial exhibition, 'The Rise of an American Architecture', Weisman left the Schuyler lead and developed the theory that was, in fact, to be a reductio ad absurdum of the principle that the elevator, and the elevator alone, had caused the vertical rise of these two buildings. In 'A New View of Skyscraper History', *The Rise of an American Architecture*, Edgar Kaufman, Jr., ed., New York/Washington/London, 1970, p. 125, he avowed: 'After much contemplation, I would like to change my earlier position. My vote for the "first skyscraper" goes to the Equitable Life Assurance Company Building raised in New York during 1868–70 by Gilman & Kendall and George B. Post. The reasons: The Equitable was the first business building in which the possibilities of the elevator were realized.' And although Weisman had to admit that with a mere five storeys and a height of only 130 feet the building could not be regarded as 'conspicuous' and 'comment-provoking' as the two later ones, it had nevertheless shown a certain 'jump' in height, which had to 'be viewed as proof that once the height barrier had been broken by the Equitable, others rose rapidly within a very few years.' This reasoning, which Weisman shared with his Chicago opponent Carl Condit, who, some ten years earlier, had expressed a similar viewpoint, could probably convince by its logic, but it yielded a monstrum of semantic misunderstanding. The Equitable (Weisman, op. cit., p. 119, figs. 3–6) might very well have 'realized the possibilities of the elevator,' but this elevator had not in the least been able to change the appearance of its three floors rather than five, Napoleon III, low-lying bulk. If the Equitable had to be regarded as the proof of anything, it had to be of the inability of the chosen terms to define a skyscraper (Fig. 1).

In the present study I will refrain from undertaking anything of the sort. A skyscraper is anything that will appear in the imagination of modern man the moment the term is communicated. Everybody knows what a skyscraper is: a thing that scrapes the sky. The clouds are not the object of its ascent, but, far more ambitious, it is the sky. Although the skyscraper's denotations hardly vary, its connotations have remained dormant. It is the purpose of this study to reactivate these connotations. Once, in

*Fig. 1. What all skyscraper-stories had in common was their ceaseless quest for the origin of this building type: 'The First Skyscraper, 1631' (from Above the Clouds & Old New York, an historical sketch of the site and a description of the many wonders of the Woolworth Building, by H. Addington Bruce, New York, 1913).*

wall.'[11] Starrett then emphatically stressed the importance of the skyscraper as 'a completely American creation'[12] 'in that it is, let me say it again, essentially and completely American, so far surpassing anything ever before undertaken in its vastness, swiftness, utility, and economy that it epitomizes American life and American civilisation, and, indeed, has become the cornerstone and abode of our national progress.'[13] This is the second element: the skyscraper is entirely un-precedented. Construction and form were invented from scratch, and there is no indebtedness whatsoever to the traditions of architecture. Reliance upon ancient styles is thought of as indecent, although the artistic subconscious of architects and builders is constantly plagued by the lurking presence of the Tower of Babel. This was acclaimed as a triumph of ancient skill and engineering, 'yet,' Starrett warned his readers, 'we must not get sentimental about the ancients and their engineering,' calling to memory the many architectural 'errors' such as the Leaning Tower of Pisa, the Campanile of Venice, the Colossus of Rhodos and St. Paul's and Westminster Abbey in London because of their 'faulty foundations'.[14]

Having done away with the classical models of academic training, Starrett hailed the new generation of self-made *builders* − a new architectural breed, somewhere between engineer and architect. Preferably they were self-taught or at least had no brilliant academic career to boast of. The ideal must have come from the same material from which Ayn Rand had fabricated her unpleasant hero of *The Fountainhead*: strong, rugged, independent and sent away from school at least once (Fig. 2).[15] This is the third element. It is evident that Starrett had selected his heroes by these criteria and so situated them on the mythical crossroads of the Western Frontier: in Chicago. Burnham had already arrived there in style and as Starrett wrote: 'Daniel Burnham alighted in that city from a cattle train from the West.' He also happened to have the right kind of educational credentials: 'he had failed to pass the entrance examinations at both Harvard and Yale, and had gone to Nevada on a mad French colonization scheme; he had remained a miner ... had run for state senator,

1975, I sketched its outlines as 'a building, clearly manifesting its ambition to look very, very, tall' (Thomas Van Leeuwen, 'De commerciële stijl', *Americana, Nederlandse architectuur, 1880–1930*, Otterlo, 1975, p. 58). And I see no reason to change my earlier position. On the contrary, the following essays are intended to reinforce this position and to provide insight into those mysterious incentives that caused commercial buildings to become 'conspicuous', 'comment-provoking' and ambitious, briefly, to become 'skyscrapers'. For a comprehensive treatment of the question of 'the first', see J. Carson Webster, 'The Skyscraper: Logical and Historical Considerations', *J.S.A.H.*, XVIII, 4, Dec. 1959, pp. 126-140.

12. Col. W.A. Starrett, op. cit., p. 1.

13. Ibid., p. 2.

14. Ibid., p. 26. See also 'Apokatastasis, or the Return of the Skyscraper', p. 40ff., and the memorable remarks by Joseph August Lux in his introduction to *Ingenieur-Ästhetik*: 'Die Allgemeinheit sieht noch immer nicht, dass die Technik unsere menschlichen Ideale verwirklicht. In der Technik geschieht nichts, was nicht vorher schon als Traum, als Dichtung, als Utopie dagewesen ist. ... Zu Babel wurde ein Turm gebaut, den man nicht fertig zu bringen vermochte. Die Menschheit träumt seither von dem Übermenschlichen des babylonischen Türmes. Aber die Techniker von heute verwirklichten diesen Traum und bauten Wolkenkratzer, gegen die die höchsten Türme der Erde zwerghaft aussahen' (Joseph Aug. Lux, *Ingenieur-Ästhetik*, München, 1910).

15. Ayn Rand, *The Fountainhead*, New York, 1971 (1943¹). Howard Roark never did make the impression that he went to school to learn; he already knew. He is dismissed from the Stanton Institute of Technology, but in order to avoid the suspicion that Roark was just not intelligent enough, it is emphasized that his professor of engineering as well as his professor of mathematics acted 'quite the crusader' on his behalf (p. 20).

16. Col. W.A. Starrett, op. cit., pp. 4/6.

17. Ibid., p. 4.

18. The fact that William Le Baron Jenney was considered to be the 'father' of the skyscraper, which, to hold on to the analogy, was 'born' in Chicago, was a persistent element in the notion of the skyscraper as being of an anthropomorphic nature. To Starrett it was immaterial whether the skyscraper had more than one father. Daniel Burnham, for example, was 'one of the fathers of the skyscraper'. Starrett, op. cit., p. 7.

19. Carl W. Condit, *The Chicago School of Architecture, A History of Commercial and Public Building in the Chicago Area, 1875–1925*, Chicago/London, 1973, pp. v–vii, 1–13; Winston Weisman, 'Carl W. Condit, The Rise of the Skyscraper, The Genius of Chicago Architecture from the Great Fire to Louis Sullivan', book review in: *J.S.A.H. (Journal of the Society of Architectural Historians)*, XII, October 1953, pp. 30–31.

*Fig. 2. The hero from* The Fountainhead *was the last of a generation of self-taught builders: strong, rugged, independent and expelled from school, once at least (Gary Cooper as Howard Roark in* The Fountainhead; *from Andrew Saint,* The Image of the Architect, *New Haven/London, 1983).*

been defeated, and eventually made his way to Chicago as best as he could.'[16] The other 'great pioneers', Starrett continued, were William Le Baron Jenney, John W. Root and William Holabird. Jenney had the misfortune to have enjoyed a 'classical education in architecture' and in order to make him acceptable as a true 'pioneer' the fact was stressed that he had taken 'a roundabout route around the Horn to join the rush of '49 to California.' He even went as far as the Philippines where, Starrett told with pride and relief, 'He was so struck with the possibilities of railroad building that he resolved to return home and study engineering.'[17] As times were more in favour of a technological interpretation of the past, Jenney in the eyes of his biographers had to undergo a professional travesty from architect to engineer. An operation which had become urgent, since meanwhile the fact was established that this same Jenney had been 'the father' of the 'first' skyscraper, the Home Life Insurance Co. Building, Chicago 1885, a monument that was as crucial to the skyscraper story as the Ka'aba is to the Islam.[18] Apart from small alterations and scholarly excursions, and in spite of differences of opinion, this was the material the skyscraper history was made of. Now it might be argued that Starrett's book was not a study to be taken too seriously. Most of his material was based on his own experience as a builder and it was only natural that he would glorify the early Midwestern scene as the cradle of his own existence. On the other hand, his facts and data were accurate enough and nothing was changed, twisted or otherwise manipulated. Everything was true and the whole story made a sound and utterly reliable impression. And although it might have seemed a bit like a western movie, it was in essence not much less scholarly than for example Carl Condit's *The Rise of the Skyscraper* from 1952. Condit's book was, of course, a much more detailed and systematic study, but the general pattern of his historical reconstruction was the same as Starrett's. So much even that Condit had decided to change the title of his book in 1964 into *The Chicago School of Architecture*.[19] A wise decision since he had been under attack from Eastern architectural historians, such as Winston Weisman, who had justifiably criticized Condit for his apparent oblivion

20. Winston Weisman, 'The Commercial Architecture of George B. Post', *J.S.A.H.*, XXXI, March 1972, pp. 176–203.

21. It is far from easy to produce a generally fitting definition of myth and mythology in the present context. For this special purpose, dealing with the question of origin of the American skyscraper, I have thought it wise to limit my scope and rely mainly on the treatment of myth and mythology in the study of culture, history of religions and cultural anthropology. I have tried to distill the main elements for a workable usage of the term 'myth' from the following sources: Ernst Cassirer, *Philosophie der symbolischen Formen*, II, *Das mythische Denken*, Berlin, 1925; Mircea Eliade, *Mythes, rêves et mystères*, Paris, 1957; Claude Lévi-Strauss, *The Raw and the Cooked (Le cru et le cuit)*, New York, 1975 (1964[1]); Claude Lévi-Strauss, *Structural Anthropology (Anthropologie structurale)*, New York, 1963 (1958[1]).
Resulting from these sources and considering the specific nature of the problem, the following elements should be taken into account:
The American skyscraper originated in an atmosphere of semi-conscious spontaneity, taking the parties involved by surprise. When after a little while reconstructions of the skyscraper's origin were tentatively produced, the causes and the nature of the occurrence were quickly provided with a fitting rationale. The resulting structure, which I have ventured to call mythical, was composed of the following elements: (1) The 'why' and 'how' of the origin had to be located and solved, even if the chaotic and disorderly past did not produce the necessary clues. (2) The disorderly and irrational was to be explained in the 'how'. (3). The advantages of explaining the 'why' in terms of 'how' are: absence of 'vague' speculations and a controllable disposition of data and facts. (4) The rhetoric of the argument resides mainly in the foolproof reliability of its smallest details. The mythical determination to convince the public abhors general statements and concentrates on conveniently arranged parts in which data and facts and the logic of cause and effect are condensed into such powerful doses that not even the greatest cynic can resist them. In other words, large and complex problems are reduced to small and simple ones. (5) Since the myth relies largely on rhetoric power, the role of the public is paramount. Therefore the problem should be presented in such a way that personal identification should be facilitated. (6) To facilitate identification, the elements of the problem should be 'humanized'; opposing powers are introduced. In art history, for example, the myth of artistic progress is represented by an 'avant-garde' and bourgeois conservatism. In architectural history the powers could be, respectively, 'engineering' and 'architecture'. (7) In its desire to please its public, which evidently is its very own creator, the myth invests occurrences with large quantities of sense and meaning. It is therefore clear that myths often communicate more about a certain culture than an orderly arrangement of its facts and data, as it once was suggested by Giambattista Vico in his *Scienza Nuova* (1728) that 'the fables of the gods are true histories of customs.'
In the present essays I did not intend to replace the myth by its opposite, or to replace the untruth by the truth. What I have tried to do was to supplant one myth by another, which I held to be more appropriate, more profound and more capable of providing insight into the problem of artistic creation, which the other myth had left untouched.

to the fact that skyscrapers had been constructed in places other than just Chicago and that the question of which skyscraper was the first one, and where and by whom, was still open to discussion. This resulted in an intensified polemic between East and West, New York versus Chicago. The discussion became focused upon matters of technology and it was up to Weisman et al. to prove that Eastern-based architects had been just as inventive, down-to-earth, no-nonsense, etc., as their Western colleagues. This led to the re-appraisal of a man such as George B. Post to whom Weisman devoted most of his attention. [20] But again the basic structure of the story did not change. What did happen was merely an internal shift of attention in the struggle for dominance remaining within the frame of the narrative. It is this basic frame that *all* skyscraper histories from Starrett to Goldberger have followed.

The object of the following essays is to demonstrate the mythical structure of what has generally been made known as 'The History of The American Skyscraper'. Sometimes this may result in a somewhat polemical tone, but this is not intended to lead to the conclusion that I should in any way not 'agree' with the way the skyscraper has been dealt with. On the contrary, in its spasmodic will to emphasize the logic of evolution, and in its determination to locate the origin of the steel-framed tall building, its mythical nature becomes more clearly manifest. [21] I will never foster the illusion that by seeking for the truth, the truth would appear, or, put in positivistic terms, the myth would disappear in order to be supplanted by history. What I am going to show is that beyond the present myth is another myth. Just as thoroughly reinforced with facts and data as the first one, and sometimes adversely related to it, but nevertheless being a myth. It was Sartre who once wrote in his commentary on Jean Genet's autobiographical *Thief's Journal*: 'He does, to be sure, tell us everything. The whole truth and nothing but the truth, but it is the sacred truth. He opens up one of his myths; he tells us: "You're going to see what stuff it's made of", and we find another myth. He reassures us only to disturb us further. His autobiography is not an autobiography; it merely seems like one; it is sacred cosmogony.' [22]

William Lethaby, undoubtedly inspired by Sir James Frazer's researches into the structure of mythological thinking, elaborated on the classic theme that the origin of architecture must be sought in man's desire to imitate nature. In the first pages of *Architecture, Mysticism and Myth* (1891) he explained this with a simple analogy: 'If we trace the artistic forms of things, made by man, to their origin, we find a direct imitation of nature. The thought behind a ship is the imitation of a fish. So to the Egyptians and the Greeks the "Black Ship" bore traces of this descent, and two eyes were painted on the prow.' [23] Lethaby extended this reasoning to the Babylonian 'ziggurats' whose origin he thought to be 'an imitation of artificial reproduction of the mythical mountain of the assembly of the stars (Ararat and Eden).' [24] The idea was not remarkable for its originality, nor was it progressive in any respect. What made it noteworthy was its archaism. In defiance of his later fame as a proto-modernist, Lethaby here introduced the mythical concept of architecture at a time most people

22. Maurice Girodias, ed., *The Olympia Reader*, New Yor, 1965, p. 326.

23. William R. Lethaby, *Architecture, Mysticism and Myth*, New York, 1975 (1891[1]), p. 4.

24. Ibid., p. 127.

25. Mircea Eliade, *The Sacred and the Profane, The Nature of Religion*, New York, 1961 (1957[1]), pp. 29–36. Myth relates to the supposed historical reality in that it creates order where there is not much reason to assume there is any; mythical thinking presupposes a logical continuum in which beginning and end are clearly determined. Most attention is devoted to the 'origin of things' for which fitting and above all convincing explanations are found (see above, note 21).

26. George Holme, 'Famous Towers', *Munsey's Magazine*, XII, February 1895, 5, p. 518.

27. Henry James, *The American Scene*, London, 1907, p. 78.

thought it to be entirely obsolete. And maybe it was, in the Old World, where a long and solidly documented tradition of history had supplanted the subtle epic of mythology.

But how about America? America had no history or at least professed to have none. Americans had escaped Europe and its history willfully, in order to create a new universe and to initiate a new time, disconnected from the immediate past. Both time and place were then conceived as the very denial of history and of Europe. The past was measured in the endless 'durées' of mythical time and as its location a non-defined territory was selected, a vaguely commercial Eden, with places like Babylon and Tyre. This was modern-times cosmogony. The concept of cosmogony is a recurrent theme in the present volume. Mircea Eliade defined it as an imitation of the paradigmatic creation of the gods, and it will be used here in reference to architecture and the establishment of order in a world that was newly found, or at least was experienced as such.[25] Architecture in the cosmogonical sense is not a practical tool to live in but the demarcation of a new beginning. The American skyscraper is such a new beginning. As a determination of its own origin affiliation with the legendary cosmopolis Babylon and its paradigmatic tower was sought. Consciously and sub-consciously Babel's archetype was dug up from the vast, but nevertheless limited, reservoir of architectural means, and fell into shape in the hands of the clients, architects and builders of skyscrapers. The following essays 'The Skyward Trend of Thought' and 'Apokatastasis' deal primarily with this problem. The fact that the Tower, 'since the days of Babel's confusion, has always stood for worldly and spiritual ambition'[26] has led in the America of the emerging skyscraper to another confusion, namely between spiritual and worldly ambition. The tallest tower in New York had always been the steeple of Trinity Church. Towers traditionally demonstrated the material claim of the church on the territory between Earth and Heaven. With the coming of the skyscraper this claim was challenged. Since 1875, when New York's first skyscraper had reached a height that was to overtop Trinity's steeple, the church has been subjected to several acts of humiliation. Henry James wrote: 'Beauty indeed was the aim of the creator of the spire of Trinity Church, so cruelly overtopped and so barely distinguishable . . . in its abject helpless humility.'[27] Its tower indeed began to be treated as a mere yardstick for any new skyscraper that was thought fit to carry that name; it was 'dwarfed' or 'eclipsed' by the new towers of worldly ambition. The ensuing battle between the two powers is the subject of the third essay: 'Sacred Skyscrapers and Profane Cathedrals'. The last two essays deal with the question of origin and creation. Being opposed to the positivistic-materialist reconstruction of the skyscraper's emergence, they propose a natural-metaphysical frame in which space is given to a combined operation of the indigenous myths of natural growth, dreams and aspirations of the clients and the perennial quest of the architects to give shape to that 'natural growth'. The first part of 'The Myth of Natural Growth' deals with the collective emergence of tall buildings on Newspaper Row, Manhattan, in the mid-1870s. The second part deals with the problem of giving shape to the skyscrapers – individually.

## The title

The title – *The Skyward Trend of Thought* – was taken from the frontispiece of Moses King's *Views of New York*, 1906 (Fig. 3). The picture shows a colossal office tower of 45 stories, designed to house the municipal offices, placed over a railroad terminal, which it is thought to be part of. The station with its low-lying mass and its odd centrally placed rococo clock-tower is apparently designed to reflect the old City Hall which is situated on the other side of the square. The caption reads:

Skyward Trend of Thought in New York – Municipal Office Building and Railroad Terminal Near the City Hall. The vastness of the business of the Corporation of the City of New York and the volume of traffic at this vortex of the city's life gave birth to a design of a great 45-story structure, 650 feet high, planned by former Bridge Commissioner Gustav Lindenthal and Architects Henry F. Hornbostel and George B. Post.

*Fig. 3. The Skyward Trend of Thought. The arch-emblem of the twisted rationale that provided the frame for the skyscraper myth. The two cartouches in the upper corners exemplify the two possible dimensions of extension (from Moses King,* King's Views of New York, 1906, *Boston, 1905, frontispiece).*

What makes this text a fascinating document is the ruthless combination of its two incompatible elements: the poetry of its romantic longing for the sky – 'the skyward trend of thought' – on the one hand, and the chill prose of statistics – 'vastness of business' and 'volume of traffic' – on the other hand. The rhetoric of its phrasing, however, lies not in a mere combination, but in the mutual support of the two elements. A strange kind of simultaneity is presupposed: skywardness is not *caused* by business and traffic, but it *is* business and traffic. The skyward trend of thought *implies* business. Who thinks business thinks skyward. There is a structural indifference to the two obvious polarities that determines the denotation of a no-nonsense business enterprise as a 'skyscraper'. The connotations are clearly predominant. There is a day-dreaming in it, and romance; there is 'that high Romance' in the sky-scraper, Sullivan once wrote, there is drama, transcendence. [28] It is the purpose of the present volume to stress this dualism by articulating the transcendental qualities and opposing them to the positivistic ones. The chosen title reflects this purpose in its own natural and unassuming way, evidently because it was there, found by accident and not invented.

### Sources

Most of the source material used for this study consists of facts and opinions taken partly from the domain of art and architectural history and partly from the domain of philosophy, history of ideas, history of religions, biology, cultural anthropology, literature and other related areas. In selecting the material emphasis has been laid on the less well-known sources. A great many books, pamphlets, brochures, postcards and the like have found their way to publicity from the informal circuit of second-hand bookstores and lawn-sales, rather than from the official circuit of university, museum or public libraries. Claude Bragdon's writings, for example, have been given a certain prominence, simply because it was about time that some light was shed upon this surprisingly interesting man. His books, numerous and highly relevant for the development of architectural theory in the first quarter of our century, have received little attention so far. Even the most ambitious modern reference book of architectural theory, Hanno-Walter Kruft's *Geschichte der Architekturtheorie, von der Antike bis zur Gegenwart*, München, 1985, remains ignorant of their existence. One of the reasons for this neglect, I believe, might be found in the circumstance that Bragdon's theoretical work was too quickly and too easily associated with the occult side of American culture. A side that was at the same time enthusiastically studied so far as it concerned the 19th century, but fearfully avoided as soon as it touched on modern-times thinking. The fact that it took almost half a century before the first serious study of Sullivan's writings got off the ground with the publication of Sherman Paul's *Louis Sullivan, An Architect in American Thought*, Englewood Cliffs, N.J., 1962, could be regarded as a case in point. Narciso G. Menocal, who in 1981 published the second, seminal, study on the subject, *Architecture as Nature, The Transcendentalist Idea of Louis Sullivan*, Madison, 1981, suggested that this late awareness of the importance of Sullivan's writings was caused by a general resistance to its arcane or vague character, fearing a relapse into 19th-century romanticism at a time when an orderly positivistic picture of the immediate past was firmly established. [29] Similarly, the improbable image of Frank Lloyd Wright as a typical 'machinistic' architect was brought to life in European, particularly Dutch architectural circles, who thought it more convenient for their cause to single out the 1901 article 'The Art and Craft of the Machine' at the expense of his other 'romantic' writings, and, in a free interpretation of its title, set out to make Wright an antecedent of modern rationalism, rather than an exponent of 19th-century idealism. [30]

28. Louis H. Sullivan, 'The Chicago Tribune Competition', *The Architectural Record*, LIII, January 1923, p. 153: 'The craving for beauty thus set forth by *The Tribune* [Chicago Tribune Building] is imbued with that high Romance, which is the essence, the vital impulse', etc. This passage was included in the 1923 luxury edition commemorating the famous Chicago Tribune Competition of 1922 (*The International Competition for a New Administration Building for the Chicago Tribune, MCMXXII*, Chicago, 1923, p. 2).

29. Narciso G. Menocal, *Architecture as Nature: The Transcendentalist Idea of Louis Sullivan*, Madison, Wis., 1981, pp. 149–151.

30. Frank Lloyd Wright, 'The Art and Craft of the Machine', *Chicago Architectural Club Catalogue of the 14th Annual Exhibition* (1901). Reyner Banham suggested that the European reception of Wright as an architect who employed the machine to his own benefit was based on a free interpretation of the title of Wright's address, without having seen the actual text (Reyner Banham, *Theory and Design in the First Machine Age*, London, 1972, p. 146).

31. See note 7.

32. 'The Skyward Trend of Thought' was read at the conference *American Architecture: Innovation and Tradition*, Columbia University, Graduate School of Architecture and Planning, New York, April 21–24, 1983, and published, in a somewhat different version in: *American Architecture: Innovation and Tradition*, David G. De Long, Helen Searing, and Robert A.M. Stern, eds., New York, 1986, pp. 57–83.
'Apokatastasis, or the Return of the Skyscraper', was presented at the conference *Athanasius Kircher e il Museo del Collegio Romano tra Wunderkammer e museo scientifico*, Biblioteca Nazionale, Rome, May 8, 1985, and subsequently published under the same title by Marsilio editori, Venice, 1986, pp. 176–195.
'Sacred Skyscrapers and Profane Cathedrals' was presented at the Architectural Association School of Architecture, London, May 1984, in two lectures which were published under the above title in the *AA Files, Annals of the Architectural Association School of Architecture*, 8, January 1985, pp. 39–57.
'The Myth of Natural Growth' was presented at the conference *L'Americanisme et la modernité*, organized by l'École des Hautes Études en Sciences Sociales, Institut Français d'Architecture and The American Center, October 23–25; publication of the proceedings is in preparation.

In order to adjust the equilibrium between the positivistic image of the American skyscraper and its metaphysical counterpart, I have decided to devote more attention to the 'vague' side than to the 'clear' side. Moreover, this 'clear' side has alrady been more than sufficiently covered by the available handbooks, reference books and a number of individual studies mentioned above. [31]

Over-engineering one's point by invoking an impressive mass of carefully selected evidence is a risk, of course, that seems to lurk on every page. Too much proof at once can seriously counteract the credibility of the argument and I am very well aware of the risks. On the other hand it should be taken into account that by looking at the skyscraper as an idea rather than as a thing it seems to detach itself from a background in which it otherwise has remained invisible. It is as with that road always travelled from A to B, which takes on a completely different appearance once travelled from B to A. I have ventured to take the liberty to assume that all those interested in the history of American architecture are already sufficiently familiar with the A to B journey.

Therefore I have seen no harm in making the journey down without first having to make it up.

That the scenery now seems unnatural, in quantity and in quality, is merely an illusion: it has been there all the time.

### The form

The present volume consists of five essays, each with its own subject of study, each conceived independently. Yet they all deal with the antithetical character of the skyscraper. Originally they were presented on several occasions as conference papers and as special guest lectures, ranging in time from 1983 till 1985. The first three have been published in a slightly different form, as magazine articles and as contributions to conference proceedings. The last two are about to be published shortly in a somewhat abridged form. [32]

New York

The heart of all the world am I!
A city, great, and grim and grand!
Man's monument to mighty man!
Superb! Incomparable! Alone!
Greater than ancient Babylon,
The giant walled! Greater than Tyre,
Sea-Queen! Greater than Nineveh,
Pearl of the East! Greater than Rome,
Stupendous reared, Magnificent!
Greater than Paris, city fey!
Greater than London, fog-enmeshed!
Greater than Venice! Vienna!
Or Petrograd! Greater than these!
That I am! Mark my high towers!

ARTHUR CREW INMAN
(from Alice Hunt Bartlett,
The Anthology of Cities, London, 1927)

W ITH A FEW exceptions, it is a generally accepted opinion that the skyscraper is an unequivocal and explicable thing: A tall commercial building. Most historical reconstruction of its origins and development served to legitimize this opinion. Its traditional structure is a narrative of deterministic and evolutionary conviction, and it is frequently called a 'story' (e.g., Thomas E. Tallmadge, *The Story of Architecture in America*, 1936, and Alfred Morgan, *The Story of Skyscrapers*, 1934; cf. Ernst Gombrich's famous *The Story of Art*, 1950). Its objective is to give credence to the second half of the title of this symposium: Innovation.

Yet I would suggest that we also introduce the first half of the title, Tradition, into the history of the skyscraper, viewing it as a late, but rightly timed, example of paradigmatic architecture; indeed as the tower of cosmogony.[1]

Numerous testimonies to this larger view can be found in the initial European responses to the American tall commercial building.

Thus the French novelist Paul Bourget, finding himself in the heart of downtown Manhattan, at the intersection of Broadway and Wall Street, in August, 1893, exclaims:

As soon as one feels oneself undergoing the total ensemble of these buildings, one experiences again and again this impression of Babylon, which indeed is splendid and, I must admit, puts a spell on you.[2]

Other foreign responses were equally romantic and enthusiastic, if of somewhat limited imagination; that is, it is significant that such commentators as Jules Huret, Karl Lamprecht, A.A. Ampère, Paul de Rousiers, and André Maurois[3] were unable, or unwilling, to evaluate skyscrapers in their own right, but always interpreted and classified them within the range of paradigmatic architecture, such as represented in the books of Athanasius Kircher (most notably, *Turris Babel*, and the more familiar *Entwurff einer historischen Architectur* by J.B. Fischer von Erlach).[4]

*. I have borrowed this title from Moses King, who used it in his 1905 *King's Views of New York*, as a slogan to accompany 'a design of a great 45-storey structure, 650 feet high, planned by former Bridge Commissioner Gustav Lindenthal and Architects Henry E. Hornbostel and George B. Post' (see also 'Introduction', Fig. 1). This paper was read at the conference: American Architecture: Innovation and Tradition, A Symposium inaugurating the Center for the Study of American Architecture, Columbia University Graduate School of Architecture and Planning, New York, April 21-24, 1983. The proceedings of this symposium have been published in: David G. De Long, Helen Searing and Robert A.M. Stern, eds., *American Architecture: Innovation and Tradition*, New York 1986, pp. 57-83.

1. Apart from the somewhat outdated study by Magda Révész-Alexander, *Der Turm als Symbol und Erlebnis*, The Hague, 1953, no general studies on the iconography, ideology and semantics of the tower have yet come to my attention. There are however some interesting studies on specific types of towers, such as: Wolfram Prinz, *Schloss Chambord und die Villa Rotonda in Vicenza* (Berlin: Frankfurter Forschungen zur Kunst, 1980), and Johann-Christian Klamt, 'Der runde Turm in Kopenhagen als Kirchturm und Sternwart', *Zeitschrift für Kunstgeschichte* 38, 1975, pp. 153-170. The commemorative tower expresses its necessary values of eternity by reaching to the heavens (see *Encyclopedia of Religion and Ethics*, James Hastings, ed., New York, 1913, p. 745); the tower of progress, on the other hand, also reaches skyward, but for different reasons. It challenges the laws of gravity rather than connecting heaven and earth. Skyscrapers like the Woolworth tower which were designed to glorify one man's achievement often embody these two motives: the building was to secure Mr. Woolworth's life after death, and at the same time was to demonstrate technological progress (see further 'Sacred Skyscrapers and Profane Cathedrals').

2. Paul Bourget, *Outre-Mer, notes sur l'Amérique*, Paris, 1895, Vol. 1, p. 39.

3. The most complete study in this field is Lewis A. Dudley, *Evaluations of American Architecture by European critics, 1875–1900*, unpublished Ph.D. Thesis, University of Wisconsin, 1962. Its field is limited, however, to architectural writers and publications specializing in architecture.

4. Athanasius Kircher, *Turris Babel, sive Archontologia*, Amsterdam, 1679; Johann Bernhard Fischer von Erlach, *Entwurff einer historischen Architectur*, Dortmund, 1978 (Wien, 1721 [1]).

5. Karl Lamprecht, *Americana*, Freiburg i.B, 1906, p. 81.

*Fig. 1. 'Liberty Enlightening The World'.*

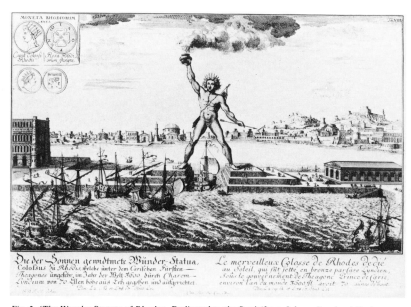

*Fig. 2. 'The Wonder Statute of Rhodos, Dedicated to the Sun' (from Johann Bernhard Fischer von Erlach, Entwurff einer historischen Architectur, Wien, 1721, fig. 31).*

In a time when visitors crossed the Atlantic by steamer, the passing of the Statue of Liberty must have seemed the preface to a picture book of architectural wonders of the past (Figs. 1, 2), and from this point on historical fantasy might flow freely. When the German historian Karl Lamprecht visited Manhattan in 1904, he envisioned immediately the many-towered city of San Gimignano and he began to draw extensive parallels between the early-capitalist fee-states of Tuscany and the high-capitalist city of New York. He illustrated his account, entitled *Americana*, with only two photographs: one of Manhattan and one of San Gimignano (Figs. 3, 4), of which he wrote: 'Do not your towers look like the skyscrapers of New York where the typewriters rattle all the way up to the twenty-fourth floor? ... New York is the San Gimignano of today, its bankers and wholesalers playing Montecchi and Capuleti which each other' (Fig. 5). [5]

*Fig. 3. 'New York as seen from the Hudson River' (from Karl Lamprecht,* Americana, *Freiburg i.B., 1906, p. 81).*

*Fig. 4. 'San Gimigniano as seen from the Rocca' (from Karl Lamprecht,* Americana, *Freiburg i.B., 1906, p. 82).*

6. Hendrik P. Berlage, *Amerikaansche reisherinneringen*, Rotterdam, 1913, pp. 6, 7, 10. I have not yet been able to trace the poet's name.

7. Rem Koolhaas, *Delirious New York*, New York, 1978, pp. 217/218.

*Fig. 5. Giuseppe Maria Mitelli, 'Sette torri famose d'Italia' (1701). The text, although strictly prosaic, has an undertone of boisterous hearsay (from* Le collezioni d'arte della cassa di Risparmio in Bologna, *Vol. I, Le incisioni, Giuseppe Maria Mitelli, a cura di Franca Varignana, Bologna, 1978, p. 404).*

The Dutch architect Hendrik Petrus Berlage, who travelled to the United States in November 1910, shared Lamprecht's 'Tuscan experience' but could not, on the other hand, suppress the resurgent image of Babel as he contemplated the skyscrapers of Manhattan; he wrote:

They seem a consummation of that dream
Of Babel's towers, these buildings that arise
And towering seem almost to touch the skies[6]

whereas later visitors like Le Corbusier and Salvador Dali saw the resurrection of the Egyptian pyramids and the city of Babel.[7]

What makes these comparisons interesting is not so much that the commentators drew parallels with the past, but that they perceived, in one way or another, a historical continuum. The skyscraper was not always, as one might have expected, experienced as a shocking novelty. New or futuristic shapes could only be imagined in a comparative relationship to the familiar. Forms of the far away past were reproduced in order to visualize the nearby future.

*Fig. 6. A brick from a 'house in Leyden' set in the south wall of the Chicago Tribune Building, Chicago.*

8. Le Corbusier, in his *Quand les cathédrales étaient blanches*, of 1937, was convinced that the skyscraper should find its own style, in spite of its architects, and that its growth could only be explained as the Tower of Babel. He wrote: 'ne possédait jusqu'ici qu'une légende: celle de la tour de Babel' (p. 62).

9. Dutch television recently presented a programme which raised several interesting points about Dutch emigration to the United States. The main argument noted the unwillingness of immigrants to admit that their expectations were not fulfilled. Even in times of hunger and poverty, the letters they sent home were filled with desperate merriment and anecdotes boasting abundance and prosperity. Clearly the immigrant's belief in the promise of material plenty triumphed over the physical realities of hunger and poverty. See also Arthur Holitscher, *Amerika, Heute und Morgen, Reiseerlebnisse*, Berlin, 1923, pp. 98ff.

10. J.W. Schulte Nordholt, *Amerika, land, volk, cultuur*, Baarn, 1965, p. 11. In the first chapter of this book the author expounds his theories on America as the continent with 'its mythical surplus value of a new world.' Especially the theories related to the notion of 'the great circle', in which America is explained as the completion of the creation, as the final realization of all preceding great cultures and as the continent of death and resurrection (John Donne: '... As West and East In all flatt Maps (and I am one) are one, So death doth touch the Ressurection'), are very enligthening (ibid., p. 10).

11. Washington Irving, *A History of New York, from the Beginning of the World to the End of the Dutch Dynasty, by Diedrich Knickerbocker*, London, 1900 (1809[1]), pp. 13, 61. Book 1, Chapter 2 of Knickerbocker's account 'Containing an account of a mighty ark, which floated, under the protection of St. Nicholas, from Holland to Gibbet Island – the descent of the strange animals therefrom – etc.', is a liberal persiflage of Genesis 9 and (partly) 10.

It must be admitted that for someone like Le Corbusier, there was almost certainly an element of jealousy; he was envious that it was not he who had created this most splendid vision of modern architecture.[8] But even this reaction shows at the same time the inevitability of the occasion: things were falling into their proper places spontaneously. And the inevitable happened, as the enactment of the fulfillment of earlier promises. These promises constitute another set of parallels: those of Genesis Rediviva and America as a New World. The expectations of the early immigrants were certainly grandiose, fed by mystical and religous impulses, and what they found when they got here was certainly not Mesopotamia or the Heavenly Jerusalem.[9] Yet their driving force, the determination to see a better world realized, makes parallels with historical, mythical, and biblical prefigurations not only apt but compulsory, even to a degree of tedium. This new world was better in the sense that it was fresh and unspoiled, like the world at the time of Creation. The Pilgrim Fathers, coming from the 'fair and bewtifull citie' of Leyden, knew that 'this is the place where the Lord will create a new Heaven and a new Earth.'[10] A brick from 'a House in Leyden, Holland, used by the Pilgrims as a church before their voyage on the Mayflower to America', is set in the southern wall of the Chicago Tribune Building (Fig. 6), together with a collection of other European relics, as if to give proof to a reality that, in the general confusion between mythology and history, might be lost. The voyage across the wild Atlantic was found to be so similar to drifting on the waters of the Deluge that Columbus could be compared with Noah, the Mayflower to his Ark, and finally America to the land of Senaar, where Noah's offspring finally settled after their descent from Mount Ararat (Fig. 7).[11]

*Fig. 7. Mount Ararat and the Land of Sanaar, showing the Wanderings of Noah's Offspring (from Athanasius Kircher,* Turris Babel, *Amsterdam, 1679, lib. 1, p. 13).*

15

American Architecture: Innovation and Tradition

*Fig. 8. The Modernistic View of The Sacred Mountain (from Poster,* American Architecture: Innovation and Tradition, *New York, 1983).*

12. Werner Oechslin, *Skyscraper und Americanismus, Mythos zwischen Europa und Amerika*, pp. 4–12 and Manfredo Tafuri, '"Neu-Babylon": Amerikanismus', *Archithese*, 20, 1976, pp. 12–15; *(Metropolis 3), Amerikanismus, Skyscraper und Ikonografie.* I am indebted to Professor Stanislaus von Moos, who was so kind as to send me this important three-volume series on American architecture. See also: Daniele Baroni, *Grattacieli – Architettura Americana tra Mito e Realtà 1910–1939*, Milano (Electa), 1979, p. 5, and above, note 11. For illustration see 'Apokatastasis', Fig. 19.

13. Assuming that their work is less well known than that of Sullivan, Ferriss and Mujica, I will mention here Claude Bragdon's *The Beautiful Necessity*, London, 1922 (1910¹), Irving Pond's *The Meaning of Architecture*, Boston, 1918, and a rare contribution by Harvey Wiley Corbett, 'America Builds Skyward', in: *America as Americans See It* (New York, 1932), pp. 44–52. It is a book expressly intended for a European public. Bragdon's remark about Ferriss is from *The Frozen Fountain* (New York, 1932), p. 32.

14. The fundamental study on this subject is: Mircea Eliade, *Le mythe de l'éternel retour*, Paris, 1949.

15. Irving Pond, *The Meaning of Architecture*, Boston, 1918, p. 11.

16. Louis Althusser, 'Les défauts de l'économie classique, Esquisse du concept de temps historique', in: *Lire le capital*, Paris, 1968, pp. 112-149 and Fernand Braudel, *Civilisation matérielle, économie et capitalisme, XVe–XVIIIe siècles*, I–III: *Les structures du quotidien, Le possible et l'impossible; Les jeux de l'échange; Le temps du monde*, Paris, 1979. Erwin Panofsky hinted at a twofold approach of historical time in his essay '"Renaissance" – Self-Definition or Self-Deception', in which he distinguished '"megaperiods" as well as the shorter ones' (originally published in 1944 and reedited in 1965 and 1970 in: Erwin Panofsky, *Renaissance and Renascences in Western Art*, London, 1970, p. 4.

17. I have borrowed the idea of 'physical time' from P.Th. Hugenholtz, *Tijd en creativiteit*, Amsterdam, 1959. I am much indebted to the philosopher Fons Elders who brought to my attention several interesting publications such as the one mentioned above.

18. The term is taken from Claude Bragdon's *The Beautiful Necessity*, London, 1922, p. 34. Bragdon illustrates the law of the opposing forces using a drawing based on a famous painting by Tiepolo.

After all, Diedrich Knickerbocker began his *History of New York* with the discovery of America by Noah, 'at the time of the building of the tower of Babel', and he had one of his heroes, 'the sage Oloffe', climb into a tree to see a vision of Babylonic New York, in a persiflage of the biblical text: 'We will build here for ourselves a city and a tower whose top shall reach into the sky' (Genesis 11).[12]

Thus the skyscraper could be approached as the realization of a higher degree of building principles than pragmatic or deterministic ones, the discovery of which requires digging into that timeless reservoir of expressive means and didactic models of revelation, eternity, and, most importantly, cosmogony, so aptly illustrated by the image of the Grand Tetons (Fig. 8).

Irving Pond, Claude Bragdon, Hugh Ferriss, Harvey Wiley Corbett, and Francisco Mujica, among others,[13] all made it their daily concern to search for what Mircea Eliade, and Henri Bergson referred to as *L'éternel retour*[14] or, as Pond formulated it, 'the constant search for the sublime essence of a spirit which has found embodiment in the great architecture of the past.'[15]

These notions of timelessness, of changeless change, seem strangely out of place in our standard art-historical treatment. The history of architecture as an evolutionary process seems radically opposed to the lifespan of the timeless types. If we want to describe their historical presence, we have to measure their lifespan by a different historical time, one that encompasses much longer units than those we employ normally.

It appears now that a good opportunity has been presented to bring to a test the division of historical time into several 'durées', as has been practised by Althusser and Braudel, from which I will reserve the 'longue durée', so-called 'geological time', for paradigmatic architecture and the timeless types (e.g., Babel, the Pyramids, Solomon's Temple, etc.), and the short time-spans for the events ('les événements') of which most of art history is made.[16] In art history (and predominantly the custom-made history by and for the modern movement), the evolution of art is made visible as a string of events, knotted together by the convincing logic of cause and effect, and made universally digestible by the organization of the cause and effect model. Thus we get one level on which events occur, brought forth in a single sweep of time, tolerating only those facts that appear as the logical constituents of such a model. These events are arranged sequentially, the only way possible within a linguistic construct, and an arrangement that in its turn affects not only the position of events but suggests a causality. *After* becomes *because of*. This system of causation relies on a multitude of natural laws, all centred around the themes of action−reaction and cause−effect.

Completing the law of causation, although not a natural law but a modus operandi in interpretive historiography, is what I will call the Law of Polarity.[18] The function of this law is to reinforce and intensify presumably opposing forces. Its method relies on the modes of short time-span, anecdotism, and polarization, as used in extremely dialectical fields like diplomatic and military history ('histoire bataille'). To be protected against the dictates of history, these modes have acquired built-in defense mechanisms.

Movements and *isms* are prefabricated and attached to the product before it even arrives.

In 1927 Walter Curt Behrendt published a bellicose pamphlet called *Der Sieg des neuen Baustils*, in which he suggested that (a) there was something like an enemy, (b) there was a battle, and (c) that battle was won by the New Builders. [19] Comparable examples of an antagonistic historical consciousness may be found naturally, but to a modest degree, in the manifestos of Le Corbusier, Giedion, and other CIAM members, and, in a much less restricted manner, in the quasi-histories of the movement, such as Hitchcock's *Modern Architecture* (1929) and Cheney's *The New World Architecture* (1930). Here we find, even more than in the European accounts, probably because of an accumulative effect of American 'new worldness' combined with European revolutionism, the most radical picture of architectural history. Architecture is seen as a military operation, ranging back all the way into the nineteenth century, where with a most convincing feeling for reality, the artists are pitched against the engineers, the traditionalists against the protomodernists, and so on. [20]

To illustrate the workings of anecdotal history and its auxiliary mechanisms I have selected the Chicago Tribune Competition of 1922 for several reasons. First, thanks to the fact that the Tribune Competition has become such a monumental cliché in art history, all of its constituent elements have been blown up to excessive proportions; second, its historical material can be interpreted in terms of the two methods that I have just expounded; and third, it is still one of the rare cases in which European conceptions and American conceptions can be observed under (almost) laboratory conditions. The Chicago Tribune Competition of 1922 offers good illustrations of the incongruity of both historical time and interpretative polarization.

The competition's programme was simple and enigmatic: 'To erect the most beautiful and distinguished office building in the world is the desire of *The Tribune*.' [21] Undoubtedly, the winner would be the one who would interpret this ultimatum the most penetratingly. The key word was 'world'. It appears no less than eight times on the first page of the introduction to the *Tribune*'s 1923 catalogue of the competition's entries and a total of twenty-one times on its first eight pages. There are two possible interpretations. The first is that 'world' was to be understood as the *Tribune*'s world, which was Chicago and the State of Illinois, possibly including the other world, of New York, merely for the sake of rivalry. [22]

This is not bad reasoning. To be the most beautiful office building it had to be more beautiful than the most beautiful building then existing within the aforementioned 'world'. General opinion agreed that this was the almost ten-year-old Woolworth Tower, designed by Gilbert in 1913 (Fig. 9). That this was so is confirmed by the statement that a fellow competitor added to one of his sketches (Fig. 10). It was the Japanese-American architect Richard Yoshijiro Mine:

My tireless search for a building design at the famous Ricker Architectural Library from end to end brought me to the Woolworth Building of New York. My conviction was, then, that it would be something. [23]

19. Walter Curt Behrendt, *Der Sieg des Neuen Baustils*, Stuttgart, 1927, p. 11.

20. The alleged animosity between architects and engineers in the nineteenth century seems to be the result of a mythical personification of architecture and construction, represented as two opposing powers (see Peter Collins, *Changing Ideals in Modern Architecture*, 1750–1950, Montreal, 1967, pp. 128–149).

21. *The International Competition for a New Administration Building for the Chicago Tribune 1922*, New York, 1980, p. 10.

22. The relative value of the term 'world' in American parlance did not remain unnoticed by Europeans. For example, Paul Bourget wrote: 'Le moindre produit est sur les annonces "the best in the world, le meilleur au monde!" Un vainqueur de boxe devient "le champion du monde", "the champion of the world". ... Où finit la naiveté? Où commence le charlatanisme?', *Outre-Mer*, I, p. 54.

23. From a letter by Mine to the curator of the Department of Architecture at the Art Institute of Chicago, John Zukowsky, dated March 23, 1979. I thank Mr. Zukowsky for helping me to establish this informative link. Copyright the Art Institute of Chicago.

*Fig. 9 (below). 'The most beautiful office building
in the world', Cass Gilbert's Woolworth Building,
New York, 1913 (from a postcard).*

*Fig. 10 (right). Richard Yoshijiro Mine, Design for
the Chicago Tribune Tower Competition, 1922
(from* The International Competition for a New
Administration Building for the Chicago Tribune,
*Chicago, 1923, pl. 82).*

Mine won one out of ten honourable mentions, but not first prize because he was too close to Gilbert's design, and a straight copy was not desired. Hood and Howells revealed their similar conclusion in a much more subtle and attractively disguised interpretation of the Gothic spirit, which was, if we may believe Frank Lloyd Wright, an irresistible topic in the Midwest: 'It is alone in an atmosphere of this nature [of the West and Midwest] that the Gothic Spirit in building can be revived'[24] (Figs. 11a & b). Thus the jury had to succumb to that wonderful gimmick of the flying buttresses balancing the spire, reminiscent of the Butter Tower in Rouen (Fig. 12).

Another interpretation of the term 'world' was probably more acute. It was made by Eliel Saarinen, who received second prize but was generally acclaimed as the real winner.[25]

One of the reasons the competition became so famous was its typical competitive character. Not only did it carry a very large sum of prize money, but also a widely and enthusiastically disputed verdict.

The fact that European modernism did not get the representation the authors of the competition had expected it to get was a sad case of miscalculation. In progressivist eyes, Chicago was the Eldorado of the 'Neue Sachlichkeit', of merciless pragmatism, unscrupulous functionalism, and, above all, a territory where 'artists' were not welcomed; was it not Giedion himself, re-quoting Bourget, who said 'Chicago [architecture] is the work of some impersonal power, irresistible, like a force of Nature,' and that 'the architect frankly accepted the condition imposed by the speculator,' and then went on to speak of 'the simple force of need as a principle of beauty'?[26]

*Fig. 11a & b. Nor were the winners of the competition, Raymond Hood and John Mead Howells, able to resist the charms of the Woolworth Building.*
*a) Entrance to the Woolworth Building (from* The Cathedral of Commerce, *1916).*
*b) Entrance to the Chicago Tribune Tower (from Raymond M. Hood, 'The Tribune Tower – The Architect's Problem',* The Western Architect, *November 1925, p. 114. Etching by Birch Burdette Long).*

*Fig. 12. 'That wonderful gimmick of the flying buttresses balancing the spire.' The Chicago Tribune Tower in Winter. Hood & Howells, architects, 1922–1925.*

24. Frank Lloyd Wright, *Ausgeführte Bauten und Entwürfe/Studies and Executed Buildings*, Berlin, 1910, Introduction, n.p.

25. 'Sullivan hailed this design as a return to, and a carrying forward of, those principles of which he had been the advocate and exemplar; Bertram Goodhue, himself a competitor, who had had an advance view of all the drawings, told me that Saarinen's design was in a class by itself and superior to all others, and such was the consensus of opinion, professional and lay.' Claude Bragdon, *The Frozen Fountain*, p. 31. See for a more detailed treatment: 'Myth II', p. 130ff. and notes 110, 111, 112.

26. Sigfried Giedion, *Space, Time and Architecture*, Cambridge, Mass., 1946, p. 303, and Montgomery Schuyler, 'Architecture in Chicago: Adler and Sullivan', *The Architectural Record*, 1895, p. 8.

And so, when the projects of Gropius and Max and Bruno Taut were rebuffed, they felt betrayed, firstly by America, but above all by *time*. What had seemed the logical continuation of the modern was not recognized, not regarded as fitting the purpose. The *future* was not part of the programme. As we shall see, it was the celebration of the *present* that was the issue. Disillusionment, mixed with resentment and indignation, fed the notion that an army of opposing forces was conspiring against the right course of history. Existing polarities such as architect versus engineer, visible construction versus 'sham' or 'bogus' decoration, nineteenth century – this time not seen as a periodization but as a being with human characteristics which was, according to Pevsner, of a 'profound artistic dishonesty' – versus the new era: all of these were amalgamated with the local American oppositions, such as East versus West, academism versus self-reliance, and so forth.[27] In the ensuing 'cold war', more than anything else the exhibition of the frame was the all-pervasive article of faith. And the frame, as Colin Rowe has said, was much more than a means to an end; it was the end itself.[28]

The voices of European paternalism made it their vocation to point out to the Americans that they were losing their faith and that in the Chicago Tribune Competition it was clearly becoming apparent that the Europeans had stuck much more faithfully to the principles of the frame. Giedion proclaimed that the 'foreign projects [were] closer to the Chicago School.'[29] In other words, American architects were handling their heritage with increasing carelessness, and it required the higher intelligence of a Gropius to make them realize this. In Giedion's view the early Chicago architects were idealized as noble savages, who created out of instinct rather than reason, and who were to be treated as natural artists, but always and exclusively in spite of themselves.

In this way modernism discovered its unspoiled Eden, and the great myth was spun around Chicago. In a Rousseau-esque effort to crown the least artistic the noblest of savages, a man like William leBaron Jenney was chosen to fulfill the role of inventor of the frame (see 'Introduction'). That this was a dramatic case of miscasting, due to a rigorous lack of evidence, did not bother anybody at the time; nor did the election of Louis Sullivan as the omnipotent representative of American progressive architecture in general stir up questions of doubt. On the contrary, Sullivan was unanimously hailed as the savage genius, the isolated conscience of artistic truth, the victim of academic conspiracy, and also the man who had been monstrously neglected by his own countrymen. This, in particular, was an excellent occasion for the Europeans to adopt him as the ideal precursor of modernism in Paradise. Paul Frankl, who professed a lively interest in the skyscraper and even designed 'skyscraper furniture', believed firmly that Sullivan was the inventor of the skyscraper: 'The credit for this innovation goes to the distinguished architect Louis Sullivan.'[30]

Wright had already conquered Europe with the Wasmuth publications in 1910 and 1911. Sullivan followed in his wake, and from 1913 on, when Hendrik Petrus Berlage had his *Amerikaansche reisherinneringen* published, Sullivan's authority was firmly established in Europe.[31] Thus it was around Sullivan that the 'Künstler-Legende' was woven. Sullivan acted as a *pars pro toto* for the Chicago School.

It was, of course, mere coincidence that when the Chicago School, for reasons of stylistic impurity, was declared clinically dead in 1922, Sullivan had to follow soon. It was all the fault of the Chicago Fair of 1893. The White City is an inevitable and vastly overrated oddity. Where other World Fairs have been treated with benevolence and even canonized like the ones in London of 1851 and in Paris of 1889, the Chicago World's Fair has been regarded with some-

27. Nikolaus Pevsner, *Pioneers of the Modern Movement, from William Morris to Walter Gropius*, London, 1936, p. 20.

28. Colin Rowe, 'Chicago Frame', *The Mathematics of the Ideal Villa, and other Essays*, London, 1967, p. 90.

29. Sigfried Giedion, *Space, Time and Architecture*, p. 314.

30. Paul T. Frankl, *New Dimensions, The Decorative Arts of Today in Words and Pictures*, New York, 1928, p. 52. For Sullivan as 'Parent and Prophet' of Modern Architecture, see Deborah F. Pokinski, *The Development of the American Modern Style*, Ann Arbor, Michigan, 1984, p. 57.

31. Hendrik P. Berlage, *Amerikaansche reisherinneringen*, Rotterdam, 1913, p. 33: '... the credit for being the forerunner of modern architecture in America belongs to Sullivan.'

thing akin to hatred. Hitchcock, taking his cue from Sullivan's *Autobiography of an Idea*, in his 1929 *Modern Architecture*, called it 'the white plague'. [32]

Yet ordinary people felt comfortably happy with it, and, as was common in world exhibitions, it disappeared after it was consumed. Therefore it was called 'the vanishing city' (Fig. 13), for it did vanish almost without a trace, but not quite: the park and the later reconstructed 'Queen of the Fair', Charles Atwood's Fine Arts Building, remained.

Atwood has never wholeheartedly been credited for his work on the Reliance Building, which rises to such heroic heights in Giedion's *Space, Time and Architecture* as to be described as having this role: 'to symbolize the spirit of the Chicago School whose swan song it was.' Thus the function of the fair in the 'stories' is that of a sort of architectural 'bête noire'. Modernists as well as many Americanists were convinced that the fair represented something evil, something America had to be protected against.

Lewis Mumford wrote in 1931 in his *The Brown Decades*, 'So low had American taste sunk in the generation after the World's Fair that people habitually characterized as an advance what was actually a serious retrogression.' [33]

Mumford believed that the fair represented a collection of 'dull and inert forces that stood in the way' of what he considered to be the natural course of architecture. [34] By general prejudice and traditional consensus, those 'forces' were usually embodied by the architects 'from the East'. About the time of the fair several pictures were made of the architects responsible (Fig. 14); later these served as snapshots of the enemy on manoeuvres ('die Gegner', as Walter Curt Behrendt called them). [35]

Thus, the same 'dull and inert forces' were observed to be demonstrably at work in the years 1922 and 1923, and it was logical and in the line of history to assume that the fair was an anticipation of the Tribune competition. Sullivan, the oracle, had said that 'the damage wrought by the Chicago Fair would last half a century.' Giedion, and Pevsner following him some seventy years later, believed that Sullivan had made an important prediction, although in fact the text comes from the 1924 *Autobiography of an Idea*, and not from 1893. Thus Pevsner wrote in his *An Outline of European Architecture* (1943): 'Chicago might have become the international centre of modern architecture had it not been for the "World's Fair" .... Of the Chicago Exhibition Sullivan said that the damage wrought by it would last for half a century. The prognostication has proved accurate.' [36]

The prognostication was only accurate for Pevsner and Giedion in terms of their ideal line of history, and their idea of what was modern and youthful. In their view, what was modern and youthful, as opposed to being dull and inert, was Sullivan and the frame. In their search for presages, oracles, and prognostications, they found that Gropius's Tribune Tower was foreshadowed in Sullivan's Carson, Pirie, Scott Store, which dates from the threshold period of transition between the nineteenth century and the New Age. In its exhibiting of the 'neutral skeleton' Sullivan's monument was well chosen, but it turned out that its architect had been guilty of certain transgressions. The plot, as set out by the modernist historians, develops as follows. First, the building is described by Giedion as the realization of the ideal of true architecture: 'The interior is still of the warehouse type, with continuous unbroken floor areas. The front is designed to fulfil its indispensable function, the admission of light.' [37] (The latter statement is, of course, an error. If there is one thing that was to be avoided in a department store, it was direct light from the street fronts.) Giedion continues: 'Its basic elements are the horizontally elongated "Chicago windows", admirably homogeneous and treated to coincide with the

Fig. 13. 'The Vanishing City', cover of a photograph guidebook to the 1893 Chicago World's Fair.

Fig. 14. 'Die Gegner': an identi-kit picture of 'the dull and inert forces' (Mumford). From left to right: G.E. Graham, E. Butler, D. Burnham, a newspaper reporter, Dr. Ch.G. Fuller, Ch. Atwood (from The Western Architect, August 1924, p. 90).

32. Henry-Russell Hitchcock, *Modern Architecture, Romanticism and Reintegration* (1929), reprinted, New York, 1970, p. 110. Was he perhaps paraphrasing a quotation of Fiske Kimball? See Dimitri Tselos, 'The Chicago Fair and the Myth of the "Lost Cause"', *J.S.A.H.*, 26, December 1907, pp. 259–268, and, more recent: Deborah Pokinski, op. cit., pp. 3-4, 20ff.

33. Lewis Mumford, *The Brown Decades; A Study of the Arts in America, 1865–1895*, New York, (1931[1]) 1971, p. 64.

34. Ibid., p. 64.

35. Walter Curt Behrendt, *Der Sieg des neuen Baustils*, Leipzig, 1927. As the title of this booklet indicates, the field of architectural development was seen as comparable to military history. Battles could be fought, victories could be won, defeats could be suffered.

36. Nikolaus Pevsner, *An Outline of European Architecture*, Harmondsworth, 1963, p. 446.

37. Sigfried Giedion, *Space, Time and Architecture*, op. cit., p. 311.

framework of the skeleton.'[38] Yet the edge where State and Madison streets converge and where 'the world's busiest corner' is situated, is elegantly curved and is therefore a blatant violation of the ideal. Giedion finds a way out. He explains that Sullivan was responding to the demands of his client: 'The owners had asked for this curvilinear addition as a reminiscence of the pavilion attached to their old store.'[39]

Apart from the fact that the curved access made most effective use of 'the world's most profitable corner', and was, as Giedion suggested himself, 'a stylistic remnant' of the owners' previous store, it seems highly inconsistent to attribute this design decision exclusively to the owners, since the Chicago style was predicated on the belief that 'true beauty' was the result of 'the simple force of need'. Wasn't the architect or engineer supposed to 'loyally accept the conditions imposed by the speculator/owner?' A similar dissimulation is evident in Giedion's attempt to downplay the use of ornament in the building: 'The windows, with their thin metal frames, are sharply cut into the façade. The windows in the lower stories are connected by a narrow line of ornament pressed into the terra cotta. Too thin to be visible in the photograph ...' (Fig. 15).[40] In fact, the worst photograph available does not obscure this ornament, and although one can see a suspicious cut running from the lower left corner through the entrance pavilion, the thin line of ornament is still very much apparent. It is more apparent in any case than in the photo Walter Curt Behrendt used for his chapter on Sullivan in *Modern Building* of 1937, where the ornament, intentionally or not, has been eliminated (Fig. 16).

Even Giedion must have realized now that he had gone too far. He had fixed the reader's attention on a line of ornament which, he said, could hardly be seen, when it could be seen quite clearly – all the more so perhaps now that he had suggested a reason not to notice it.

For Behrendt, a year or so earlier, in his discussion of the Carson, Pirie, Scott Store, had taken a different approach. He too had noticed the discrepancy (especially for a European modernist) between the bareness of the upper storeys and the exuberant detailing of the two lower storeys. But instead of dissimulating it, he focussed the reader's attention on it: '... the urge and pleasure of self-expression, never put fully to rest in an artist, is worked off on the two lower stories, the only ones which are really visible at a glance from the street.' Yet in their symptomatic mistaking of functionalism for pure aesthetics, both men had a blind spot when it came to seeing functionalism as a system of finding optimal answers to specific needs, such as those of American business. Whereas Giedion in his excitement entirely forgot that the building was intended as a department store, Behrendt half-apologetically acknowledged that the prime need of the building was to attract window-shopping buyers who were not at all interested in those surfaces of the building beyond their range of vision. On the contrary, as every shopkeeper knows, the shopper's interest is almost exclusively directed to the windows at eye level; and it is precisely for this reason that the fanciful and – certainly for that time – wild ornament lines the windows like seductive eyelashes.

Quite rightly Behrendt noted the 'obvious similarity to the abstract ornament of the Art Nouveau movement.'[41] There can be little doubt that a client who borrowed its image so freely from the famous Parisian stores must have been quite pleased with a local architect who could design in the vein of men like Frantz Jourdain, who at that time was applying to the La Samaritaine Department Store a rich Art Nouveau ornamentation. Behrendt even went so far as to see a certain artistry in Sullivan's design, albeit still within the tradition of the nineteenth century, and when he considered the fact that he was judging the product of a culture in transition he could also forgive Sullivan's more regressive tendencies to a degree.

38. Ibid., p. 311.

39. Ibid., p. 312.

40. Ibid., p. 311–312.

41. Walter Curt Behrendt, *Modern Building*, New York, 1937, p. 110.
Juan Pablo Bonta demonstrated quite entertainingly in his *Architecture and its Interpretation*, New York, 1979, how photographs of buildings became the means of illusionistic manipulation in several cases of architecture in the process of canonization. The Carson, Pirie, Scott Store is presented as a classic case of its genre. William Jordy was the first to show oblique views of the upper storeys so that otherwise invisible ornaments could be seen in the recessed mouldings framing the windows (*American Buildings and Their Architects*, Vol. 3, *Progressive and Academic Ideals at the Turn of the Twentieth Century*, Garden City, New York, 1976, pp. 140–141).
The cracked photograph Giedion reproduced as figure 183 on p. 311 was most probably taken from Morrison's book from 1935 (see note 51) on which Giedion based his own account of Sullivan.

42. Walter Curt Behrendt, *Der Sieg des neuen Baustils*, p. 121; Sigfried Giedion, *Space, Time and Architecture*, op. cit., p. 312.
It was Hugh Morrison's idea to transfer the responsibility for the decoration to Elmslie, who, after all, was Morrison's 'chief source of information'. See also William Jordy, *American Buildings and Their Architects*, op. cit., Vol. 3.

43. Hendrik P. Berlage, *Amerikaansche reisherinneringen*, op. cit., pp. 34–35.

44. Ibid., p. 35. Cf. Tom van Leeuwen, 'De commerciële stijl', *Americana*, Otterlo, 1975, p. 78.

Not so Giedion. It was not that he was more committed to the movement than Behrendt, but he was more committed to the idea of Sullivan as a leader, and as such Sullivan had to be infallible. Therefore he had to be 'cleansed', and so Giedion wrote: 'George Elmslie, whom we have already mentioned as one of Sullivan's staunchest collaborators, was the designer of most of the ornamentation in his building.' And he went on to dispute Behrendt's lax judgment: 'It was not influenced by the contemporary Art Nouveau.'[42] (One must bear in mind that Art Nouveau was considered the most lethal of all nineteenth-century diseases.)

Nor was Berlage much impressed by Sullivan's ornamentation. In his Travel Recollections of 1913 he called him 'too much of a decorator', especially in the Bayard Building in New York and in the Carson, Pirie, Scott Store.[43] Berlage too noticed the discrepancy between the undisguised mass of the building and the 'superfluity of ornament',[44] but in the end he was not able to see clearly the essence of Sullivan's ornament, and it seems that his admiration for him was rather indiscriminate and without much real understanding. As a tribute to the great man, Berlage included in his book a picture of a typical Sullivanesque building, of which he wrote: 'Masonic Temple at Chicago –

*Fig. 15 (below). 'A narrow line of ornament, . . . too thin to be visible in the photograph' (from Sigfried Giedion,* Space, Time and Architecture, *Cambridge, 1941, fig. 183).*

*Fig. 16 (right). 'The two lower stories, the only ones which are really visible at a glance from the street' (from Walter Curt Behrendt,* Modern Buiding, *New York, 1937, p. 110b).*

Architect Sullivan' (Fig. 17, right). It should not be alarming that even a foreigner as knowledgeable as Berlage could mistake a well-known Burnham & Root building for one by Sullivan, but it remains rather odd that Berlage should have accepted unquestioningly the hipped roof and the pointed gables as characteristic of Sullivan. Even odder is the way Berlage set out to manipulate his photographic material. On plate 6 he introduced one of the less known and less distinguished products of Chicago architecture: the University Club (Fig. 17, left). Berlage reproduced this illustration without apparent reason. It does not relate to the text and it is identified merely as 'A Club — in Chicago'. Why then did he include the picture? There are several answers to the question. The first possibility is that Berlage had a photograph of the building, where he had had lunch one day — as can be read from the text — but he did not quite know what to do with it. The name of the architect (the building could be identified as the Chicago University Club by Burnham & Co.) had obviously escaped him, but by comparing it with other pictures in his possession, he must have noticed a certain similarity with the Masonic Temple, which he believed was by Sullivan (Fig. 17, right). The handling of the Tudor details in the two buildings is stylistically similar, and so, by way of a clever juxtaposition — the two illustrations are on facing pages — he made a nice set of what he thought were buildings by the legendary Louis Sullivan. But there is yet another possible explanation for the inclusion of the University Club. For the progressive taste a far more relevant ensemble appears in the right-hand corner of the photograph: the famous Gage Group by Holabird and Roche, and, of course, by Louis Sullivan, who had designed the façade of the building at the extreme right (Fig. 18). It would have been quite understandable if Berlage's host at the time, the architect William Gray Purcell, who used to work for Sullivan, would have provided his guest with some in-

*Fig. 17 left & right. An attractive ensemble of two friendly Tudor gables facing each other (from H.P. Berlage,* Amerikaansche reisherinneringen, *Rotterdam, 1913, figs. 6 & 7).*

CLUBGEBOUW        TE CHICAGO

DE TEMPEL DER VRIJMETSELAARS        TE CHICAGO

45. Sigfried Giedion, *Space, Time and Architecture*, p. 312. In their apparent failure to understand the artistic libertinism and tolerance of the preceding periods, Mumford, Pevsner, Giedion and Morrison believed that the nineteenth century was a time of 'confusion' and of 'inner conflict'. Giedion was convinced that France was full of inner contradictions. He wrote: 'On the one hand it is the country of obstinate academism, . . . on the other, the course of painting and construction is inconceivable without France' (Sigfried Giedion, *Mechanization Takes Command, A Contrubiton to Anonymous History*, New York, 1969, p. 496). The use of the term 'inconceivable' is characteristic of their line of historical thinking. Carl Condit, the most loyal of Giedionists, continued this thought in *The Chicago School of Architecture*, Chicago/London, 1964, pp. 1–13.

*Fig. 18. A classic case of art-historical amputation. A comparison between two modes of appreciation (compare fig. 17 left) (from Carl W. Condit,* The Chicago School of Architecture, *Chicago, 1964, p. 31).*

teresting photographs of some typical works, including that stretch of Michigan Avenue showing the Gage Group. What Berlage might have done with it, is up to the reader to guess. However, it is to be feared that Berlage had cropped off the two uninteresting box-like structures at the right and that he composed the nicely picturesque pair of hipped roofs. Whatever could have been the true reason for this artistic interference, it nevertheless throws an interesting light on Berlage's notion of Sullivan's architecture. It also proves how widely the interpretations of the great forerunner could differ, even when they come from the propagators of modernism themselves.

Thus it appears that both Giedion and Berlage were influenced by the authority of Sullivan's name and reputation, but when it came to recognizing his style and ideas, they failed dramatically. In Giedion's case this meant an unpleasant complication. His anecdotal-positivist treatment of history did not allow for insignificant or inexplicable occurrences, and therefore the conflicting character of Sullivan's architecture had to be resolved. So Giedion concluded in the mellow and understanding tone of the psychoanalyst:

Even when architects of Sullivan's generation pressed on towards new solutions, they sometimes found themselves held back by nineteenth-century traditions. They suffered from a split personality. . . . The split personality of the nineteenth-century architect makes itself felt in Sullivan's Carson Pirie Scott building.[45]

A recurrent theme in the appreciation of the frame by the European modernists is the connotation of youth. The framed building is the image of the new age and the vehicle for new generations to express their youthfulness. But why? What makes the frame so easily understood as denoting youth? There seems to be no unequivocal explanation of this meaning, but there are enough instances to suggest a common conception. An enlightening commentary is to be found in the Dutch architectural magazine *Bouwkundig weekblad* of 1923, written by J.J.P. Oud, precisely on the case of the Chicago Tribune Competition.

Most Dutch competitors were, unlike their French and Italian colleagues, of a modernist inclination and their reflections on the competition's results were a mixture of old-world arrogance and modernist indignation. Dutch indignation, habitually more indignant than justified, concentrated itself upon a rigorous rejection of Hood and Howells' winning design and a fanatical rehabilitation of a Danish modernist design that was not even entered: Knut Lönberg-Holm's icon of the frame, with dominating horizontals and two Wrightian light-fixtures near the top (Fig. 19). In his 'oratio pro domo' Oud favoured Lönberg-Holm's project and disapproved of Hood's as well as Saarinen's, writing:

[Hood's design is] a 'pseudo-morphosis': modern requirements petrified in traditional, gothicising, counter moulds . . . . The Finn's design is a hybrid between American mercantilism and the devotional surrender to the 'sublime' in the religious sense of the Western world.[46]

In the appraisal of the Holm entry that followed, Oud wrote: 'It is so much fresher and younger than the "petrified" designs of "those two elderly gentlemen" [i.e. Hood and Saarinen].'[47] Equating 'petrified' architecture with 'old', he coupled 'fresh' and 'young' with the diaphanous frame of Holm. In doing so he echoes a notion that pervades the cosmology of many cultures, that 'man is created with a body that was diaphanous, and . . . a counterforce tries to destroy it by progressive petrification.'[48] Another equally important connotation of the frame, besides its well-known analogy to the vertebrae, is the analogy to the psychical interior; modernism regarded the frame as 'the true self of architecture'. Freudians like Giedion called it 'the subconscious of architecture'.[49] Truth, they thought, could be measured in the exposing of the frame.

In terms of our subject of the skyscraper it is important to know that this moral-theological criterion determined the distinction between skyscrapers and true skyscrapers. The skyscraper might be nothing more than a very tall building, for unless it had a steel frame it was not a *true* skyscraper. The skyscraper's truth was located in its interior. All this has to do with the question of the first skyscraper, authoritatively solved decades ago in favour of the 1885 Chicago Branch Building of the New York Home Insurance Company, by

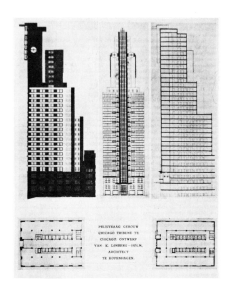

Fig. 19. Knut Lönberg Holm, Design for the Chicago Tribune Tower Competition, 1922 (from J.J.P. Oud, 'Bij een Deensch ontwerp voor de Chicago Tribune', De bouwwereld, XXXXIV, no. 45, 10 November 1923, p. 457).

Fig. 20. With the religious fervour of St. Thomas the Incredulous he poked his finger into the wounds of the dying building (from The Origin of the Skyscraper, Chicago, 1931).

46. J.J.P. Oud, 'Bij een Deensch ontwerp voor de Chicago Tribune', *Bouwkundig weekblad*, Nov. 10, 1923, p. 457.

47. Ibid., pp. 457–458.

48. Jacob Needlebaum, ed., *The Sword of Gnosis*, Harmondsworth, England, 1974, p. 148.

49. Sigfried Giedion, *Space, Time and Architecture*, op. cit., p. 24.

50. *The Origin of the Skyscraper, Report of the Committee Appointed by the Trustees of the Estate of Marshall Field for the Examination of the Structure of the Home Insurance Building*, Chicago, 1931. Tallmadge was chairman of the committee, which consisted of the architects Graham, Shaw, Schmidt, Reed and Rebori. See also: Thomas Eddy Tallmadge, *The Story of Architecture in America*, New York, 1936, pp. 180–181.
This quest for the first skyscraper is comparable to the somewhat naive optimism of the 'esprits simples' who thought that the origin of architecture could be revealed in the reconstruction of the primitive hut. See Joseph Rykwert, *On Adam's House in Paradise – The Idea of the Primitive Hut in Architectural History*, New York, 1972.

51. *The International Competition for a New Administrative Building for the Chicago Tribune 1922*, New York, 1980, p. 3.

William Le Baron Jenney, which is not very much a skyscraper from a visual point of view. From an ethical point of view, however, it was sufficiently true to be acknowledged as the nation's first.

Thus, with almost religious fervor Thomas Eddy Tallmadge in 1931 poked his finger into the wounds of the dying building to ascertain that in the lifeless remains lay what he could not see in the living thing: the first skyscraper (Figs. 20 & 21). [50]

With the strong emphasis on the frame the other aspects of the skyscraper – its awesome tallness, its towering presence, in brief, all the meanings that refer to sublimity and divinity – were neglected. The anecdotal history of cause and effect did not take these factors into consideration. The meaning of the word 'world' in the competition programme was aptly interpreted by Hood

*Fig. 21. St. Thomas the Incredulous (detail). Michelangelo da Caravaggio, 1598–1599.*

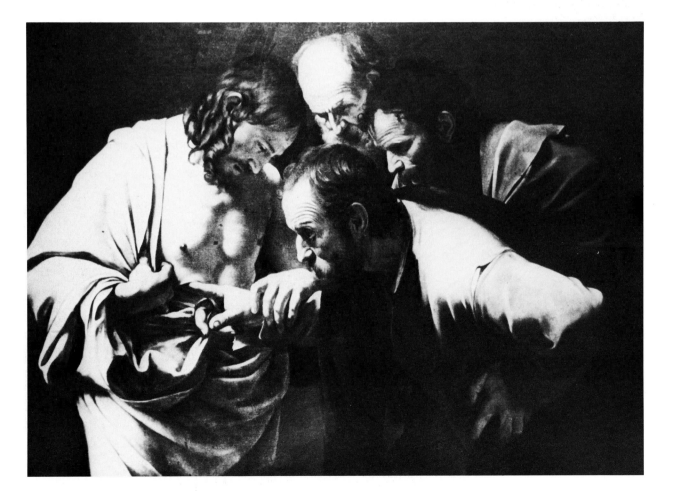

*Fig. 22. Eliel Saarinen, Design for the Chicago Tribune Tower Competition, 1922 (from* The International Competition for a New Administration Building for the Chicago Tribune, *Chicago, 1923, pl. 13).*

52. Dutch architect H.J.M. Walenkamp wrote in *De bouwwereld*, Vol. 23, No. 20, 1923, p. 1: 'He [Saarinen] had designed a tower, as the towers of the Old World ought to be.'

53. J.J.P. Oud's response was in the same vein (see note 44).
J. Huizinga, *Mensch en menigte in Amerika*, Haarlem, 1918; and J. Huizinga, *Amerika – levend en denkend*, Haarlem, 1926.

54. J. Huizinga, *Amerika – levend en denkend*, op. cit., pp. 173–174. See especially Roland van Zandt, *The Metaphysical Foundations of American History*, The Hague, 1959, p. 34: 'The deepest assumption of the American mind, ... is an assumption that is strangely at odds with itself and tries to deny its own reality. It is the grand assumption of philosophical dualism that there is division between theory and practice, mind and action, idea and fact. ...'

55. Ibid., p. 174.

and Howells, but it was Saarinen whose response was most accurate and intuitive (Fig. 22). Saarinen sensed that phrases like 'the building of a world-city in a new world' could refer to a different level of time.[51] Thus, 'world city' meant *cosmopolis, cosmic city*; and 'new world' was not simply the United States of America, but indeed a *new* world. Everything had to have a meaning both in terms of Creation (cosmogony) and in terms of evoking geological time ('longue durée').[52] Further, this world had to be understood and experienced in terms of radically different conceptions of time and space: as Heaven upon Earth, as the Pilgrim Fathers had foreseen, as the Heavenly Jerusalem.

On first consideration it may seem that such unworldly ideas are irrelevant in the context of the skyscraper, being a business structure and not a palace or a temple, the immediate result of commercial transactions. Indeed, business and businessmen dictated the programmes out of which skyscrapers grew, their form as well as their decoration. In many cases it can be said that the creative power of the businessmen was more responsible for final results than that of the architect or the contractor. Nevertheless, although it always seems to be purely functional, business – and in particular big business and still more so American big business – contains a highly paradoxical and metaphysical element, in which extreme oppositions alternate, in which the practical and the frivolous, efficiency and waste, fight for priority and surprisingly often coexist harmoniously. In the American skyscraper, poetic imagination and brutal materialism are perfectly welded, and it would be a mistake to think that these two aspects are in contradiction; they are not. Dreams, while rooted in business, are the cornerstones of the skyscraper.

This seeming contradiction of motives was noted by the Dutch historian Johan Huizinga, author of *The Waning of the Middle Ages*, who wrote about America and its culture in two small volumes, published in 1918 and 1926.[53] Huizinga wondered how it could be that Americans had such a religious, mysterious, and even atavistic nature, but at the same time placed enormous emphasis on the practical and not, as would have been logical, on the metaphysical. He was an exceptionally well-read man, with a thorough knowledge of American culture, including the writings of William James and John Dewey, whom he frequently quoted, and he had no difficulty understanding American pragmatism, behaviourism, and the like. But what he could not understand was the violence with which the pragmatic attitude was professed. In the last chapter of his *Amerika, levend en denkend* (America, Living and Thinking) of 1926, he elaborated on what he called 'the anti-metaphysical attitude of the American.' After quoting one of the more irreverent and striking passages from J.B. Watson's *Behaviorism* ('No one knows just how the idea of a soul or the supernatural started. It probably had its origin in the general laziness of mankind. etc.'), he went on to wonder whether America had returned to the eighteenth century.[54] He then quotes from the 'young American sociologist Elizabeth Ephrussi' to explain the mystique of American materialism:

It would be a mistake to think that America is materialistic because of its strong proliferation of big business, which is so manifestly embodied in its skyscrapers. The substance of this reality is materialistic, no doubt, but so vehemently, so insistently, so fervently materialistic, that the very ardor of the devotion vouchsaved to the material rises to a new kind of spirituality. The impulse, overreaching itself, becomes transcendent.[55]

Transcendent materialism is indeed a most dominant constituent of the skyscraper story. The two-sidedness of Sullivan did not seem contradictory to his American public, even though it was an unsurmountable obstacle to his European interpreters. So it was with Chicago architecture in general. The early or

*Fig. 23. Vignette of Saarinen's Chicago Tribune Tower design in a halo of the rising sun (from cover of Thomas Eddy Tallmadge,* The Story of Architecture in America, *New York, 1936).*

56. This historical cliché does not need explanation. A slight refinement could be the construction, in which 'Derivative and eclectic architecture very nearly reached its end in the Tribune, but the passion for classical and medieval styles was to survive for two more years before finally spending itself.' Carl Condit, *Chicago 1910–1929, Building, Planning and Urban Technology*, Chicago, 1973, p. 114.

57. Sheldon Cheney's *The New World Architecture*, New York, 1930, refers not to America, but to the modernist's Utopia in general. The book was not widely publicized on the European continent.

58. Thomas Eddy Tallmadge, *The Story of Architecture in America*, New York, 1936, p. 292.

59. Ibid., pp. 293–294.

60. Since Saarinen's victory as a loser, *The Western Architect* sported a new vignette of Saarinen's design against a backdrop of a rising sun (see Fig. 23).

'heroic' period was canonized for its uncompromising materialism, and was seen as clearly distinct from the following or 'decadent' period inaugurated by the Chicago Tribune Competition.[56]

But to such staunch chauvinists as Tallmadge, the dividing line was only a superficial one. Naturally, Tallmadge was too much of a mythographer not to make use of cause-and-effect anecdotism, and so his account of 'the progress of the New Architecture' is completely in line with contemporary American progressives like Mumford (1931), American modernists like Cheney (1930), and European modernists like Behrendt (1937) and Giedion (1941) (1938).[57]

But unlike them he does not emphasize rupture and opposition but continuity. Instead of contrasting Hood's design to Saarinen's in terms of old to new, eclectic to modern, as is generally done, he singled out the Saarinen entry as the most logical and natural continuation of the Chicago spirit in the modern era. In his view, the hard-core matter-of-factness of the 1880s and 1890s was subtly transformed into the metaphysics of the 1920s. Tallmadge quoted Louis Sullivan to the effect that the Saarinen tower was like a tree of stone and steel that had sprung forth from 'some titanic seed, planted deep in the earth,' most probably planted there by himself in the late 1880s.[58]

Tallmadge also stressed the importance of the process of creation. He loved to picture Saarinen 'tracing those fairylike outlines on some icy eyrie by the flashing lights of the Aurora Borealis or in a glacial grotto with myriad elves all about him, all busily engaged in making the thousands of curious little lines which gave his drawings a most uncanny feeling of enchanted inspiration and of superhuman assistance.'[59] In other words, where the beauty of the older Chicago architecture resided mainly 'in the simple force of need', the accent had imperceptibly shifted to enchanted inspiration and superhuman assistance. Even if the 'true skyscraper' could have been erected with only the help of simple technology and Midwestern self-reliance, the 'true tower' had to be resurrected from the 'reservoir of ideas', guided by divine mediation. The divine origin of Saarinen's 'true tower' is frequently suggested in drawings and vignettes in which the tower appears in a halo of the rays of the rising sun, as for example on the cover of Tallmadge's *The Story of Architecture in America* and as the new vignette of *The Western Architect* (Fig. 23).[60]

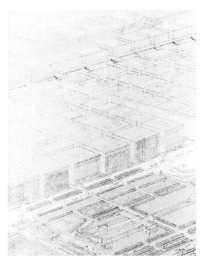

*Fig. 24 (right). Frank Helmle and Harvey Wiley Corbett, Reconstruction of the Temple of King Solomon; rendering by Hugh Ferriss, 1925 (from* Pencil Points, *VI, November 1925, p. 79).*

*Fig. 25 (extreme right). The Plan of Chicago, 1909. Proposed Boulevard and Park Way on Michigan Avenue and Pine Street. Rendering by Chris U. Bagge (detail). 'The chaotic primeval city with its irregular skyline is razed as if by a gigantic lawn-mower; the private skyscrapers are castrated and reduced to, and consequently represented by, a single, collective, artificial mountain' (see figs. 24–28) (from John Zukowsky, et al.,* The Plan of Chicago, 1909–1979, *Chicago, 1979, pl. 114).*

61. 'Dr. John Wesley Kelchner's Restoration of King Solomon's Temple and Citadel, Helmle & Corbett, Architects', *Pencil Points*, Vol. 6, no. 11, 1925, pp. 69–86.

62. The idea of linking Ferriss's drawings to those of John Martin is not new. See Oechslin, *Skyscraper und Amerikanismus*, op. cit., n. 12, pp. 6–7.

63. Mircea Eliade, *The Sacred and the Profane*, New York, 1961, pp. 20ff.

64. Eliel Saarinen, 'Project for Lakefront Development of the City of Chicago', *The American Architect and the Architectural Review*, 134, 1923, pp. 487–514. See also Manfredo Tafuri, 'La montagna disincantata – Il grattacielo e la city', *La città Americana dalla Guerra Civile al New Deal*, Rome, Bari, 1973, p. 453; and Mario Manieri-Elia, 'Trois architectes européens en Amérique: Eliel Saarinen, Mendelsohn, Neutra', *Archithese*, 17, 1976, *Metropolis* I, pp. 16–17. Eliel Saarinen, *The City, Its Growth, Its Decay, Its Future*, New York, 1943, p. 193.

65. Thomas Adams, *Regional Plan of New York and its Environs*, Vol. 2, *The Building of the City*, New York, 1931, pp. 384–385 (Swales), p. 387 (Price).

66. Athanasius Kircher, *Turris Babel*, op. cit. Kircher followed the descriptions of Strabo and Herodotus.

Saarinen was not the only one who was superhumanly assisted in recreating a monumental architecture. A few years later, in 1925, Frank Helmle and Harvey Wiley Corbett were asked to carry out the reconstruction of the temple and citadel of King Solomon, according to the instructions of a certain John Wesley Kelchner, 'who, inspired by religious zeal, has made the reconstruction of the Temple his chief object in life for over thirty years' (Fig. 24).[61] As was also the case with the well-known multitowered Monument to the Republic by Erastus Salisbury Field of 1876 (see p. 50, Fig. 18), the project was meant to add luster to that celebration of American achievement, the Philadelphia Exhibition of 1926. Once more it was the Babylonian example that was taken up by Kelchner's architects Helmle and Corbett in their design for the forecourt of the Temple of Solomon, this time in a reconstruction of John Martin's Belshazzar's Feast (1821)[62] (see p. 55, Figs. 24 & 25).

Whereas the 'true skyscraper' was merely a building of non-descript appearance in a non-defined location in the chaos of the primeval commercial city, the 'true tower' was destined to be a conspicuous beacon, to define space and to bring order into chaos. As such it was the perfect *axis mundi*.[63] In the 1909 Chicago Plan, the chaotic primeval city with its irregular skyline is razed as if by a gigantic lawn mower (Fig. 25): the private skyscrapers are castrated and reduced to, and consequently represented by, a single, collective, artificial mountain. The Saarinen design is the exact fulfillment of that idea, as it was actually proposed in his plan of 1923 for the Chicago Lakefront (Fig. 26).[64] Francis Swales and, to a lesser degree, Chester Price, followed Saarinen's concept in their recreation of City Hall Square for the Committee of the Regional Plan for New York City in 1931.[65] Swales's sketch of the 'proposed building for the Civic Center' is certainly dependent on the Lakefront Grant Hotel (Fig. 27), but more importantly, it tries to amalgamate the Nemrod-Babel archetype into a crushing Leviathan, composed of the traditional eight zones.[66]

Fig. 26 (below). Eliel Saarinen, Sketch for Tower,
Chicago Lake Front Plan, 1923. '... the predomi-
nating spirit is one of lightness, an upreaching and
aspiring strength' (from Albert Christ-Janer, Eliel
Saarinen, Finnish-American Architect and Educator, Chicago/London, 1979, p. 50, pl. 59).

Fig. 27 (right). Francis S. Swales, 'A Monumental
Building is Proposed as the Dominant Feature of
The Civic Center' (from Thomas Adams, et al.,
Regional Plan of New York and Its Environs, Vol.
II, The Building of The City, New York, 1931, p.
384).

*Fig. 28a. 'Bologna at the time of Dante − a city of early skyscrapers' (from Francis S. Swales, 'The Architect and the Grand Plan', Pencil Points, II, March 1931, p. 167).*

*Fig. 28b. 'Bologna ai tempi che vi soggiornò Dante' (postcard; Italian, early 20th century).*

*Fig. 29. Francis S. Swales, 'Upper Manhattan from University Heights, A Conception of the Future' (from Thomas Adams, et al., Regional Plan of New York and Its Environs, Vol. II, The Building of The City, New York, 1931, p. 25).*

Swales presented himself as a man enamoured of the grandeur of the Ancients. In his 1931 article 'The Architect and the Grand Plan', he praised the great mythic and historical examples, from 'the unified or monumental or civic plan, beginning in Egypt, extending to Babylon, Greece, Carthage, Rome . . . to Bologna at the time of Dante, a city of early skyscrapers'[67] and strongly advocated these examples to those engaged in reorganizing the chaotic American cities (Fig. 28).

The closest Swales ever got to his ideal was probably in his design for Upper Manhattan – 'A Conception of the Future', which features a central pyramidal (Fig. 29) monument, centaph, or temple, obviously dependent on examples from Boullée and Ledoux, but more importantly inspired by the *Spectacula Babylonica* from Fischer von Erlach's *Entwurff einer historischen Architectur* of 1721 (Fig. 30). Fischer, once called the 'father of modern art history', likewise influenced European planners on the 'grand scale', like Bruno Taut in his *Stadtkrone* of 1919 (Fig. 31).[68] Just as Kircher and Fischer von Erlach entertained a common fascination for the great buildings of the golden age of architecture and even frequented the same circles (they participated in

*Fig. 30. Johann Bernhard Fischer von Erlach, 'Spectacula Babilonica' (from* Entwurff einer historischen Architectur, *Vienna, 1721, p. 16, plate III).*

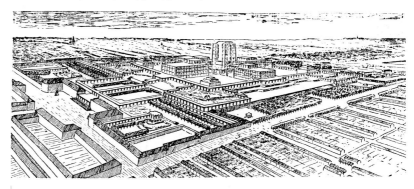

*Fig. 31. Bruno Taut, 'Die Stadtkrone' (from* Die Stadtkrone, *Jena, 1919).*

67. Francis Swales, 'The Architect and the Grand Plan – An Important Discussion of a Vital Topic', *Pencil Points*, Vol. 2, no. 3, March 1931, pp. 166–177. Passus quoted: pp. 167–174.

68. David Watkin, *The Rise of Architectural History*, London, 1980, p. 1. Bruno Taut, *Die Stadtkrone*, Jena, 1919. Although he did not mention Fischer von Erlach, the source appears to be quite evident.

Fig. 32. 'An alternative design for a civic center building with ample setbacks and courts.' The drawing shows McKim, Mead & White's Municipal Building (New York, 1913) being dwarfed by its own reflection, aggrandized to Babylonic proportions in the proposed civic center by Chester B. Price in collaboration with Thomas Adams (from Thomas Adams, et al., Regional Plan of New York and Its Environs, Vol. II, The Building of The City, New York, 1931, p. 387).

69. Hans Aurenhammer, J.B. Fischer von Erlach, London, 1973, pp. 19–20, and Harald Keller, Johann Bernhard Fischer von Erlach, Entwurff einer historischen Architectur, Dortmund, 1978 (Vienna, 1721[1]), n.p. ('Nachwort').

70. Adolf Behne, 'Wiedergeburt der Baukunst', in: Taut, Die Stadtkrone, op. cit., p. 1160.

71. Taut, Die Stadtkrone, op. cit., p. 93, figs. 60–61.

the cultural life around Queen Christina of Sweden), architectural thinkers like Bruno Taut found in Irving Pond, Claude Bragdon, and, to a lesser degree, Louis Sullivan, coeval spirits in the United States.[69] In all their writings they stressed the importance of continuity rather than change, 'the cosmic being opposed to the anecdotal', as Adolf Behne put it in his contribution to Taut's book.[70]

It was the cosmic inspiration of a civilization to crown its 'world cities' with one large tower or a cluster of towers which Taut illustrated with forty examples from the past and several from contemporary America, including the McKim, Mead and White Municipal Building of New York and the southern tip of the Manhattan skyline (Fig. 32).[71] It is in this light that what are usually interpreted as predictions or images of the future can now be seen as symptoms of an architectural continuum, the same vision that one finds in the city of towers described by Washington Irving or in the image of a skyscrapered Manhattan described by Edgar Allen Poe in 1849. Poe's story takes place

*Fig. 33. Thomas Nast, Clustered skyscrapers on the tip of Manhattan, cartoon for* Harper's Weekly, *1881 (from Charles Lockwood,* Manhattan Moves Uptown, *Boston, 1976, p. 277).*

72. Edgar Allen Poe, 'Mellonta Tauta', *Tales*, III, New York, 1914, p. 341, originally published in *Godey's Lady's Book*, February 1849. It was Antoine Bodar who directed my attention to the important passage.

73. From a reproduction in: Charles Lockwood, *Manhattan Moves Uptown*, Boston, 1976, p. 277. The cartoon was probably made a year earlier, in 1880. See William Bonner, *New York, The World's Metropolis*, New York, 1924, and Albert Bigelow Paine, *Th. Nast, His Period and His Pictures*, Princeton, 1904, p. 444.

74. See note 50.

after the year 2050, the year the New York area is destroyed by an earthquake. Archaeologists find that nine-tenths of Manhattan was covered with churches, or churchlike buildings. It explains that the 'Knickerbocker Tribe' was 'by no means uncivilized':

It is related of them that they were ... oddly afflicted with a monomania for building what, in the ancient Amriccan, was denominated 'churches' – a kind of pagoda instituted for the worship of two idols that went by the names of Wealth and Fashion. [72]

Similarly, when Tom Nast made his 'visionary' print of the clustered skyscrapers on the tip of Manhattan in 1881, it was probably less visionary than we are inclined to think (Fig. 33). [73] The question of the first skyscraper, so eighteenth-century-like in character, now becomes less and less relevant. [74] So does the overpowering emphasis on Yankee technology and on the skyscraper as a constructional invention.

*Fig. 34. 'Urbs Turrita' (from Athanasius Kircher,* Mundus Subterraneus of De onderaardse wereld, *Amsterdam, 1682, lib. VIII, p. 29).*

By now I have made it sufficiently clear that the skyscraper was not an invention, and certainly not an exclusively technological one. The 'eternal return' of the tower was not dependent on mere technology. Whoever does not believe this has only to look back to the late 1950s and early 1960s, when that other perennial dream, the voyage to the moon, was finally realized with technological means hardly more sophisticated than the bullet Jules Verne had imagined for his moonshot. Even in the years during which we watched on television those poor, lame astronauts in their cramped iron lung, shot a mere 240,000 miles from the earth, we were shocked by the primitiveness of the operation.

A last point I want to stress is the position of the idea of the future within the perennial dream. Hegel was right to say that the future could never be a real future because it always had to be at least part of the present. In other words, the future can only be imagined in the terms of either the present or, however paradoxical, the past. The farthest one can get if one *believes* in the future is to visualize it with the help of pre-future images. In this sense the skyscraper realized two functions: it signified an optimistic belief in the future, and it did so with the help of a familiar significant image. In this way, belief in the future was transformed into confidence in the future. Cesar Pelli has said in a recent interview that the mainspring of present skyscraper building is 'to express a strong confidence in the future'.[75] Apparently, opinion has not changed over the last hundred years; the *Real Estate Record and Building Guide* of November 1875 states, in reaction to the appearance of two well-known proto-skyscrapers: 'Look at the overgrown and oppressive Western Union and Tribune and Equitable buildings − types of unbounded confidence in our future, without regard to our present ability to pay.'[76] This proves that skyscrapers are built especially in times of economic depressions: 1875, 1929, 1982. They seem to serve as magic totems to ward off the evil turn of the economy.

75. Jan Rutten and Hans Wijnant, 'Wolkenkrabbers zijn uitdrukking van vertrouwen in de toekomst' (Skyscrapers are the Expression of Confidence in the Future), an interview with Cesar Pelli, *Bouw*, Vol. 30, no. 11, 1983, special issue, *Wolkenkrabbers in New York*, p. 25.
Nothing could illustrate this attitude better than the feverish building activity in Hong Kong, continuing with unyielding faith in the future even with the end of the crown colony in sight. For a little less than a billion dollars the Hong Kong and Shanghai Bank has commissioned the British architect Norman Foster to build a skyscraper destined to become Hong Kong's tallest building for its headquarters (Peter Brusse, *De Volkskrant*, 15 December 1984, Saturday Supplement, p. 1; Colin Amery & David Dodwell, 'Monument to Money', *Financial Times*, April 5, 1986, weekend F.T., p. 1).

76. *Real Estate Board and Builders' Guide*, Vol. 16, no. 402, November 27, 1875, p. 776.

77. Athanasius Kircher, *Mundus Subterraneus of De onderaardse Weereld*, Amsterdam, 1682, book 8, p. 29.

*Fig. 35. Hugh Stubbins & Associates, CitiCorp Building, New York, 1977.*

This reference to totemism brings us to a wonderful gem from Kircher's collection of rarities, the *Mundus Subterraneus*, or *De onderaardse weereld*, of 1682. In this most curious book, Kircher exhibits pages profusely illustrated with intriguing images engraved on amber amulets and dug out of the Inner World, sometimes by innocent passers-by, sometimes by official prospectors, and brought to the attention of the author. The Inner World was considered to be the apocalyptic vault of creation, the place where all mysteries were revealed. On the wondrous ambers were messages containing clues to age-old problems as well as predictions of important things to come. One of Kircher's ambers contains the image of an Urbs Turrita, a towered city (Fig. 34). [77] Looking at this enigmatic picture, can anybody deny that the Citicorp Building was prognosticated a long, long time ago? (Fig. 35).

'It is a far cry from the ziggurat architecture of the Plains of Shinar to the setback skyscrapers of New York, though in some respects there is a striking similarity.
Even if you went to Nineveh and Tyre for your new and 'modernistic' architecture, and there are those who do so, you are not yet at the root of the matter, for the primitive efforts of man in architecture lie so far back in the experience of the race that recorded history does not note them and the dim haze of antiquity leaves them shrouded in the mists of time.' – CASS GILBERT, Reminiscences and Addresses, New York, 1935, p. 50.

'Psyche and the Pskyscraper.
If you are a philosopher you can do this thing: you can go to the top of a high building, look down upon your fellow men 300 feet below, and despise them as insects. ... The philosopher gazes into the infinite heavens above him, and allows his soul to expand in the influence of his new view. He feels that he is the heir to Eternity and the child of Time. ... And when the philosopher takes the elevator down, his mind is broader, his heart is at peace, and his conception of the cosmogony of creation is as wide as the buckle of Orion's summer belt.' – JOHN O'HENRY. [1]

# APOKATASTASIS OR THE RETURN OF THE SKYSCRAPER*

IT HAS BEEN the habit of architectural historians to begin the history of architecture at the beginning. And although the logic of the statement seems to pass the borders of tolerable banality, the problems generated by this harmless intention have proven to be manifold. Most questions could be roughly classified into three groups: 1) what should be understood as architecture?; 2) what is history?; and 3) how shall we deal with the concept of time? Yet, supposing that these questions could be adequately answered, the object of study can in quite a few cases generously avoid them. The ways to define the art of building are wildly diverse and neither architecture nor its theorists have taken them much into consideration. History then, as a way to reconstruct the past with the help of its dominant time axis, is a discipline designed to articulate change rather than permanence, which nevertheless is the essence of architecture.

It would be interesting to take some distance from the matter and reflect upon the occasionally suggested comparison between the Tower of Babel and the American skyscraper.

Joseph August Lux, for example, German critic and architectural writer, wrote in the introduction to his *Ingenieur-Ästhetik* (München, 1910), that modern-times technology was nothing but the realization of ancient dreams and visions:

In der Technik geschieht nichts, was nicht vorher schon als Traum, als Dichtung, als Utopie dagewesen ist. 'Wenn ich ein Vöglein wär ...', singt die alte Sehnsucht. Zu Babel wurde ein Turm gebaut, den man nicht fertig zu bringen vermochte. Die Menschheit träumt seither von dem übermenschlichen des babylonischen Turmes. Aber die Techniker von heute verwirklichten diesen Traum und bauten Wolkenkratzer, gegen die die höchsten Türme der Erde zwerghaft aussahen. [2]

Skyscrapers, in other words, were the fulfilment of the Babylonian promise; the realization of both its technical enigma and its utopian-cosmopolitan objective. The following essay tries to reconnoiter the possible extents of this proposition.

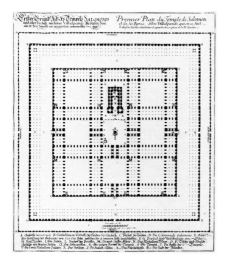

Fig. 1. Johann Bernhard Fischer von Erlach, Plan of the Temple of Jerusalem after Villalpando (from Entwurff einer historischen Architectur, *Vienna, 1721, p. 10, plate 1).*

*. Apokatastasis is, like the Eternal Return, a term to indicate the general repetition of things in the course of time. Jorge Luis Borges provided the term, originally derivative from the Acts of the Apostles, III, 21, in his *Historia de la Eternidad* (1936). In this case the Dutch translation, *Geschiedenis van de Eeuwigheid*, Amsterdam, 1985, p. 82, was used. See also: Mircea Eliade, *Le Mythe de l'Éternel Retour, Archetypes et Répétition*, Paris, 1949.

The present essay is a revised version of a paper presented at a conference devoted to Athanasius Kircher and the Collegio Romano (Athanasius Kircher e il Museo del Collegio Romano tra Wunderkammer e Museo Scientifico), Rome, Biblioteca Nazionale Centrale, May 8, 1985. The conference was endowed and organized by the following institutions: Ministero per i Beni Culturali e Ambientali, II Università di Roma, 'Tor Vergata', Dipartimento di Ingegneria Civile e Edile, and II Università degli Studi di Roma, 'La Sapienza', Facoltà di Scienze Matematiche, Fisiche e Naturali.

The conference papers were published in: Maristella Casciato, Maria Grazia Iansiello, Maria Vitale, eds., *Enciclopedismo in Roma Barocca, Athanasius Kircher e il Museo del Collegio Romano tra Wunderkammer e museo scientifico*, Venezia, 1986. The present essay appeared under the same title but in a slightly different version on pp. 176–194.

1. John O'Henry, 'Psyche and the Pskyscraper' (1910), *The Complete Works of O'Henry*, Garden City, New York, 1953, p. 1564/5.

2. Joseph Aug. Lux, *Ingenieur-Ästhetik*, München, 1910, p. 1.

3. David Watkin, *The Rise of Architectural History*, London, 1980, p. 1.
It must be borne in mind that Fischer entertained an active relationship with Giovanni Pietro Bellori, whose collection of coins he had studied for the purpose of reconstructing lost architecture. The Abbot Bellori was well at home at the court of Queen Christina, and so was Father Athanasius Kircher.

## Apokatastasis

Johann Bernhard Fischer von Erlach has been held to be the first to have written a history of architecture.[3] But his *Entwurff einer historischen Architectur* of 1721 is no history, in the sense that it deals with architecture historically. Fischer certainly had collected his examples of great architecture from the available sources of the past – the Greek and Roman travellers, chroniclers, and historians of antiquity – but the order in which he brought them together was not the order of time: his order was the hierarchy of excellence. The great example with which the book opens is the Temple of Jerusalem, not the first building of mankind but the most perfect one (Fig. 1).[4] The fact that the Temple was the only building on earth designed and ordained by God, as mediated through Solomon and, later, through Ezekiel, made it not merely the model of all architecture but architecture itself.

Instead of defining architecture verbally in order to make a clean beginning with its intended history, Fischer simply prefaced his first book with the Temple of Jerusalem and thus defined his subject.[5]

The power of the Temple, in addition to its divine origin, lies in its didactic qualities – its capacity to show and to explain the cosmos.[6] Dimensions and plan were understood as the material with which order was made out of chaos and, consequently, the perfect design could be approximated as close as was theoretically possible. The perfect square of the plan lived as the type and model for all other near-perfect square plans.[7]

The didactic qualities of the Temple were shared by other types and models of architecture which comprise what is commonly known as the Seven Wonders of the World. Marcello Fagiolo has pointed out, following the interpretation of Gregory of Nazianzus, that the wonders were not so much of the 'world' but rather of 'life' itself.[8]

The walls of Babylon became '*the* wall', the colossus of Rhodos '*the* statue', the hanging gardens of Queen Semiramis '*the* gardens' and so on. Interpreted in this way the marvels could reach such a level of abstraction as to serve as the essential elements of any design. The city of Babylon then was reduced to the general principles that served as the matrix of all ideal cities to follow.

Fischer von Erlach had based his reconstructions of the great works of antiquity on serious source material and in that respect he behaved as a trustworthy antiquarian, but at the same time he made it appear as if these would be situated in his present-day environment. The circular temple of Nineveh, reconstructed on the basis of a coin from the collection of the Roman antiquarian Giovanni Pietro Bellori, is drawn into a square formed by an ensemble of contemporary buildings. The idea, it seems, was to provide a convincing setting for the marvel which was otherwise vaguely located, in time as well as in place.

It was admittedly not a marvel in the proper sense, but was introduced into the first book for reasons that it would 'please the eyes of the cognoscenti'.[9] Whereas at first glance the combination of ancient and modern architecture seems an insult to our ideas of historical correctness, it is a perfectly normal way of representation for those who want to express the timelessness of the type, which in this case is the circular plan of a temple, apparently dedicated to the sun, inscribed in a perfect square, symbolizing the cosmic duality of heaven and earth, such as is known through the wide varieties of mandalas (Fig. 2; cf. Fig. 3).[10]

In a similar way the Spectacula Babylonica (Fig. 4) shows an unlikely juxtaposition of seventeenth-century garden design with an archeological correctness that, surprisingly enough, equals the findings of an early twentieth-century archeologist like Robert Koldewey.[11]

Although the time of archeological positivism was still to come, Fischer was

*Fig. 2. Mandala Vasudhara; Nepal AD 1504; British Museum, London (from Arnold Toynbee,* A Study of History, *New York, 1972, plate 5).*

For the present dealing with ideas, archetypes, types and models, Bellori's authoritative neo-platonic treatise 'L'Idea del Pittore, Dello Scultore e Dell'Architetto, Scelta Dalle Bellezze Naturali Superiore Alla Natura', being the introduction to *Le Vite de' Pittori, Scultori et Architetti Moderni*, Roma, 1672, is naturally of the greatest importance. For the concept itself, see the classic study of Erwin Panofsky, *Idea, A Concept in Art Theory* (1924), New York, 1968. The role played by Athanasius Kircher in the history of architecture has not yet been seriously considered.

4. René Taylor, 'Architecture and Magic, Considerations on the Idea of the Escorial', *Essays in the History of Architecture Presented to Rudolf Wittkower*, London, 1976, p. 90; Joseph Rykwert, *On Adam's House in Paradise, The Idea of the Primitive Hut in Architectural History*, New York, 1972, p. 120; Robert Jan van Pelt, *Tempel van de Wereld, de Kosmische Symboliek van de Tempel van Salomo*, Utrecht, 1984, pp. 42ff.

5. The authoritative power of Solomon's Temple apparently was so great that even the so-called 'Brazen Sea', the legendary vessel standing in the forecourt of the Temple as described in the Book of *Kings*, 7: 23–26, could act as a pictorial preface to Fischer's fifth book of the *Entwurff*, titled 'Divers Vases Antiques, Aegyptiens, Grecs, Romains & Modernes', the same way the Temple itself had figured in the first book on architecture.

6. Van Pelt, op. cit., p. 59ff.

7. Taylor, op. cit., p. 81.

8. Marcello Fagiolo, 'Le Meravigle e il Meraviglioso', *Psicon*, III, 7, 1976, p. 3/4.

fully aware of his own free handling of his material. He therefore stated unambiguously that in most cases he had only vague indications at his disposal and that it was beyond his knowledge to give precise representation of details such as ornament, but that this should not discourage the attentive reader, since the main thing that mattered in architectural study were the general principles – 'Dass aber dennoch in der Bau-Kunst, aller Veränderung ungeachtet, gewisse allgemeine Grund-Sätze sind, welche ohne offenbahren Übelstand nicht können vergessen werden'.[12]

Fischer's notion of what should be seen as historical was a combination of what belonged to the past and what was not affected by the course of time. The highest quality a work of art, and in a single case a work of nature, could have was its quality of eternity. Those works that had this quality in common were consequently arranged not in the ineffective chronological order, but as types and models, demonstrating their respective typological elements: the square, circular and rectangular plans; the tower; the pyramid; the statue; the tomb; and the temple. They were arranged in the comparative manner, irrespective of time and place, a practice common in academic educational circles and later made famous by J.N.L. Durand in his *Recueil et parallèle des édifices de tout genre, anciens et modernes, remarquables par leur beauté, par leur grandeur ou par leur singularité* of 1800 (Fig. 3; cf. Fig. 2).

These types of architecture (in this I am following the academic use of the terms archetype, type and model, as for example in the case of the Tower of Babel, where the cosmic mountain is the archetype, the Babylonic Tower the type, and any other tower which could be copied literally the model[13]) have played a role in cultural history which far outweighed their relevance to architecture alone.

The Tower of Babel and the Ark of Noah represented not only the beginnings of that which Christopher Wren in his manuscript *Discourse on Architecture*[14] called 'civic' and 'naval' architecture respectively, but also the beginnings of civilization (Fig. 5; cf. Fig. 4).

*Fig. 3. 'Tombeaux Romains' (from J.N.L. Durand,* Recueil et Parallèle des édifices de tout genre, anciens et modernes, etc., *Paris, 1800, plate 20).*
*Perfect squares and circles as ideal plans for the architecture of eternity.*

*Fig. 4. Johann Bernhard Fischer von Erlach, 'Spectacula Babylonica' (from* Entwurff einer historischen Architectur, *Vienna, 1721, p. 16, plate III). Fischer's print was based on the 'Babilonia Muris' in Kircher's* Turris Babel *(see Fig. 6).*

*Fig. 5. 'The City of Babylon', from Christopher Wren,* Discourse on Architecture, in: Parentalia *etc., London, 1750. This plate which C. Decker originally made for Kircher's* Turris Babel *had been recycled for this posthumous publication of Wren's* Discourse. *Decker's signature had been erased and the round tower had been replaced by a square-based one. This latter interpretation followed the description Herodotus had given in the* Histories, *Book 1, p. 181.*

9. Fischer von Erlach, *Entwurff einer historischen Architectur*, Vienna 1721, p. 36 and 37.

10. The mandala has seemingly been reintroduced by Carl Gustav Jung as an interplay between circle and square denoting the cosmos in the mid-twentieth century, but in the architecture and architectural theory of the Western world it has always been an integral part. See for example Hermann Kern, 'Abbild der Welt und heiliger Bezirk. Labyrinthstädte', *Daidalos*, 15 März 1982, 2, pp. 10–25.

11. Robert Koldewey, *Das Wiedererstehende Babylon*, Leipzig, 1925; Walter Andrae, *Babylon. Die versunkene Weltstadt und ihr Ausgräber Robert Koldewey*, Berlin, 1952.

12. Fischer von Erlach, op. cit., 'Vorrede', p. 4a.

13. Mircea Eliade, *Images et Symboles, Essais sur le Symbolisme Magico-Religieux*, Paris, 1952, pp. 54ff. Anthony Vidler, 'The Idea of Type: The Transformation of the Academic Ideal', *Oppositions*, Spring 1977, 8, pp. 95–115.

14. 'Discourse on Architecture. By Sr. C.W.', *Parentalia, or the Memoirs of the Family of the Wrens*; viz. of Sir Christopher Wren (etc.), compiled by his son Christopher; now published by his grandson, Stephen Wren, London, 1750 (facsimile reprint, 1965), pp. 1–3.

15. Athanasius Kircher, *Turris Babel, sive Archontologia*, Amsterdam, 1679.

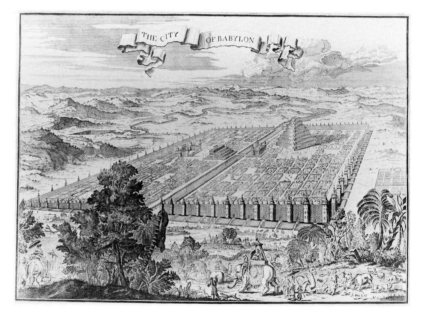

The inviting possibilities of establishing clean-cut demarcations in the history of creation were enthusiastically accepted by synthetic thinkers and in particular by the Jesuit syncretist Athanasius Kircher, who saw an excellent opportunity to weave his pan-Christian construct of micro- and macro-cosm upon those patterns.

Kircher, being an inventive linguist, titled and sub-titled his work on the Tower of Babel: *Turris Babel, sive Archontologia: a study into the origins of existence.* [15]

It has been noted before that our studies of the history and culture of the New World offered strong parallels with those of the beginnings of the Old World. John Locke's famous dictum that 'In the beginning all the world was America' clearly illustrated the assumption that America offered a contemporary look into the creation of the world under almost laboratory conditions: he who studies America, studies Genesis! [16]

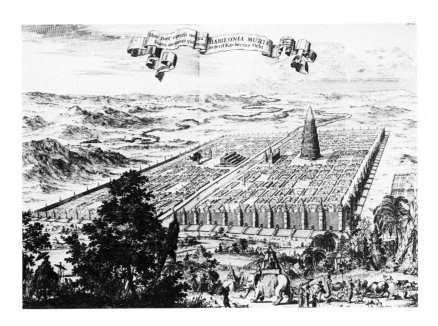

Fig. 6. 'Haec ruet eversis nunqua Babilonia Muris',
C. Decker, inv. et fec. (from Athanasius Kircher,
Turris Babel, *Amsterdam, 1679, p. 52) (compare
figures 4 and 10)*.

16. R.W.B. Lewis, *The American Adam, Innocence, Tragedy, and Tradition in the Nineteenth
Century*, Chicago/London, 1975, p. 42.

17. Washington Irving, *A History of New York
from the Beginning of the World to the End of the
Dutch Dynasty, ... by Diedrich Knickerbocker*,
London, 1900 (1809), p. 6.

18. Ibid., p. 14.

19. Ernest Lee Tuveson, *Redeemer Nation − The
Idea of America's Millennial Role*, Chicago/
London, 1968, ch. IV and more in particular pp.
94−97. See also below, note 42.

20. A selection of descriptions of famous buildings:
Graybar Building: 'These are signs that the architecture of these huge towers of Babel will more and
more symbolize the energy responsible for their existence, and for the growth, prosperity, and enterprise
of the time in which we live.' S.J. Vickers, 'The
Graybar Building', *Architectural Record*, LXII,
1927, p. 189; Singer Building: 'Thousands of Trav-
elers came to New York to see this modern "Tower
of Babel".' W. Parker Chase, *New York − The
Wonder City*, New York, 1932, p. 184; Flatiron
Building: 'In 1902, the Flatiron Building, the first
real skyscraper in the world since the days of Babylon, rose on Twenty-third Street ... .' Charles A.
Beard & Mary R. Beard, *The Rise of American
Civilization*, London, 1949, Vol. II, p. 818; The
Woolworth Building: 'Der moderne Thurm zu
Babel. Das Wunder von Gestern wird zum Selbst-
verständlichen von Heute.' *New York Staatszeitung*,
Sonntagsblatt, 23 Juni, 1912, Heinrich Reinhold
Hirsch, 'Der Moderne Thurm zu Babel'. Architect
Harvey Wiley Corbett was co-author with W.K. Ol-
tar-Jevsky of *Contemporary Babylon*, New York,
1933. Hugh Ferriss, *Metropolis of Tomorrow*, New
York, 1929, was not very different from a modern-
times Babylon. Ferriss wrote: 'It is not a little dis-
turbingly reminiscent of the Tower of Babel' (p. 62).

It is therefore perfectly understandable that the American skyscraper was so
often related to the Tower of Babel. Both represented the markings of metropolitan cultures, constituted not by one, but by many different peoples with
just as many different languages, who had been brought together, indeed unified, by the common ambition, namely to found Paradise on Earth.
Washington Irving, alias Diedrich Knickerbocker, conceived his *History of
New York* (1809) as 'from the Beginning of the World to the End of the
Dutch Dynasty', and accordingly he began with 'Cosmogony or Creation of
the World'. [17] The role Noah and his offspring had played in the founding of
Babylon was transferred to America by having Noah himself discover the bib-
lically non-existent continent. Irving had for that reason called in the help of
two learned Frenchmen, Marc Lescarbot and the Jesuit Charlevoix, who apparently were the first to have felt the necessity to cover up the omission of
Genesis 10:

Who can seriously believe that Noah and his descendants knew less than we do, and the
builder and pilot of the greatest ship that ever was should be ignorant of the art of sail-
ing on the ocean? Therefore they did sail on the ocean; therefore they sailed to
America; therefore America was discovered by Noah! [18]

Although written in a jesting fashion, poking fun at bigotry and all too literal
readings of the Scripture, Knickerbocker's text nevertheless reflects an attitude
of manifest destiny that pervaded Anglo-American utopian expectations from
the late seventeenth century on to our present day. Dualistic as it was, this
awareness of America's role as a fulfilment of apocalyptic prophecies ran two
courses: a 'moral' one, professing strict adherence to the Millennial doctrine;
and a 'natural', or worldly one, which was based upon the conviction that
finally the empire of civilization would have to settle in the New World on its
apparent course westward. In this latter 'translatio imperii', Babylon, the city
of cities, played its role as forerunner, or as St. Augustine wrote, as 'the first
Rome', marking the beginning of the worldly cosmopolis, of which Rome was
the splendid intermediary and the American metropolis its logical finaliza-
tion. [19] In this vein it became habitual to describe the American metropolis, in
casu New York, in Babylonic terms (Fig. 17). [20]

*Fig. 7. '"Building a Babylon" from a drypoint by Martin Lewis' (from* Pencil Points, *October 1930).*

*Fig. 8. 'Modern Ziggurats'. – For his* Metropolis of Tomorrow *architectural draughtsman Hugh Ferriss used the Babylonian example throughout. Terraces became 'hanging gardens' and set-back skyscrapers were 'ziggurats'. Whether Ferriss was familiar with the illustrations of Kircher's* Turris Babel *remains to be seen; the elephants are there alright. (from Hugh Ferriss,* The Metropolis of Tomorrow, New York, *1929, p. 98, Fig. 99).*

In his *Metropolis of Tomorrow* architectural draughtsman Hugh Ferriss had brought together, between 1923 and 1929, a collection of Babylonian compositions with which he had intended to shape the city of the future (Fig. 8). [21] Encouraged by the New York Zoning Law of 1916 he had designed monumental groups of interlocking multi-levelled towers and hanging gardens suggesting the forms of the Rockefeller Center, 'The New Babylon' of the 1930s. [22] In harmony with the intentions the set-back skyscrapers that had emerged from under the Babylonian moulds were called 'ziggurats' (literally: 'cosmic mountains'). [23] Consequently these 'ziggurats' were decorated with Assyrian-Babylonian motives, such as for example the French Building (1927: Fred. French & H. Douglas Ives) (Fig. 9); even the city as a whole came alluringly close to being a replica of the original City of Marvels (Fig. 15). Bird's-eye views of both cities (Figs. 6 & 10) reveal their similarities. The picture C. Decker drew for Athanasius Kircher's *Turris Babel* (Fig. 6) represented Babylon in its official quality as world wonder, contained within its legendary walls: 'Babylonia Muris'. The plan is a square divided into a rectangular grid in which space is reserved, in multiples of rectangles, to house its most important monuments. The Hanging Gardens and the Tower fulfil their tasks as city park and civic centre, acting as individual marvels within the collective marvel of its walls. The Tower is represented in a completed state, as is regularly done in Kircher's work, indicating a corrective implementation, suggesting sympathetic admiration for its builders. Contrary to the usual representations the city is not embraced by the Euphrates and the Tigris, but rather divided by one river, filling the surrounding moat with its waters. To the right a miniature reflection of itself is represented as a formal garden; a botanic test tube of cosmopolitanism. [24]

Kircher and his Netherlandish illustrators refrained from depicting Babylon in its habitual state of decomposition, but preferred its preceding phase of quiet magnificence, enabling it to perform its duties as urbanistic paradigm, rather than as an admonition to hybris.

In all the large prints, including the frontispiece, the work is not only shown in unhampered progress, but also in a state of completion, to such an extent that it even remains visible to where the work had proceeded until the intervention of Genesis 11: 8. The remaining storeys were added in a demonstrably corrective fashion.

Gerard de Lairesse's frontispiece, engraved by J. van Munnichuysen (1679), dealt with this problem in an interesting way (Fig. 11). The page should be read in a downward spiralling movement beginning at the top on the central axis, with the eye of divine wisdom, surrounded by a screen of clouds casting its rays of inspiration downwards, guided by the gestures of two cherubs to the only one worthy to be inspired by that light, the godly Nemrod, king of Babylon and descendant of Noah. Nemrod is shown in the act of transferring his idea, rather *the* idea of the tower to his master builder, the 'archi-tekton' who had prepared a perspective drawing, naturally in completed state, held by an assistant in such a way that it supports the gesture of the architect who points slightly backwards to the tower which is nearing completion. Following the spiralling movement upward, however, some streaks of lightning are drawn to indicate the oncoming disaster.

Posing as a scientist rather than as a theologian, Kircher endeavoured to refute the feasibility of Nemrod's, and later Queen Semiramis's designs by proving that a tower that would have to reach into heaven never could have been realized. Not only because it would have taken too long, or used an improbable amount of bricks, but also because a structure so tall would unbalance the earth in such a way that it would literally make it capsize. [25]

21. Hugh Ferriss, *The Metropolis of Tomorrow*, New York, 1929. See: Jean Ferriss Leich, *Architectural Visions – The Drawings of Hugh Ferriss*, New York, 1980, pp. 23–26. G.H. Edgell, *The American Architecture of To-Day*, New York/London, 1928, published already some Ferriss drawings and wrote of them: 'Babylonian compositions of terraces and ziggurats' (pp. 371–375).

22. Rem Koolhaas, *Delirious New York, A Retroactive Manifesto for Manhattan*, New York, 1978, pp. 173–176; 'The Hanging Gardens of Babylon: A Vision of What the Future May or May Not Bring', *Literary Digest*, June 14, 1924, p. 31; 'The Hanging Gardens of Manhattan', in: Earle Shultz and Walter Simmons, *Offices in the Sky*, Indianapolis/New York, 1959, pp. 172–179.

23. Mircea Eliade, *The Sacred and the Profane, The Nature of Religion*, New York, 1961 (1956), p. 40/41.
'Ziggurat' became another term for 'set-back skyscraper' right after the introduction of the type. Francesco Mujica in his *History of the Skyscraper*, New York, 1929, quoted H.D. Ives in *The Voice* o February 1927, concerning the architecture of the French Building (see Fig. 9): 'As the likeness of the mass of the French Building recalled strongly the form of the Assyrian Ziggurats, or observation towers, such as the Tower of the Seven Planets at Babylon, ...' (p. 36). Incidentally, Frank Lloyd Wright had accompanied his design for the upside-down truncated Tower of Babel with the motto 'Ziggurat' (see: *Daidalos*, V, 15 September 1982, p. 13).

24. In his brilliant *Delirious New York* (1978), Rem Koolhaas had observed that Coney Island entertained a comparable relation to Manhattan: 'At the junction of the nineteenth and twentieth centuries, Coney Island is the incubator for Manhattan's incipient themes and infant mythology. The strategies and mechanisms that later shape Manhattan are tested in the laboratory of Coney Island before they finally leap toward the larger island. Coney Island is a foetal Manhattan' (p. 23).

25. Athanasius Kircher, *Turris Babel*, Lib. II, cap. IV, p. 51.

Fig. 10. 'The Face of the City'. Bird's-eye view of Manhattan 'showing treatment of Battery Park proposed by Mr. Eric Gugler.' (from Thomas Adams et al., The Regional Plan of New York and Its Environs, Vol. II, The Building of the City, New York, 1931, frontispiece). Note the monumental sun-dial termination of the island with its gigantic obelisk.

Fig. 9. The French Building; Fred. French & H. Douglas Ives, 551 Fifth Ave., New York, 1927.

Yet, fascinated by the tower in its many 'archontological' functions, he had it restored and preserved for coming generations to be used as the type onto which they could model their 'ziggurat'-centred cosmopoles.[26]

## 'The Final Cosmetropolis'

At certain intervals Americans felt irresistibly attracted to the arch-cosmopolis for a variety of reasons. Town planning and Babylonian rigidity came to America as inducements of remorse. What had grown spontaneously in the wilderness of uncontrolled settlement had to be cut away and stitched up again, leaving spotless towns and slums. The classical clean-ups in Chicago of 1893 and 1909 and in New York of 1930 were model cases of plastic surgery provided by academically trained architects who redesigned the cities with Haussmannian 'percées' and Babylonian 'civic centres'.[27]

Concurrent with this ran the confident conviction that America was the chosen successor to the greatest civilizations of the past and that it was uniquely responsible for the progress of civilization. Thomas Hart Benton, a senator from Missouri, put forward the notion of a gradual progression in space of civilization, moving in a westward direction from the earliest centres of the Old World, Babylon, Nineveh, Tyre, to Athens and Alexandria, to Rome, to Paris, Amsterdam and London, and finally across the Atlantic to settle in the continent that was 'last' discovered, America.[28]

With the discovery of America, and the founding of its capitals, the Great Circle of Civilization was closed. The final consummation of the World had been arrived at. Part of this notion was used by the man who gave it its greatest notoriety: Frederick Jackson Turner, who, in a famous speech at the World's Columbian Exhibition – a fitting occasion – , Chicago, 1893, expounded his theory of 'The Significance of the Frontier in American History'. 'American social development,' he claimed, 'had been continually beginning over again at the frontier. This perennial rebirth, this fluidity of American life, this expansion westward with its new opportunities, its continual touch with the simplicity of primitive society, furnish the forces dominating American character. The true point of view in the history of this nation is not the Atlantic coast, it is the Great West.'[29]

*Fig. 11. Gerard de Lairesse, Frontispiece for Athanasius Kircher,* Turris Babel, *Amsterdam, 1679. Divine wisdom enlightens King Nemrod while instructing the chief architect.*

26. See: Giuliano Gresleri and Dario Matteoni, *La Città Mondiale: Andersen, Hébrard, Otlet, Le Corbusier*, Venezia, 1982, in particular Andersen's and Hébrard's design for 'an international world centre' of 1912, pp. 21–36, and Le Corbusier's 'Mundaneum' (1928), pp. 161–196. See also: Stanislaus von Moos, *Le Corbusier: Elements of a Synthesis*, Cambridge/London, 1979 (1968), pp. 243–245. Von Moos observed rightly that the Babylonian Tower Le Corbusier had designed for the 'World Museum' had been inspired by the Helmle, Corbett, Ferriss and Kelcher project (ibid., p. 244, n. 12).

27. Best examples could be found in Thomas Adams, *Regional Plan of New York and Its Environs: The Building of the City*, Vol. II, New York, 1931. Special notice should be given to the unmistakably Babylonian ensembles by Francis S. Swales. For example: pp. 384, 385, 387, 419, 465.

28. J.W. Schulte Nordholt, *Amerika*, Baarn, 1965, p. 15. The idea was certainly not new, being an adaptation of the ancient notion of 'translatio imperii'.

29. Frederick Jackson Turner, *The Frontier in American History*, New York, 1921, p. 2/3.

30. George Berkeley, *The Works*, III, Oxford, 1871, p. 231. The original 'Verses on the Prospect of Planting Arts and Learning in America' were published in Berkeley's *Miscellany* in 1752. See also: Ernest Lee Tuveson, op. cit., pp. 92–95.

31. The sequence *Course of Empire* by Thomas Cole, painted between 1833 and 1836, was recently published in: Robert Geddes, 'The Forest Edge', *Architectural Design*, 52, no. 11/12, 1982, pp. 2–23. The five states are: the Savage State, the Pastoral State, Consummation, Destruction and Desolation. References to the idea of the Great Circle or Berkeley's poem are not given.

But this new notion of the Great Circle coming to a close in the West was not a new one. Bishop Berkeley had pointed the way in his famous verse:

Westward the course of Empire takes its way;
The first four acts already past,
A fifth shall close the drama with the day;
Time's noblest offspring is the last. [30]

The tragic consequence was that the last discovered would have to be the first to enter the final stage of creation. The final closing of the circle meant that the land of hope and promises necessarily had to be the continent of death.

The Hudson School painter Thomas Cole illustrated a comparable, though temporally restricted, construct in a series of five allegorical paintings, titled *Course of Empire*, painted about 1835 (Figs. 12 & 13).[31] Walt Whitman stressed the inescapability of this logic in his *Passage to India* from 1871:

Lo, soul, seest thou not God's purpose from the first?
The earth to be spann'd, connected by network,
The races, neighbors, to marry and be given in marriage,
The oceans to be cross'd, the distant brought near,
The lands to be welded together.[32]

*Fig. 12. Thomas Cole, 'Consummation'; the third stage of the sequence 'Course of Empire', 1833–1866. New York Historical Society, New York (from* Architectural Design, *52, nos. 11/12, 1982).*

*Fig. 13. Thomas Cole, 'Destruction'; the fourth stage of the sequence 'Course of Empire', 1833–1866. New York Historical Society, New York (from* Architectural Design, *52, nos. 11/12, 1982).*

In the beginning of the poem Whitman drew parallels between the new wonders of technology, such as the Suez Canal, the Transatlantic and the Pacific cables, and the transcontinental railroads, with the seven ancient marvels, underlining, as he thought, the theory of purposeful succession in the development of creation. Whitman elucidated his poem by saying: 'There's more of me, the essential ultimate me in that than in any of the poems. There is no philosophy, consistent or inconsistent, in that poem ... but the burden of it is evolution − the one thing escaping the other − the unfolding of cosmic purposes.'[33]

In 1883 *The Century Magazine* published a remarkable essay by William C. Conant entitled: 'Will New York Be The Final Metropolis?' Conant acknowledged the paradigmatic importance of the Chaldean cities and elaborated on their capacity to have transformed cosmic chaos into what he called 'world-organization', saying that: 'The past inchoate stages of world-organization, provisional, partly abortive (Babylon!), but every time progressive, stand out boldly in the historical retrospect, mainly three: Babylon, Rome, London.'[34]

Then, following the Berkeley lead, Conant continued: 'The Old World has left many of its once imperial centers literally buried in the track of the westward moving vortex. ... a movement that would reach its final destination in America, − and that consequently the American metropolis must be the great city of the future, we might here take for granted without further discussion.'[35]

Also taken for granted was history's selection of the city of New York as the rightful successor to the paradigmatic trinity, notwithstanding the then loudly professed claims from the quickly growing cities of the Middle West, particularly from Chicago. New York, Conant could prove, was not even the final 'metropolis', nor the final 'cosmopolis', but the 'final *cosmetropolis*'![36]

32. Schulte Nordholt, op. cit., p. 16; Walt Whitman, *Leaves of Grass*, edited by Sculley Bradley & Harold W. Blodgett, New York, 1973 (1965), p. 412.

33. Walt Whitman, op. cit., editorial note, p. 411.

34. William C. Conant, 'Will New York Be The Final Metropolis?', *The Century Magazine*, XXVI (new series, IV), 1883, p. 688.

35. Ibid., p. 689.

36. Ibid., pp. 690, 693.

*Fig. 14. 'I love it! It says city!' Cartoon by Bernard Schoenbaum for* The New Yorker, *January 19, 1981. With didactic clarity the essential quality is shown of Manhattan, 'the citiest of cities'.*

---

37. Louis Sullivan recalled in his *Autobiography of an Idea*, New York, 1956 (1924), that the first building to be called 'skyscraper' was the Masonic Temple by John Root and Daniel Burnham in Chicago, 1891: '... until the Masonic Temple by John Root had raised its head into the air and the word "skyscraper" came into use' (p. 316). The Masonic Temple, though, was quite un-Chicagoan in its appearance; it had hipped roofs and it was profusely decorated. Champions of the 'functionalistic' unadorned Chicago School of Architecture, such as Sigfried Giedion, preferred to ignore it, notwithstanding its being the tallest building of its time (Sigfried Giedion, *Space, Time and Architecture*, Cambridge/London, 1946, p. 301, fig. 177). Giedion's ideological follower Carl Condit went as far as to say that Root in this design was 'not at home with the skyscraper', and that he had gotten much closer to its true expression in the flat-roofed Monadnock and Great Northern Building (Carl Condit, *The Chicago School of Architecture*, Chicago/London, 1973 (1956), p. 106).

38. The use of the term 'illud tempus' is derived from Mircea Eliade, *The Sacred and The Profane*, New York, 1961 (1957), p. 70ff.

39. Athanasius Kircher, *Mundus Subterraneus*, 1682; Dutch translation: *De Onderaardse Wereld*, Amsterdam, 1682, lib. VIII, p. 29.

40. Helen Rosenau, *Boullée and Visionary Architecture*, London/New York, 1976, p. 7, n. 5.

41. Francisco Mujica in his *History of the Skyscraper*, New York, 1929, p. 35, wrote: 'In the history of architecture in the United States there have been three opportunities for a renaissance by developing primitive architectural styles of America: the first vanished with the beginning of colonization; the second was just after the period of decadence following American independence; and the third is the present which is more propitious than any preceding period. Primitive American architecture has approached us miraculously through modern skyscrapers, because architects are seeking inspiration in alien styles of architecture closely resembling our primitive style.'

## 'I love it! It says city'

This controversy between Chicago and New York was of particular interest for the role of the American skyscraper as a successor to the paradigmatic tower. Although Chicago architects had produced numerous tall, commercial buildings, they only occasionally designed what properly could be called a 'skyscraper', which should be understood as a piece of architecture that universally could meet the semiotic requirements of its connotations. [37] The New York type, with its tall, sky-piercing towers, its brilliant white and coloured cladding and its 'ziggurat' outlines, was easily recognized as giving substance to the idea of 'city'. New York, it has often been said, is 'the citiest of cities', whereas other American cities, however hard they tried and regardless of their size or success, could never pass beyond the status of 'runner-up' or 'second city'. The main ingredient of New York's 'cityness' seems to lie in its fairytale, even banal, cartoonesque, sawtooth silhouette of towers.

A most apt illustration of this point is presented by the splendid cartoon (Fig. 14) by Bernard Schoenbaum for *The New Yorker*, January 19, 1981, in which a pair of rather loud arrivés feast their eyes on the skyline of Manhattan through a panoramic window of oversized dimensions, which functions as the frame for a gigantic picture that presents in didactic clarity the essential metropolis. Both seem well pleased with the spectacle, but it shows the artist's keen understanding of the semiotic process (as most cartoonists do) that he has given the key line – 'I love it! It says city' – to the woman. By transmitting the message of cityness through her as the medium, the idea is reinforced that messages like these do affect the subconscious, in casu 'female intuition', rather than reason.

The worldliness of the scene, the vulgarity of its protagonists, contrasting with the poetic subtlety of the message, reflects suggestively the paradoxical existence of the terrestial paradise. The tense relationship between the terrestrial and celestial paradises, as demonstrated in the Babylonian case, is again made manifest in the new 'paradise-on-earth', America, with New York as its cosmopolis; materialism and pragmatism are held in delicate balance by a fine sense for the metaphysical. The towers of Manhattan are outgrowing the concrete level of the streets to the abstract level of the skyline. It is here that the level of abstraction is achieved, necessary to connect the skyscraper to its forerunners from 'illo tempore'. [38] The degree of abstraction is that of the Wonders of the World, being no particular models, but acting as paradigms of a particular state of order (Fig. 15).

When Athanasius Kircher published that remarkable *amber*, selected from one of the Roman curiosity cabinets in which stones with mysterious images were collected, showing the irregular skyline of a city of towers, *Urbs Turrita*, in the *Mundus Subterraneus* of 1682, he must have been aware that this was not just an amusing picture of a freak of urbanism, but that it contained a revelation from the subterranean world, communicated by the wondrous ambers

*Fig. 15. 'New York – the Wonder City'; Souvenir book, published by the Interborough News Co., New York, 1945.*
*The American 'cosmetropolis' has proclaimed itself to be 'the city of marvels' or 'the wonder city', i.e. the collective depository of the modern successors to the ancient wonders of the world. New York was a marvel, like Babylon, that contained in its turn other marvels. Most appropriately a phrase by John Milton is printed on the inside cover: 'Towered cities please us then, And the busy hum of men.'*

*Fig. 16. 'Urbs Turrita'; the towered city as revealed in an amber from the collection of Athanasius Kircher (from Athanasius Kircher,* Mundus Subterraneus/De Onderaardse Wereld, *Amsterdam, 1682, Lib. VIII, p. 29).*

*Fig. 17. 'Annuit Coeptis – Novus Ordo Seclorum – 1776'; reverse side of the one-dollar bill. The Divinity approves of the new order of ages: America.*

which were held to transmit wisdom and to reveal mysteries (Fig. 16).[39] The image of the *Urbs Turrita* therefore possessed a status that lifted it over the level of anecdotism to the level of general truth, in being not *a* city of towers but *the* city of towers, acting as a symbol of that specific state of order the towered city represented.

The recognition of that truth is experienced throughout the ages, over and over again, without ever losing its original meaning. This is so whether we turn to Filarete, who elaborated upon it around the middle of the fifteenth century to develop his ethical and didactic models of the towered cities of Sforzinda and Zogalia in the *Trattato d'Architettura* (1451–1464), to Étienne-Louis Boullée, who, by the way, himself owned a copy of Kircher's *Turris Babel*, and who submitted his ideal communities to buildings of colossal dimensions, such as the spiralling tower of 1784, which in fact was a modernized and streamlined version of Kircher's Babylonic Tower, or to the lady with the 'I love it! It says city' *Erlebnis* in her Manhattan apartment.[40]

Most designs of European architects, such as the ones by Filarete, Jacques Perret, Boullée and Bruno Taut, remained within the realm of plans and projects. American planners on the other hand could take a fresh start, which in this context must be read in the terms of Frederick J. Turner, as 'to return to primitive conditions' and to partake in 'the perennial rebirth'.[41]

### Re-invention of architecture

When in 1776 America entered a *Novus Ordo Sec[u]lorum*, as the one-dollar bill unflaggingly instructs us (fig. 17),[42] its intentions to 'return to primitive conditions' were, in spite of the pyramid and the divine eye that accompanied the motto, not as urgent as they became at about the time of its centennial celebration. Thomas Jefferson's argument that the national American style should be based upon the Maison Carrée which was 'allowed without contradiction to be the most perfect and precious remain [sic] of antiquity in existence,' as well as upon the undisputed authority of Andrea Palladio, did not only speak for the aesthetic false start that American architects deplored so deeply at the close of the 19th century, but also of the relentlessly pragmatic side of the American material-metaphysical polarity.[43] A hundred years later the opposite side showed itself strongly in the *Historical Monument of the*

42. For a Millennial explanation of the Great Seal on the one-dollar bill see: Ernest Lee Tuveson, *Redeemer Nation – The Idea of America's Millennial Role*, Chicago/London, 1968, p. 119: '... the fact that the latter eagle [i.e. the heraldic eagle of the United States] carries in one talon the arrows of war and in the other the olive branch of peace might symbolize the two ways in which millennialists thought the way was prepared for the earthly Kingdom – by violent "overturning and breaking" of evil and by peaceful progress. The motto on the reverse of the Great Seal, "Annuit Coeptis Novus Ordo Seculorum," could with no difficulty be given a millennial significance.' The Millennial doctrine is based on the belief that a period of great prosperity will come, in which Satan will be bound and Christ will reign on Earth during a thousand years, as was predicted in the Book of Revelations, XX, 1–5. The Millennial ideology was strongly represented in the United States, in particular by communitarian sects like the Shakers, the Harmonists, the Oneida Perfectionists and the Latter-Day Saints or Mormons (see: Dolores Hayden, *Seven American Utopias: The Architecture of Communitarian Socialism, 1790–1975*, Cambridge, Mass./London, 1976).

43. James Early, *Romanticism and American Architecture*, New York etc., 1965, p. 14.

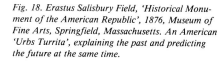

*Fig. 18. Erastus Salisbury Field, 'Historical Monument of the American Republic', 1876, Museum of Fine Arts, Springfield, Massachusetts. An American 'Urbs Turrita', explaining the past and predicting the future at the same time.*

44. Propagandists of New York were never shy about comparing their achievements to those of Babylon in its most magnificent moments. As early as 1857 *The New York Times*, quoted by *The History of Architecture and the Building Trades of Greater New York*, Vol. II, New York, 1899, p. 184, wrote: '... the commercial metropolis of the New World will be very nearly a fulfillment of the vision of Nebuchadnezzar. So said *The New York Times* of April 3, 1857.' At the time of this quotation Moses King was publishing his famous 'Views of New York'.

45. Washington Irving, op. cit., p. 61.

46. Preoccupation with the search for a national style of architecture begins to take on serious dimensions at the time of James J. Jarves, *The Art-Idea: Sculpture, Painting and Architecture*, New York, 1864; and Horatio Greenough, *The Travels, Observations, and Experience of a Yankee Stonecutter*, New York, 1852. With the emergence of the American architectral magazines, such as the *American Architect and Building News*, established in the year of the Centennial, 1876, articles with nationalistic overtones, as for example 'The Search for an American Style', *American Architect and Building News*, Vol. XXI, January 8, 1887, pp. 16–17, appeared with a certain regularity. In November 1885 the Western Association of Architects held its second convention at St. Louis, on which occasion several lectures were delivered dealing with the necessity of a national style. Best known is Louis Sullivan's 'Characteristics and Tendencies of American Architecture', published in: *Kindergarten Chats and Other Writings*, ed. Isabella Athey, New York, 1976 (1947), pp. 177–182.

47. How seriously this obligation of originality was taken was clearly demonstrated by the declination of the American government, in the person of Herbert Hoover, then Secretary of Commerce, to participate in the Paris 1925 Exposition Internationale des Arts Décoratifs et Industriels Modernes, for reasons that it was felt that America did not produce anything that could live up to the standards formulated by the organizing committee of modernity and originality (Rosemarie Haag Bletter in: Cervin Robinson and Rosemarie Haag Bletter, op. cit., p. 45, n. 25).

48. The question of the un-precedented was of course of the greatest concern to the theoreticians of evolutionism, such as Herbert Spencer, who exclaimed in his *The Principles of Biology*, London, 1864, Vol. I, p. 406: 'How comes there a wish to perform an action not before performed?'

*American Republic* by Erastus Salisbury Field, painted at the occasion of the Centennial Exhibition in Philadelphia of 1876 (Fig. 18). Here, as in a colossal *Urbs Turrita*, seven towers were assembled on a rectangular grid, reaching into the skies as if to provide the proper platform for a crown of angels arranged upon what in skyscraper terms would be called 'observation decks'. Field has provided us with a multivalent image. On the one hand it is a memorial of the American past in which the towers perform functions related to that of mausolea of 'tombeaux romains' as illustrated by Durand in fig. 3. On the other hand it can be read as an allegory of the American nation of the present and, furthermore, to judge from the futuristic elevated railroads connecting the tops as in Moses King's fantastic *Views of New York*, as a prefiguration of the future, in which the towers should be interpreted as Babylonic ones. [44] In the latter case they might as well have acted as the redemption of Washington Irving's vision of New York as a city of 'domes and lofty spires' as he had given the Sage Oloffe to see, when he had climbed '... up the top of one of the tallest trees ... and he fancied that the great volume of smoke assumed a variety of marvellous forms, where in dim obscurity he saw shadowed out palaces and domes and lofty spires, all of which lasted but a moment and then faded away' (Fig. 19). [45]

At the time that Field was busy designing his didactic tableau, most of the American architectural world was frantically searching for what might properly be called an American style of architecture. [46]

Those who felt the burden of responsibility for America's contribution to the great circle of civilizations were actively digging into that vast reservoir of images and symbols to which I shall, in Jungian terms, refer as the 'collective subconscious of architecture'. The intention of this search was clear: if America was to present itelf as the *Novus Ordo Seculorum* it had to come up with an architectural style worthy of its position as the successor to the 'old order of ages'.

Petty copies of Palladio or other exercises in European-based eclecticism had to fall hopelessly short. Even a restaging of the Babylonic city would lack the originality and integrity necessary to a nation that was about to lead the world into the future. [47] The only way out of this predicament was to *re-invent* architecture from the very beginning. [48]

The obvious simplicity of this task presented certainly the greatest, the most insoluble, of all artistic problems of creativity. In fact, it forces man to remember what he has forgotten since the beginnings of mankind. He has to remember the immemorable.

About the time that Sir James Frazer had written *The Golden Bough* and the search for the forgotten past was in full swing, William Lethaby published his *Architecture, Myth and Mysticism* in 1891. Lethaby stressed the importance of the essentials of architecture and fixed the attention of his readers on the inevitable recurrence of the architectural types with only slight modifications: 'It has rightly been the habit of historians of architecture to lay stress on the differences of the several styles and schools of successive ages, . . . but, in the far larger sense, all architecture is one, when traced back through the stream of civilizations.[49] And although the advice contained sufficient wisdom, it did not incite those who were seeking to go beyond where they already were. Sir Reginald Blomfield in one of his lectures (1913) hinted at interesting leads when he attempted to provide, as Hans Sedlmayr[50] would do somewhat later, new explanations for the sudden and mysterious emergence of the Gothic cathedral. Quoting Lucas Champronnière Blomfield wrote: '. . . our thoughts and discoveries frequently are merely the résumé of observations of the past, not only of that past from which we directly derive our instruction, but of a past of which we have no conscious knowledge.'[51]

This non-conscious knowledge or intuition is probably what the old tower builders and originators of the first American skyscrapers had in common: an enthusiastic, non-rational, desire to build high in celebration of something that probably they were not aware of. John Ruskin described this feeling in his first Edinburgh lecture on architecture of 1853: '"Go to now. Let us build a tower whose top may reach unto heaven." From that day to this, whenever men have become skillful architects at all, there has been a tendency in them to build high; not in any religious feeling, but in mere exuberance of spirit and power — as they dance or sing — with a certain mingling of vanity — like a child builds a tower of cards.'[52] Ruskin admitted that all towers, naturally, harked back to the paradigmatic Tower of Babel, but he made it just as clear that the impulse of all tower building was pre-architectural in the sense of Albertus Magnus's 'Universalia ante res'[53] so that even the tower builders had to design from scratch, with no other references than the pertinent will to elevate themselves and a vague idea of a mountainous pile of which the architectural terms were not yet developed. And indeed, the urge to build towers presupposes a sense of the adventurous, testing the limits of the familiar and exploring the unknown. This consequently precludes the habitual and the traditional and requires therefore the absence of model and type as a necessary condition. The builders of the first tower had set out to transgress the limits of knowledge, propelled by a curiosity similar to that of Icarus and Prometheus.[54] Yet, the unknown was never the barren territory it may have seemed to be. During the building process the architect was guided by the archetypal image which lent the form to the will of the designer to express what he wanted to express. De Champronnière's 'past of which we have no conscious knowledge' must then be understood as the common realm of platonic ideas, which the 19th-century Americans as well as the Babylonians had shared and from which they had derived their ambitions as well as their concept of verticality. The notion that the New World and the Old World were to meet in the completion of the great circle of eternity, is illustrated by its iconic representation: the snake biting itself in the tail. The artistic imagination of both cultures might be located exactly there where eternity shows its *caesura*, where head and tail and old and new meet. The present meets the past in what is known as the Eternal Return; just as Whitman's 'lands were welded together,'

*Fig. 19. 'And Oloffe bethought him, and he hastened and climbed up to the top of one of the tallest trees, and saw that the smoke spread over a great extent of country; and, as he considered it more attentively, he fancied that the great volume of smoke assumed a variety of forms, where in dim obscurity he saw shadowed out palaces and domes and lofty spires.' Illustration by Maxfield Parrish for* A History of New York . . . *by Diedrich Knickerbocker, London, 1900. Frontispiece.*

49. William R. Lethaby, *Architecture, Mysticism and Myth*, New York, 1891, pp. 2/3.

50. Hans Sedlmayr, *Die Entstehung der Kathedrale*, Zürich, 1950. Both Blomfield and Sedlmayr opposed the constructivist theories centred around Viollet-le-Duc in which the sudden emergence of the Gothic style was explained predominantly in terms of structural improvement. Resistance to Sedlmayer's theory was uncommonly fierce. Reviews in: *Kunstchronik*, 4, 1951, 14; 78, 84, and 304, 323, the author's rebuttal.

51. Sir Reginald Blomfield, *The Touchstone of Architecture*, Oxford, 1925, p. 93.

52. John Ruskin, *Lectures on Architecture and Painting*, Vol. XII of *The Works of John Ruskin*, edited by E.T. Cook and A. Wedderburn, London, 1904, p. 37.

53. Jorge Luis Borges, op. cit., p. 27.

54. Carlo Ginzburg, 'Hoch und Niedrig — Erkenntnisverbote im 16. und 17. Jahrhundert', *Freibeuter*, X, 1981, p. 17. Prof. Anton Boschloo provided me with this rare source.

so was time. What seemed to be long forgotten presents itself as an unprecedented novelty, the Apokatastasis. In a slightly different reading of the habitual definition, the Eternal Return in the creative sense could mean something like:

That, in the process of creation, which necessarily has to be unprecedented, always a precedent wedges itself between the creator and his product and thus guides it into its final shape.

Those involved with the creation of the American city were often thought to have been guided by the Wonders of the World. Samuel Philips Day related that 'Penn had the celebrated City of Babylon in view, when he planned his American town, and from the draft given by that learned divine, the idea, as far as regularity is concerned, appears to have been well founded. It would seem also that Penn wished, or thought it practicable, to emulate at least the size of the Chaldean capital, ....'[55]

Even William Le Baron Jenney, whom art history had traditionally assigned the role of the noble savage of the Chicago school of commercial building, was in real life a neat bourgeois academician who had taught at the University of Chicago 'a short course of popular lectures on the history of the different styles of architecture that have arisen, flourished and passed away, embracing the savage tribes, Egypt, Assyria, Greece, Rome and the Middle Ages.' It was subsequently popularized further in an amusing, but on the whole thoroughly French academic manner, as a series for the first volume of *The Inland Architect and Builder* of 1883.[56] At the time he was working on his Home Life Insurance Co. Building, Jenney was said to have remarked that 'we are building to a height to rival the Tower of Babel.'[57]

It was not found to be at all eccentric that the Empire State Building has presented itself as the Eighth World Wonder, following the steps of the Mausoleum of Halicarnassus and the other six (Fig. 20).[58] And it must have been ac-

55. Samuel Philips Day, *Life and Society in America*, London, 1880, p. 175.

56. William L.B. Jenney, 'Lectures delivered at the University of Chicago', *The Inland Architect and Builder*, Vol. 1, no. 2, 1883, p. 18. The material Jenney presented was mainly derived from E.-E. Viollet-le-Duc, in particular from his *Histoire de l'Habitation Humaine*, Paris, 1875.

57. Donald Hoffmann, *The Architecture of John Wellborn Root*, Baltimore/London, 1973, p. 27, n. 11.

58. Theodore James, Jr., *The Empire State Building*, New York, etc., 1975, pp. 158–161. The text to the picture of the Empire State Building reads as follows: 'The 8th wonder of the world. The tallest and most famous building of all time – the Empire State Building. This triumph of architectural and engineering genius – the Eighth World of the World – soars 1,472 feet into the sky – as high as all the original Seven Wonders piled one on top of the other. A city in itself – virtually a city of marvels – the Empire State Building has a population of 16,000 persons working in the building plus 35,000 visitors daily – totaling more visitors in a single year than the combined totals of all who visited the original Seven Wonders of the World' (p. 161). A text that was probably more boasting than all the boasts of the original Seven Wonders of the World had ever boasted.

59. Eugene Clute, 'Dr. John Wesley Kelchner's Restoration of King Solomon's Temple and Citadel; Helmle and Corbett Architects', *Pencil Points*, Vol. VI, no. 11, 1925, pp. 69–86 (p. 69).

60. Manfredo Tafuri, '"Neu-Babylon": das New York der Zwanziger Jahre und die Suche nach Amerikanismus', *Metropolis 3, Archithese* 1976, Vol. 20, pp. 20/21.

TOMB OF KING MAUSOLUS    THE 8TH WONDER OF THE WORLD

*Fig. 20. 'The Empire State Building – The Eighth Wonder of the World. The tallest and most famous of all time ... – as high as all the original Seven Wonders piled one on top of the other. A city in itself – virtually a city of marvels.' Eight panels of the Marvels of the World, designed for the Empire State Building by Roy Sparkes (from Theodore James Jr.,* The Empire State Building, *New York, etc., 1975, p. 161).*

cepted as the logical consequence of this line of thought that in a time that set-back – 'zigurrat' – skyscrapers were transforming Manhattan into Mesopotamia, another marvel was to be recreated in the minutest details: the Temple of Jerusalem.

Harvey Wiley Corbett and his partner Frank Helmle had produced the plans for a monumental restoration of King Solomon's Temple, following the idea of a biblical scholar named John Wesley Kelchner, a name that could not be more meaningful for our present subject. The renderings were done by Hugh Ferriss, who at the time was busy, in conjunction with the same firm of Corbett & Helmle, drawing the famous set-back zoning-law envelopes for skyscrapers, which evidently bore resemblances to the proposed Great Porch of the Temple which was meant to 'rise 300 feet in white and gold against the sky as a set-back tower of majestic effectiveness' (Fig. 21).[59]

Skyscrapers with 'ziggurat' silhouettes and Assyrian-Babylonian – or as Tafuri suggested 'anti-European' – decorations were fashionable at the time and it seems an inviting thought that this smooth blending of archeological accuracy and architectural modernity were to be taken as proof of the genetic affinity between the paradigmatic Jerusalem/Babylon and the modern-time America (Fig. 22).[60]

This short-circuiting of 'illud tempus' and the present was another symptom of the need to base the beginnings of the nation and its matching architecture upon the authority of the ancient marvels. Field had designed his tableau of

*Fig. 21 (below). 'The Great Porch' of the Temple of Jerusalem, which was intended to rise 300 feet in white and gold against the sky as a set-back tower of majestic effectiveness. Design for a reconstruction of the Temple of Solomon by Frank Helmle, Harvey Wiley Corbett, and Dr. John Wesley Kelchner. Rendering by Hugh Ferriss (*Pencil Points, *VI, no. 11, November 1925, pp. 79, 86).*
*The shape of the Tower of Babel had infiltrated into the ideology of the Temple of Jerusalem in order to become a set-back skyscraper.*

*Fig. 22 (right). The Hotel New Yorker; Sugarman & Berger, architects; 34th Street at 8th Avenue, New York, 1930.*
*The proof of genetic affinity between paradigmatic Babylon/Jerusalem and modern-time America (postcard).*

*Fig. 23. Transamerica Building; William Pereira & Associates; 600 Montgomery Street, San Francisco, 1972.*
*A dramatic structure just there where it runs the greatest risk. A pyramid which is meant to be its own obelisk.*

61. Eugene Clute, op. cit., pp. 69/71.

62. It appears that the project never has been realized. Plans and drawings, though, have achieved wide publicity. They were exhibited at the *Ausstellung neuer Amerikanischen Baukunst*, Akademie der Künste, Berlin, January 1926, and correspondingly at The Architectural League of New York, New York. References to the project in recent publications are to be found in: Cervin Robinson & Rosemarie Haag Bletter, op. cit., pp. 11/12, n. 21; Manfredo Tafuri, op. cit., pp. 12–13, n. 7; Alison Sky & Michelle Stone, *Unbuilt America*, New York, etc., 1976, pp. 128–131; Jean Ferriss Leich, *Architectural Visions – The Drawings of Hugh Ferriss*, New York, 1980, pp. 22, 31.

63. Cervin Robinson & Rosemarie Haag Bletter, op. cit., p. 12.

64. Eugene Clute, op. cit., pp. 70/71.

towers for the centennial, while Helmle, Corbett, Ferriss and Kelchner had contributed theirs to the sesquicentennial celebration of the events of 1776. Since 'as we know, Solomon's Temple was built during a period of peace and prosperity which followed the turbulent days of war under King David,' it was found fitting that the model could serve to mark the establishment of a completely original style of architecture, based on a common-source collate with the establishment of a new world order.[61]

In reconstructing the Temple, Kelchner cum suis made their contribution to a long living tradition of architectural interpreters of the vision of the prophet Ezekiel, joining their more illustrious predecessors Juan Bautista Villalpando, Claude Perrault and, of course, Johann Bernhard Fischer von Erlach.[62]

Partly as a realistic analogy to the destruction of the Temple, and partly as a reference to the discontinuation of the Tower of Babel, to which especially the Great Porch bore a striking resemblance,[63] the complex was designed to temporarily eradicate itself: 'It is intended to incorporate in the structure a system of pipes through which, when the building is empty of visitors, it will be possible to force volumes of gas which will envelope the structure to its full height presenting, in conjunction with other means, an impressive spectacle of the destruction of the Temple.' Reassuringly it was added that 'when the clouds of gas drift away the structure will be found unharmed.'[64]

Whether this exhibition of an architectural death-wish could be ascribed deeper meanings than the superficial analogies it pretended, is dependent on the importance one is willing to ascribe to the notion of America sitting on the welding seam of creation and destruction. For example, the location of San Francisco on one of these seams, the San Andreas Fault, has given the builders of skyscrapers the irresistible urge to put up the most dramatic structures just there where they run the greatest risks. The presence of William Pereira & Associates' Transamerica Pyramid (1972) is an alarming case in point (Fig. 23). Catastrophe movies such as *Towering Inferno* (1974) and *Earthquake* (1974) are the logical consequence of this inclination.[65]

Creation and destruction have lived in a tense symbiosis, from Brahma and Visnu, and Zarathustra's dualism to Colonel W.A. Starrett who wrote in his *Skyscrapers and the Men Who Build Them* (1928), 'Building skyscrapers is the nearest peace-time equivalent of war. In fact, the analogy is startling, even to the occasional grim reality of a building accident where maimed bodies, and even death, remind us that we are fighting a war of construction against the forces of nature.'[66]

The fusion of the antithesis destruction–construction was a necessary constituent in the world of skyscraper building: 'The tearing down and building that is forever going on here, at the heart of things, give evidence of vigor and vitality that will continue to demolish and create,' wrote Earle Shultz and Walter Simmons in their *Offices in the Sky*.[67]

War and destruction were the constituent elements of the act of making order out of chaos in the histories of creation. Building skyscrapers as an act of violence is the primordial act of establishing order in the built environment. The smoke that erupted from the Temple joined the divine Jerusalem with the mundane Babylon, the set-back-shaped Great Porch with the Tower, and the Hall of Pillars (Fig. 24) with the Palace of Belshazzar, as it was depicted by John Martin in his *End of Babylon* (Fig. 25).[68]

What at first sight would seem an innocent attraction, aimed at those who were familiar with the phantasmagoric world of Lunapark,[69] became, in the hands of those who created the skyscraper, the atavistic reenactment of cosmogony, following the same principles Kircher had in mind when he wrote his *Turris Babel, sive Archontologia*.

*Fig. 24. 'The Hall of Pillars' of the Temple of Jerusalem; Design for a reconstruction of Solomon's Temple by Frank Helmle, Harvey Wiley Corbett and Dr. John Wesley Kelchner. Rendering by Hugh Ferriss (from* Pencil Points, *Vol. VI, no. 11, November 1925, p. 80).*
*Again the divine Jerusalem joins up with the mundane Babylon (compare fig. 25).*

*Fig. 25. John Martin, 'Belshazzar's Feast', 1821 (from Jean Seznec,* John Martin en France, *London, 1964, plate 2).*

65. The building of skyscrapers has often been seen as an act of recklessness, usually challenged by the presence of the impossible. Col. William A. Starrett regarded the skyscraper as the fulfilment of 'It can't be done' (see below, note 66, p. 63). European observers recognized this tendency to perform the impossible as a typical American characteristic: 'To any protest of the break with tradition, of the impracticality of a new proposal, the response has always been: "Why not?"' (Geoffrey Gorer, *The Americans, A Study in National Character*, London, 1948, p. 152).

66. Col. William A. Starrett, *Skyscrapers and the Men Who Build Them*, New York/London, 1928, p. 63.

67. Earle Shultz and Walter Simmons, *Offices in the Sky*, Indianapolis/New York, 1959, p. 320/321.

68. An interesting early reference to John Martin's work is by Emerson: 'From London in 1847, Emerson describes to his wife the "dusky magnificence" of the West End Buildings, which makes his walking "dreamlike", and which he compares to John Martin's picture of Babylon – "light, darkness, architecture and all".' Quoted from: Vivian C. Hopkins, *Spires of Form, A Study of Emerson's Aesthetic Theory*, Cambridge, 1951, p. 88.

69. Coney Island's 'Fighting the Flames' and other series of 'simulated disasters' such as the Fall of Pompei and the San Francisco Earthquake, belonged to the most drastic forms of public amusement in the active years of Dreamland and Lunapark. See: Rem Koolhaas, op. cit., pp. 42, 47/48.

70. Friedrich Nietzsche, *Thus Spoke Zarathustra – A Book for Everyone and No One*, Harmondsworth, 1983 (1892[1]), p. 178.

## Epilogue

'Behold this gateway, dwarf!' I went on: 'it has two aspects. Two paths come together here: no one has ever reached their ends. This long lane behind us: it goes on for an eternity. And that long lane ahead of us – that is another eternity. ... The name of the gateway is written above it: "Moment".'
'But if one were to follow them further and even further and further: do you think, dwarf, that these paths would be in eternal opposition?'
'Everything straight lies,' murmured the dwarf disdainfully.
'All truth is crooked, time itself is a circle.' ...
'Behold this moment!' I went on. 'From this gateway Moment a long eternal lane runs *back*: an eternity lies behind us. Must not all things that *can* run have already run along this lane? Must not all things that *can* happen *have* already happened, been done, run past?' – FRIEDRICH NIETZSCHE, Thus Spoke Zarathustra.[70]

*Fig. 1. 'Religion' (from Hugh Ferriss,* The Metropolis of Tomorrow, *1929).*

ALTHOUGH there was an enticing variety of building types in America at the turn of the century, the introduction of the skyscraper created a stir. Its uneasy reception was caused mostly by unfamiliarity and fear of unknown consequences. Some were shocked by the unprecedented heights, others feared problems of urban instability. These were natural reactions – the unknown tends to cause anxiety, even on a continent where it was still a common experience. It is therefore interesting that another reaction was caused by the exact opposite: familiarity. With their pointed tops lifting above the amorphous skyline of Manhattan, the skyscrapers resembled the churches which had dominated medieval cities (Figs. 1 & 2). Some even provoked the title 'cathedral' – because of its stepped-back silhouette, the Paramount Building (1926) in New York was called the Cathedral of Motion Pictures (Fig. 3). Names which use the cathedral as a metaphor are not uncommon, for example the Cathedral Spires of Yosemite (Fig. 4). Usually the comparison is to the cathedral's structure and interior, as in Le Corbusier's reference to the Galerie des Machines (1889) as 'cette cathédrale de fer'.[1] Or it may provide some clues to serious analysis, as in the Green Cathedral, the centre court of Wimbledon. Although Wimbledon's centre court has nothing to do with a Gothic church, to most people it is still a thoroughly appropriate metaphor, perhaps because it characterizes the public's devotion to its heroes. In some cases the relationship must remain obscure, as in the Cathedral of Restaurants.[2] Usually, however, there is at least a formal resemblance. But innocence must end when formal and ideological elements are concocted in such a way that it seems to point at an impersonation of the most impudent kind. And such, it was felt, was the case with the Cathedral of Commerce.

*Fig. 2. 'Skyscrapers, Medieval and Modern-Time's Reversal of Sacred and Profane.' (from Claude Bragdon,* The Frozen Fountain, *New York, 1932.)*

SACRED SKYSCRAPERS
AND
PROFANE CATHEDRALS

## 'Not a church enters into it'

It has frequently been observed that the Americans are a religious people and that they go to church in great numbers every Sunday: 'In fact, if you would use your eyes only, the first attribute you would ascribe to the Americans would be that of a churchgoing people.'[3] Church-goers there were indeed in great numbers, in the nineteenth century, but so were there many different denominations. Each promising new interpretation of the Scriptures would have its own followers, and it is possible to say, with exaggeration, that there were as many sects as there were opinions. Opinion, interpretation and exegesis are the keys to explaining this unusually rich selection of religious establishments. The main difference between the European and American attitudes, Paul de Rousiers noted in his *La vie américaine* (1892), was that

*Fig. 3. 'The Cathedral of Motion Pictures': The Paramount Building, New York, by C.W. & G. Rapp, 1926 (postcard).*

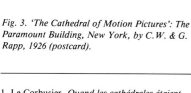

1. Le Corbusier, *Quand les cathédrales étaient blanches* (Paris, 1937), p. 102. This book contains by far the most persuasive analysis of the metaphorical relationship between the Gothic cathedral and the New York skyscraper.

2. I once came across a postcard depicting the facade of a restaurant with the boast that it was 'the cathedral of restaurants.' It might have been part of the St. George's Hotel, Brooklyn.

3. Edward Dicey, *Six Months in the Federal States* (London, 1863), II, 204. Quoted in Richard L. Rapson, *Britons View America: Travel Commentary, 1860–1935* (Seattle and London, 1971), p. 145.

4. Paul de Rousiers, *La vie américaine* (Paris, 1892), pp. 650–1.

5. James Bryce, *The American Commonwealth* (New York, 1922), II, 770.

6. Ibid., II, 781.

7. Montgomery Schuyler, 'Architecture in Chicago: Adler & Sullivan', in *American Architecture and Other Writings*, edited by William H. Jordy and Ralph Coe (Cambridge, Mass., 1961), II, 378–9. The article was originally written in 1895.

8. Ibid., II, 377.

9. Ibid., II, 378.

10. De Rousiers, op. cit., p. 655.

11. Although Sigfried Giedion greatly admired Chicago commercial architecture, he had no eye for skyscrapers. He included, in *Space, Time and Architecture* (1947) a dramatic full-page photograph of Randolph Street taken some time after 1892 and featuring the Ashland, Schiller and Masonic buildings, which he captioned thus: 'Chicago in the early nineties: Randolph Street about 1891. The large buildings here are the offices, built by Burnham and Root in 1891.' The Masonic Temple, by far the tallest building of its time, is not mentioned. Although it must be said that in Giedion's time Root's work was not yet fully appreciated, disapproval of the Masonic Temple as well as the Woman's Temple is typical of the circles of American, and more specifically mid-Western, architectural historians operating in Giedion's ideological wake. Carl W. Condit, for example, was unhappy with the two because they were not in line with the canonic flat roof and suppression of ornament (*The Chicago School of Architecture* (Chicago, 1964), pp. 105–7).

*Fig. 4. 'The Cathedral Spires of Yosemite' (postcard). Verso: 'One spire rises 700 feet above the rock.' This is exactly the height of the Metropolitan Life Tower, and 92 feet less than that of the Woolworth Building.*

Americans experienced religion more as a literary or quasi-philosophical exercise than as devotion. Most churches created among their congregations a bond of reason rather than that of a cult, and so, he argued, they often could better be characterized as dissenting clubs rather than places of devotion.[4]

To foreigners it was also instantly apparent that, although the nation was teeming with churches of every imaginable denomination, there was a conspicuous absence of a national religion. James Bryce, who echoed Alexis de Toqueville in declaring that he was impressed by the religiosity of the Americans, was less troubled by this absence than, say, de Rousiers. He felt quite at ease with the conclusion that it was in fact this surprising diversity which constituted what one might call 'the national religion'.

Nevertheless, the thought of a church on the grand scale never left the minds of those who felt themselves responsible either for the religious welfare of the Americans or for edifying their cultural conscience. Although the very thought of a state religion was a heresy, and contrary to the letter of the Constitution, fantasy was constantly stimulated by suggestions that splendid churches ought to be erected in the centres of prospering cities. The point was not so much to establish places of worship as it was to furnish these cities with monuments to their prosperity and civic pride.[6]

For a long time the western settlements had had to make do with wandering evangelists and humble shacks for Sunday preaching, but, the moment they started to thrive, civic pride had to be reckoned with. In 1895, Montgomery Schuyler related the amusing story of 'the inhabitant of a boom town further West, who was bragging about the hotels and the saloons and the "opera house" of it to a stranger, who at last inquired about the churches. "Well, no", *Occidentalis Gloriosus* had to own; "there was some talk about one, but the boys thought it would look too dudish".[7] This was more or less the case with Chicago when Schuyler wrote that 'It is indeed curious how the composite image of Chicago that remains in one's memory as the sum of his numerous impressions is made up exclusively of the sky-scrapers of the city and the dwellings of the suburb. Not a church enters into it.'[8] It seemed to him that Chicagoans were reluctant to spend money on churches because they considered it 'a little frivolous and dilettante'.[9]

It is a pity that Schuyler was unaware of the observations of visitors from abroad because, though there were no 'official' churches, no church buildings in the traditional sense, he might have noticed that there were at least two colossal buildings of the type that de Rousiers had described as 'religious clubs', which comprised a chapel surrounded by a library, Sunday-school rooms, a billiard room, and rooms for tea parties and theatrical performances – 'à la fin j'ai eu une forte envie de lui demander: "Et le bon Dieu, dans tout cela, qu'en faites vous?".'[10] These were the Woman's Temple (1890–2) (Fig. 5) and the Masonic Temple (1890–2), both by the firm of Burnham and Root. It took a native American to overlook them. That the two temples were not regarded as churches is understandable, but not consistent. After all, the Woman's Christian Temperance Union, a powerful institution which was largely responsible for Prohibition, was a full-fledged daughter of the Methodist Church. Although the building it commissioned was to be devoted primarily to administration and other business, it nevertheless included a sanctuary at street level and, though it was never executed, a flèche in the French Gothic style. Schuyler had been misled by the hybrid character of these two prototypes, however brief their existence (they were torn town in 1922 and 1938 respectively), of the American metropolitan 'revenue church'. Nor was he much impressed by their architectural merits, an odd lapse of taste that he shared with later critics.[11]

When Schuyler declared 'that this is not a cathedral building country', he meant cathedral-cathedrals and nothing of the kind Edgar Allen Poe hinted at when he wrote that extraordinary example of perspicacity *Mellonta Tauta*, a scenario of New York in the twentieth century: 'It is related of them [the 'Knickerbocker Tribe', or the New Yorkers] that they were oddly afflicted with a monomania for building what in the ancient Amrrican [*sic*], was denominated "churches" – a kind of pagoda instituted for the worship of two idols that went by the name of Wealth and Fashion' [12] (Fig. 6). Whether this description of Manhattan, written in 1849, was the result of a magical insight, or of the collective imagination, which has the habit of depicting the city of the future as a city of towers, is of little interest here. What makes this text remarkable is the fact that all towers, in other words the skyscrapers of the coming century, are called 'churches'. The worldly powers have conquered the city, and they rule it in the robes of the Church.

### The Cathedral of Commerce

In 1913 this travesty was in fact enacted in a splendid New York skyscraper, conceived by its owner, Frank W. Woolworth, designed by his architect, Cass Gilbert, and realized by their contractor, Louis Horowitz. It was an ingenious whim; the building looked very much like one of the twin towers of a French Gothic cathedral but it was entirely devoted to commerce. It was called The Cathedral of Commerce (Fig. 7), [13] and indeed it was officially christened as such by the noted divine Dr S. Parkes Cadman.

*Fig. 5. The Woman's Temple, Chicago, by John W. Root, 1891 (from W.H. Birkmire,* Skeleton Construction in Buildings, *1894).*

When seen at nightfall bathed in electric light or in the lucid air of a summer morning, piercing space like a battlement of the paradise of God, which St. John beheld, it inspires feelings even for tears. The writer looked upon it and at once cried out 'the Cathedral of Commerce' – the chosen habitation of that spirit in man which, through means of change and barter, binds alien people into unity and peace. [14]

It seems obvious that the appellation 'cathedral' was prompted by its Gothic style and form, but at the same time other analogies were competing for priority. This is apparent in existing texts which, with an uncommon feeling for propriety, hint at a diverse and complex body of references.

The Cathedral of Commerce was designed as a place of worship; but the question still remains, the worship of what? Commerce alone will not do – there is much more to it. And what, in any case, was meant by 'commerce'? Dr Cadman wrote, 'Just as religion monopolized art and architecture during the Medieval epoch, so commerce has engrossed the United States since 1865.' [15] Thus it might be said that, since commerce and religion had been brought to the same level of comparison, they were regarded as comparable.

Long before Woolworth had entrusted the realization of the building to his architect Cass Gilbert and his contractor Louis J. Horowitz, of the Thompson-Starrett Company, he had already thought out the building, hazily in architectural terms, but most clearly in the ideological sense. Horowitz, a feudal major-domo representing, more or less, the interests of his lord, who worked closely with his client as an intermediary between him and the architect, was very much aware of this. 'Whoever would try to find a reason for this tall building' and did not take into account 'that Woolworth's ego was a thing of extra size', Horowitz warned, 'would reach a false conclusion.' [16]

12. Edgar Allen Poe, 'Mellonta Tauta', *Tales* (New York, 1914), III, 341, originally published in *Godey's Lady's Book* (February 1849). I wish to thank Antoine Bodar, who directed my attention to this important passage.

13. The expression was not entirely new. Emile Zola described, in his *Au bonheur des dames* (1883), the paradigmatic department store Au bon Marché (1873–6) as follows: 'C'était la Cathédrale de Commerce Moderne, solide et légère, faite pour un peuple des clientes.' There is reason to believe that the name 'cathedral' had already been suggested by Woolworth during early negotiations with contractors. Paul Starrett, competing with Horowitz, made a point of talking Woolworth out of using terracotta for the cladding of the frame. Instead he strongly urged the application of stone because 'all great cathedrals which were the inspiration of his building were built of stone' (Paul Starrett, *Changing the Skyline* (New York and London, 1938), p. 167).

14. 'The Cathedral of Commerce' (New York, 1916), Foreword. There were at least four different editions of this booklet, in 1916, 1917, 1920 and 1921.

Fig. 6. 'Templum Americanum': Worshipping two idols in one and the same temple seems to have been normal practice for Americans – in Athanasius Kircher's observation from the mid-seventeenth century they are the sun and the moon, rather than Poe's 'wealth and fashion' (from Athanasius Kircher, Oedipus Aegyptiacus . . . , 1652).

a. 'when seen at nightfall bathed in electric light'

b. 'or in the lucid air of a summer morning, piercing space like a battlement of the paradise of God'

Fig. 7a&b. 'The Cathedral of Commerce': The Woolworth Building, New York, by Cass Gilbert, 1913 (postcards; texts from The Cathedral of Commerce, 1916).

15. Ibid. Woolworth was not the only one to have conceived of his building in religious or rather Christian terms.

Joseph Pulitzer, owner of the New York *World* newspaper (see 'Myth' I, p. 102ff.) dedicated his new building with the following message, sent by cable from Wiesbaden, Germany, October 10, 1899: 'God grant this structure be the enduring home of a newspaper forever unsatisfied with merely printing news ... forever aspiring to be a Moral Force, forever rising to a higher plane of perfection as a Public Institution ....' The compiler of the Dedication Brochure added: 'There is a sermon in these stones; a significant moral in this architectural glory, ... a persistent aspiring to loftier Ideals' (*The World, Its History and Its New Home: The Pulitzer Building*, New York, 1899 (?), n.p.) (see also 'Myth' I, p. 96, 'the American press as ethical standard').

An even clearer case of usurping the functions of the church was presented by an address delivered by the historian William Henry Atherton at the convention of the Metropolitan Life Insurance Company of New York in 1915, in which he remembered the erection of the firm's record-breaking tower on Madison Square, 1909. The tower was modelled after the campanile of St. Mark's, Venice, was designed by Napoleon le Brun & Sons and was, with 48 storeys and 680 feet, briefly the tallest building in the world (Fig. 15A). Atherton said: 'You and your Directors were well advised in the choice of your symbol. For a tower with its light and its belfry has always been a source of inspiration . . . Thus your Tower partakes of the character of the ancient towers of refuge and defence . . . Your high tower should, therefore, be *a symbol of God* to you and others, standing out boldly and erect as a plea for righteousness and purity in business corporations, and as monumental protest against the exploitation of the poor' (William Henry Atherton, *The Metropolitan Tower: A Symbol of Refuge, Warning, Love, Inspiration, Beauty, Strength*, New York 1915, pp. 2, 4, 6; quoted by Kenneth Turney Gibbs, *Business Architectural Imagery: The Impact of Economic and Social Changes on Tall Office Buildings, 1870-1930*, unpublished dissertation, Cornell University, Ithaca, NY 1976, p. 174. Gibbs noted that the Metropolitan Tower also was characterized 'as a metaphor for 'the religion of business', ibid.).

*Fig. 15A. The Metropolitan Life Insurance Company Building, New York, 1909, by Napoleon Le Brun & Sons, architects. Modelled after the Campanile of St. Mark's, Venice, it was 'A Symbol of God' (postcard).*

## The transcendence of materialism

Woolworth's motives are worth examining, because they could equally be applied to other founders of skyscrapers since they reflect quite clearly the almost tragic condition of those who had set out to 'make good'. To most Europeans making money was an evil activity, which the Americans had pursued far beyond the acceptable limits of decency. According to the Scriptures, Christianity was predominantly incompatible with business, yet the Americans, thanks to their diverse interpretations of Christianity and the resulting multiplicity of opinions, treated the subject with great inventiveness and a conspicuous lack of dogmatism. Working with the sole intention of making money was held in high esteem as the democratic answer of the New World to the inequality of the feudal Old World.

George Santayana located the 'unshared essence of Americanism' in its total absorption with work, combined with liberty of spirit. Work was equated with business, and business became the object of attention; all else was regarded with indifference. [17] The Americans' feverish pursuit of money and things was a constant preoccupation of foreign visitors, and it elicited condemnations and stern warnings, particularly from Rudyard Kipling and Matthew Arnold. [18] But what they overlooked in their categorical disapproval of materialism was the ideology behind it. Theories of business such as Andrew C. Carnegie's *Empire of Business* (1902) were neither factual nor theoretical, but on the contrary overflowed with morality, mysticism and piety. A quasi-religious rationale for business was expounded in quaintly edifying books like *The Imperial Highway, or the Road to Fortune and Happiness, with biographies of Self-Made Men, their Business Traits, Qualities and Habits* (Chicago, 1888), and the very popular *Success* (1897) and *Pushing to the Front* by Orison Swett Marden.

Success in business was the equivalent of deliverance – the acquisition of money made man independent and liberated him from his former condition of servitude. As Alexis de Toqueville wrote in 1834, democracy was another word for equality. [19] Following this line of interpretation, James Bryce wrote in 1893, 'Democratic government has in reality not much to do with it ... More must be ascribed to the equality of material conditions.' [20]

It is this same curious deviation from the current understanding of democracy that made Frank Lloyd Wright's use of the word in 'a democratic architecture' so puzzling to the non-American reader. What he meant, in fact, was an individual, non-conformist architecture which would suit the equally non-conformist, uniquely individual Self-Made Man. No phrase is more revealing than this; it is the archetypal American notion of the man who created himself, who had to invent and re-invent himself and his environment, competing with other self-made men (all starting with the proverbial equal opportunities) to grab as many riches as there were lying around in that richly stocked primordial garden. Those who grabbed the most were regarded as not only most successful but also the most individual and the most 'democratic'.

Sooner or later this process of auto-creation would bring the self-made man face-to-face with the Creator. This confrontation would usually take place at what could be characterized as the point where the acquisition of wealth comes to a halt and where the dispensing of it begins. If the acquisition of wealth was vested with social obligation and moral responsibility, so too was the dispensing of it. Carnegie considered it immoral to sit on one's fortune: 'The epitaph which every rich man should wish himself justly entitled to is that seen upon the monument to Pitt: 'He lived without ostentation, And he died poor.'' Such is the man whom the future is to honour, while he who dies in old age retired from business, possessed of millions of available wealth, is to die unwept, unhonoured and unsung.' [21]

*Fig. 8. Paedomorphic architecture: James Stirling and his Babylonian sand-castle (from* The Sunday Times Magazine, *17 August 1980).*

16. Louis Horowitz and Boyden Sparkes, *The Towers of New York: The Memoirs of a Master Builder* (New York, 1937), p. 120.

17. Richard Colton, editor, *Santayana on America* (New York, 1968), p. 240.

18. Richard L. Rapson, *Britons View America: Travel Commentary, 1860–1935* (Seattle and London, 1971), p. 12.

19. Alexis de Toqueville, *De la démocratie en Amérique* (Paris, 1864), I, 85–7.

20. Bryce, op. cit., II, 887.

21. Andrew Carnegie, *The Empire of Business* (London and New York, 1902), pp. 144–5.

22. Edward W. Bok, *Dollars Only* (New York and London, 1926), p. 157.

23. Arthur Koestler, *Janus – A Summing Up* (London, 1978), pp. 216–218.

24. Ibid., p. 219.

25. Jacques Hermant, visiting Chicago on behalf of the *Gazette des Beaux-Arts* in 1893, was much impressed by the Chicago skyscrapers' single, simple and brutal statement of tallness. He analyzed this phenomenon, combined with what he called 'primitive ornament' (possibly referring to the organic decoration of Sullivan), as 'la vraie création d'un peuple nouveau, primitif en art, inconscient de ses propres forces, qui bégaye [babbles] et ne sait que ce que les autres lui ont appris' ('L'Art à l'exposition de Chicago', *Gazette des Beaux-Arts* (1893), vol. X, 3e série, pp. 245–6).

26. Lewis Mumford, *The Condition of Man* (London, 1944), p. 59.

27. Carnegie, op. cit., p. 18.

## Paedomorphosis

The ritual of making money honourably obliged its participants to begin with nothing and to end with nothing; the intermediate phase was simply proof of the ability to 'make good'. It might be assumed that the most logical solution would be to refund the fortune to those who had, wholeheartedly or reluctantly, contributed to it, but this idea was rejected as prodigal, despite an eloquent appeal by Edward Bok, editor of the *Ladies' Home Journal*, for a system of 'moving back of wealth to its sources', the motto being 'If I had the gift to make money, why can't I acquire the gift of giving it away?'[22]

This process of artificial impoverishment is related to the atavistic act of rejuvenation. In evolutionary theory it is called 'paedomorphosis', a 'retreat from the adult to a juvenile stage as the starting-point for the new line'. At certain critical stages, evolution can, in the words of Arthur Koestler, 'retrace its steps, as it were, along the path which led to the dead end and make a fresh start in a new, more promising direction.'[23] Paedomorphosis generally occurs in the creative process, when the mind reverts to 'primitive modes of ideation, followed by a creative forward leap'.[24] In the history of art, especially in what is called 'modern' art, this phenomenon can be observed in the retreat to primitive models in the work of Brancusi, Picasso, Klee and others. The American skyscraper also has roots in a paedomorphic inversion of the mature refinements of civic architecture into the crude, archetypal pre-Babylonian Tower. This was significantly demonstrated by James Stirling when he sculpted a sand-castle for *The Sunday Times Magazine* of 17 August 1980 (Fig. 8).[25]

Complementary to this principle of 'reculer pour mieux sauter' were numerous religious notions, of not only Christianity but also American transcendentalism, of the inevitability of death and the obligation to favour the conditions of new life. Emerson compacted this philosophy into the aphorism 'Life only avails, not the having lived.'[26] Similarly, the conduct of business must not be impeded by retrospection and it should be resuscitated periodically by the removal of its burden of sufficiency. Sufficiency was regarded as the main impediment to a successful career in business, hence President Garfield's famous dictum, 'The richest heritage a young man can be born to is poverty.' In an address of 1885 to students in Pittsburgh, Carnegie went so far as to 'congratulate poor young men upon their being born to that ancient and honourable degree which renders it necessary that they should devote themselves to hard work.'[27] A slightly modified version of this pattern may be found in the life histories of some of the greatest American artists, for example Louis Sullivan and Frank Lloyd Wright, in which the artist is deprived of a solid upbringing and education and, as an autodidact, recreates himself.[28] But 'success' and 'survival' in the field of business were uniquely dependent, not on education, but on the ability to compete.

## Competition

The natural condition of business is competition, in which free and independent individuals engage in battle with total commitment to the laws of nature. The rules of the battle are few but relentlessly clear. As Geoffrey Gorer, 'Control over people – authority – is always morally bad; [but] control over things, or abstractions envisaged as things (natural resources, goods, services, money, chattel) – power – is morally neutral and even, within certain ill-defined limits, highly praiseworthy.'[29]

28. Ibid., p. 125; also Paul Starrett, op. cit., note 13, p. 14. The highly successful Starrett brothers all began their careers after an aborted high-school education: 'Theodore was about to graduate from Lake Forest, but old Dr. Gregory, the president, said he couldn't get a diploma until he made up a biblical course which he had flunked. Theodore decided to use that as an excuse to quit school and go to work. Ralph and I decided to quit, also, and we did. Theodore was eighteen, I was sixteen. Ralph was fourteen. That was the last of school for the three of us. We all got jobs in Chicago.' A telling story. Doubtless a good education for all, one of the ideals of American democracy, was still held in high esteem, yet working was regarded as manlier and a sign of self-reliance, therefore morally superior. A strong specimen of the anti-educational ideology is Orison Swett Marden's chapter on 'The Help Yourself Society', in his book *Success* (Boston, Mass., 1897), pp. 140–68.
The mistrust of education among American architectural historians was, and still is, such that they have treated the Columbian Exposition of 1893 as an act of treason, by a bunch of effeminate European-educated gentlemen, against the original and self-sufficient Chicago School. It is impossible to find an exception to this rule, just as it would be difficult to single out any of the architectural histories as most exemplary in illustrating this train of thought. Wayne Andrew's *Architecture, Ambition and Americans* (1947) (New York and London, 1964) is a parody of its kind: for the glorification of Sullivan's tragic failures in higher education, see pp. 214–217; for Wright, who 'was only eighteen when he quit the School of Engineering at the University of Wisconsin to look for work', pp. 230–1; for Holabird, who 'failed to graduate from West Point', p. 210; for the 'pernicious' influence of the gentlemen from the East, pp. 220ff. Ayn Rand's *The Fountainhead* (New York, 1943) remains unsurpassed in its infantile heroization of the above-mentioned characteristics. Very enlightening, on the other hand, is Ernst Kris and Otto Kurz's *Die Legende vom Künstler: Ein geschichtlicher Versuch* (Vienna, 1934), p. 26.

29. Geoffrey Gorer, *The Americans; A Study in National Character* (London, 1948), p. 26.

30. Ralph Waldo Emerson, *Essays: 1st & 2nd Series* (1841) (London, 1906), p. 33.

31. Horowitz and Sparkes, op. cit., p. 119 (see above note 13).

32. John K. Winkler, *Five and Ten: The Fabulous Life of Frank W. Woolworth* (Bantam Books, 1957), p. 120. Dr. Louk Tilanus was kind enough to provide this book.

33. *The Imperial Highway*, pp. 166ff.

34. Horowitz and Sparkes, op. cit., p. 120. The most obvious source for Woolworth's Napoleon cult must have been the popular illustrated magazines of the time, particularly *The Century Magazine* of New York, which featured, from November 1894 to October 1896, a lavishly illustrated series called 'The Life of Napoleon Bonaparte', by William Sloane. Some of the prints are likely to have served as models for Woolworth's executive office.

35. Winkler, op. cit., pp. 184–5.

Success was the measure of right. In his celebrated essay on 'Self-Reliance' (1841) Emerson expounded the unity of independent action and the laws of nature, and so prepared the way for the 'self-helping' man who would find the laws of nature on his side as long as he held fast to his integrity: 'Power is in nature the essential measure of right.'[30]

The power which Frank W. Woolworth had accumulated by 1900 was embodied in fifty-nine stores with annual sales of five million dollars and in a palatial mansion on 'Millionaires' Row', Fifth Avenue, New York. Following the rules of the myth, Woolworth was the product of a modest upbringing, he had grossly neglected school, and he had developed a taste for vulgarity. In his palace on Fifth Avenue he installed the first of a series of increasingly grandiose mechanical pipe organs, about which Louis Horowitz respectfully recalled:

His favourite toy was an electrical reproducing pipe organ, the ducts of which were cunningly placed throughout the palace-like interior. Many times I watched him at the organ. Other minds, other skills conceived the music, but his was the will to control the speed and the volume. He told me that this playing gave him exquisite pleasure; when he was tired or vexed he would play for hours, not stopping until he was relaxed and easy in his mind.[31]

What Horowitz did not mention was the extraordinary light-shows and 'artistic' visual effects that accompanied the music. 'Just before the opening of a great orchestral classic,' Woolworth's posthumous biographer John K. Winkler wrote, 'with the room in darkness, a magnificent oil portrait of the composer – Wagner or Beethoven, Liszt or Mendelssohn – would appear in a panel on top of the wall, at first faintly, then growing clearer and clearer until the vision was developed in light.'[32]

Owing to a lack of proper schooling and a self-imposed exile from the world of high culture, the self-made man finds himself, at a certain point, facing a higher state of life, to which he feels obliged to respond. But the problem is that, because of his ethos of individualism, the self-made man has no tradition, let alone a cultural tradition, to fall back upon. The logical consequence is that, if there is to be a culture, it has to be an instant, self-made culture.

## Self-culture

This condition has been discerned and diagnosed in preceding periods as 'self-culture'.[33] There is no theory of what constitutes self-culture but, if it had to be constructed, it ought to contain at least three ingredients: an insistence on resurrecting juvenile fantasies and dreams; an inclination to justify the current mode of life by identifying with famous self-made men of the past; and an edge of insanity.

Woolworth's infernal pipe-organ made him 'relaxed and easy in the mind' whenever he was 'tired or vexed'. (This confidence in the therapeutic effects of his infernal machinery he shared with fictional 'vexed' organists such as Count Dracula and Captain Nemo.) Not so eccentric, and indeed traditional, was Woolworth's awakening ambition to be Napoleon. On the fortieth floor of his building were his private and executive offices. The latter, called the Empire Room, was furnished as if it were Napoleon's own room. Horowitz described it as follows: 'His marbled office in the completed building gave a clue to how the Woolworth Building's owner felt (Fig. 9). The furnishings were all French Empire things; upon the wall just where his gaze would fall most often was a full-length portrait of Napoleon in his coronation robes and, beside him, Josephine'.[34] Woolworth's candidness about his 'kingly afflic-

*Fig. 9. 'The Empire Room', Frank W. Woolworth's office in the Woolworth Building (from* The Cathedral of Commerce, *1916).*

tion', as Horowitz called it, is touching. In a letter of 20 February 1914, which he dispatched to all his stores, he described his new habitat. Apart from the portrait of Napoleon, 'copied directly from the picture at Versailles', there were a life-size bust of him and an ink-well 'that was bought in Paris and represents Napoleon on horseback in bronze. A smaller figure of Napoleon is a paper weight, 100 years old.' And so on.[35] The parallels to Woolworth's own career were irresistible: Napoleon was also a self-made man and, moreover, he had built, in the shortest possible time, a vast empire, with little more than his own genius.

Despite professing to be a democracy, America had — and still has — a perverse weakness for its role as an empire. Bishop George Berkeley had predicted in the early eighteenth century:

Westward the course of empire takes its way;
The first four Acts already past,
A fifth shall close the Drama with the day;
Time's noblest offspring is the last.[36]

The Hudson School painter Thomas Cole had illustrated it in the sequence 'Course of Empire' of 1830.[37] And whoever invented the name Empire State for the State of New York must have acknowledged this ideal. Naturally, the Empire State Building was intended as the ideological capitol of its own mystic realm.[38]

### 'Gloria de' Prencipi'

Competition in business results not necessarily in the humiliation of the defeated but rather in the material gain of the victor. When Woolworth entered into competition with his equals and defeated them, he was content to let his balance-sheet speak for itself. The satisfaction and glory, on the other hand, he sublimated into his impersonation of Napoleon. He was not the only businessman who had undergone this metamorphosis at the summit of his career.

36. George Berkeley, *The Works*, III, Oxford 1871, p. 231. See also 'Apokatastasis', n. 30.

37. The sequence was recently published in *Architectural Design*, 52 (November/December 1982).

38. See Lewis Mumford, *Sticks and Stones, A Study of American Architecture and Civilization* (New York, 1955), pp. 55–69. Mumford called the period 1890–1910 'the Imperial Age' (p. 71). See also Henry S. Commager, *The American Mind: An Interpretation of American Thought and Character Since the 1880's* (New Haven, 1950), p. 11.

*Fig. 10. The Foshay Tower, Minneapolis, by Wilbur Foshay and Magney & Tusler and Hooper & Janusch, 1929 (postcard).*

39. Winkler, op. cit., p. 232.

40. Paul Starrett, op. cit., p. 115.

41. Gorer, op. cit., pp. 127ff.

42. Henry James, *The American Scene* (London, 1907), p. 96.

43. Leopold Eidlitz, *The Nature and Function of Art, More Especially of Architecture* (New York, 1881), p. 333.

44. John Ruskin, *The Seven Lamps of Architecture* (New York, 1885?), III, 170.

45. Cesare Ripa, *Iconologia* (Roma, 1593 [1]); see also Edward A. Maser, editor, *Baroque and Rococo Pictorial Imagery: The 1758/60 Hertel Edition of Ripa's Iconologia with 200 Engraved Illustrations* (New York, 1971). Joseph Mascheck's unpublished dissertation, 'Irish Church-Building Between the Treaty of Limerick and the Great Famine' (New York, 1973), led me to this interpretation of obelisk-shaped buildings.

Woolworth's successor in the firm from 1919–32 'too, became obsessed with ideas of Napoleonic grandeur',[39] and Paul Starrett, the contractor and colleague of Horowitz, noted in his memoirs: 'Harry Black, my boss, had a Napoleon complex. Like Napoleon, and those Napoleons of my day, Harriman, Jim Hill, J.P. Morgan, Black loved to amalgamate and to expand.'[40] Although this behaviour might be interpreted as epidemic mental regression, it should be regarded rather as the usual pattern of self-culture at the high tide of a millionaire's fulfilment. Its complement is the rejection of power over people and its transfer to things.[41] This is perhaps one of the most important aspects of the American skyscraper phenomenon: if power could be transferred to matter, this matter could then be transformed into buildings.

*Fig. 11. Anthropomorphic architecture: a yellow-ribbon 'bow-tie' around the 'neck' of the Foshay Tower (photo: Stormi Greener, from* Time *magazine, 2 February 1981).*

*Fig. 12. 'Gloria de' Prencipi' (from Cesare Ripa,* Iconologia, *1611 (1593¹).*

The archetypal and anthropomorphic tower, with its resemblance to the human form and its dominating presence, was the ideal symbol of its master. Skyscrapers acted as architectural mercenaries in the battle of competition. (In *The American Scene* of 1907, Henry James described the skyscrapers of downtown Manhattan as 'mercenary monsters'. [42])

The final element of the passion which inspired Woolworth to erect his stupendous tower on Broadway at City Hall Park was a desire for immortality. The architect Leopold Eidlitz wrote, in his influential theory of architecture *The Nature and Function of Art, more Especially of Architecture* (New York, 1881), that 'The origin of architecture must be thought in the desire of man to live after death. This short life of ours is devoted to live as long as we can ... After this we desire to connect our individuality with the cosmic spirit, that it may outlast our body and become immortal.' [43] The idea of architecture as a data bank of the past is best known through Victor Hugo's *Notre-Dame de Paris* and John Ruskin's 'The Lamp of Memory' ('for it is in becoming memorial or monumental that a true perfection in architecture is attained by civil and domestic buildings'). [44]

In 1929 Wilbur Foshay, a kitchen-utensils magnate from Minneapolis, Minnesota, converted his fortune into an office building in the shape of an obelisk (Fig. 10). He had his name engraved on the four sides of the building, at about the same height where, to speak in anthropomorphic terms, a tennis player's headband displaying the name of his sponsor would be. Hardly anybody now knows to whom or what the name Foshay refers. Wilbur Foshay the man is forgotten, but the monument which carries his name is alive and well and popular enough to appear, wearing a yellow bow-tie around its 'neck', in a *Time* magazine special report of 2 February 1981 on the homecoming of the Iranian hostages (Fig. 11).

Foshay, who ruined himself with this breathtaking project, and ended up in jail, had two objectives: one was immortality and the other was to be George Washington. The means he used to achieve these were as simple as they were effective. The erection of an obelisk had been a traditional means of commemorating princely rulers (see Cesare Ripa's *Iconologia* of 1611 (1593¹)) (Fig. 12). [45] George Washington, the first president of the last empire – to paraphrase Berkeley – had been immortalized by the Washington Monument, an outsized obelisk 550 feet high. Like the sorcerer's apprentice, Foshay followed the magic formula step by step: first he had himself transformed into a building that would bear his memory into the future – his name had to be etched into the stone so that it could never be erased; then he constructed the building in the form of an obelisk resembling the one that represented his worshipped hero; and the two converged, as if in an Ovidian metamorphosis. A local poet jingled accordingly:

A symbol of that other shaft
Revered the nation thru
The vision of a dreaming lad
In stone and steel come true.

The complex explanation which accompanied the Woolworth Building included a claim that it was 'a monument to small things' and that it was 'the colossal and enduring gift to civilization of a trueborn, patriotic American, Frank W. Woolworth, and it stands unique in the history of great buildings throughout the world in that it is without a mortgage or dollar indebtedness.' The building was conceived, in other words, as a memorial to the means by which its owner had assembled his fortune, namely nickels and dimes, the

*Fig. 13. Cass Gilbert holding a model of the Woolworth Building – Woolworth Building, ground-floor arcade.*

*Fig. 14. Bust of Peter Parler in Prague Cathedral (from John Harvey,* The Master Builders, *1971).*

46. The average commercial skyscraper erected in the business centres of the so-called boom-towns was usually the product of speculative building and development. The tall buildings of Chicago from the early 1880s onward are a case in point. The Boston firm of Peter and Shepard Brooks was the most prolific of this type of developer. See Carl W. Condit, *The Chicago School of Architecture* (Chicago and London, 1973), pp. 51ff., and Earle Shultz and Walter Simmons, *Offices in the Sky* (Indianapolis and New York, 1959), pp. 20ff.
Speculative building was not always favourably received. Charles Harris Whitaker, in his *The Story of Architecture from Rameses to Rockefeller* (New York, 1934), made a point of condemning anything that even resembled a skyscraper as a pernicious

'atomic elements' of capitalism. But it also represented Woolworth's preparations for the hereafter: the money was being returned to the public in the form of a building that was without the sin of usury. [46]

The enduring nature of Woolworth's 'gift' is symbolized by its medieval style, and its architect, Cass Gilbert, holding a model of the building, is sculpted as the *magister operis* (Fig. 13), in the tradition of Peter Parler's bust in the triforium of Prague Cathedral (Fig. 14). In the same vein is the luxuriously presented dedication booklet of 1913, which bears the title 'The Master Builders'. (It should here be noted that the skyscrapers of the 'heroic' period, 1875–1929, were exclusively 'hand-made' and never, as is so often misunderstood, or wilfully misinterpreted, in the machine-age-type textbooks, prefabricated or factory-made products.)

It is here that the metaphor of the cathedral makes its appearance. Once money and power have been accumulated, and the days of Napoleon are past, it is time for charity – the building is a public instead of private palace. And since Woolworth wanted to be no less a prince than Napoleon, he would be no less a prelate than Christ himself. High on the building, where the tower soars upward, is the figure of a pelican, the symbol of self-sacrifice and of the Redeemer (Fig. 15). The Cathedral of Commerce becomes a kind of Jacob's ladder, a connection between heaven and earth, an *axis mundi*. As Le Corbusier so rightly observed, 'Face au vieux continent elle [New York] à installé l'échelle de Jacob des temps nouveaux. Un choc dans le ventre qu'on encaisse en ouragan.' [47]

## The Cathedral of Learning

When Colonel W.A. Starrett, another macro-contractor from the Starrett family, wrote that 'building skyscrapers is the nearest peace-time equivalent to war', [48] he was hinting at, amongst other things, the destructive forces that could be generated by these juggernauts. As mythology teaches us, war and destruction are constituents of the act of creating order, [49] thus the destructive force of the skyscraper was called forth to create order in the American wilderness. Which it did: the image of the medium-sized town clustered around a skyscraper – where in the old days there would have been a church or a town hall – is familiar enough. On the other hand, this destructive force could also strike out at its maker. Building costs were often prohibitive, loans and taxes could swallow millions, and many builders of skyscrapers perished by them or with them. [50] This is exactly how it went with the 'Cathedral of Learning'.

The Cathedral of Learning was as blatant an example of recycled Gothic as the Cathedral of Commerce. Designed by the architect Charles Z. Klauder and the Chancellor of the University of Pittsburgh, John G. Bowman, it was built between 1926 and 1937 (Fig. 16). The programme was as simple as it was profound: 'to express the meaning of a University by a great high building.' [51]

This was not a new idea, nor one that was necessarily inspired by the possibilities of skyscraper construction. Antonio Averlino, called 'Il Filarete' (he who loves virtue), had already designed and described, in the mid-fifteenth century, a tower of learning, which he named the House of Virtue. Into it he incorporated a De Sade-like philosophy, in which the highest level of wisdom could be achieved only after an initial period of bawdiness, followed by the progressive accumulation of virtue. This path of gradual detachment from material things is expressed in successive levels of the building. On the ground floor are brothels and drinking saloons; on the second floor, dormitories for prostitutes and the police headquarters; on the third floor the revels end and the studies begin; and from the fourth floor upward there is the usual array of liberal arts, until the observation platform is reached, where the art of astronomy is used to explore all of Creation, Heaven as well as Earth.

*Fig. 15 (above). A gargoyle on the Woolworth
Building: the pelican, symbol of charity and of the
Redeemer (from* The Master Builders, *1913).*

*Fig. 16 (right). The Cathedral of Learning,
Pittsburgh, by Charles Z. Klauder, 1926–37.*

contribution to civilization. Writing in the aftermath
of the Crash of 1929, he characterized the skyscraper thus: 'Skyscrapers are ... buildings, the first
purpose of which is to enable the individual, or
group, to cash in on land' (p. 287), and 'Against the
rising billions of debt that rested on nothing but human congestion, skyscrapers rose endlessly' (p. 295).
Against this it is important to realize that Woolworth wanted his skyscraper to be as 'clean' as
possible.

47. 'Facing the old Continent, New York has installed the Jacob's ladder of modern times. We have
to take that as a punch in the stomach.' (Le Corbusier, op. cit., p. 59) On Jacob's ladder as the *axis
mundi*, see Mircea Eliade, *The Sacred and the Profane: The Nature of Religion* (New York, 1961),
pp. 26, 37.

48. Colonel W.A. Starrett, *Skyscrapers and the Men
Who Build Them* (New York and London, 1928),
p. 63. Alvin Boyarsky kindly lent me his copy of
this remarkable book. See also Shultz and Simmons,
op. cit., pp. 320–1: 'The tearing down and building
up that is forever going on here, at the heart of
things, gives evidence of vigor and vitality that will
continue to demolish and create.'

49. Eliade, op. cit., p. 55.

50. Whitaker, op. cit., pp. 286 ff.; Shultz and Simmons, op. cit., p. 74; Horowitz, op. cit.,
pp. 117-118: 'The truth is that every extremely tall
building seems to be a solid refutation of the notion
that they may be good investments.'; George F.
Warren and Frank A. Pearson, 'The Building
Cycle', *Fortune*, XVI, 84–8, 136, 140; Alfred C.
Bossom, *Building to the Skies: The Romance of the
Skyscraper* (London, 1934), p. 106: 'The early skyscrapers rarely showed a profit on the investment.'

*Fig. 17. A skyscraper of learning by Jacques Perret (from Jacques Perret,* Des fortifications et artifices d'architecture et perspective, *1601).*

51. John G. Bowman, *The Cathedral of Learning of the University of Pittsburgh* (Pittsburgh, Penn., 1925), pp. 5–6: 'The spirit of achievement, which is the aim of the University, is also a provincial or distinctive development of Pittsburgh itself. It follows, then, that if by a great high building we could express the meaning of the University, we could also interpret the spirit of Pittsburgh both to itself and to the world.' See also p. 8: 'Height Tells Idea'.

52. Joseph Ponten, *Architektur die nicht gebaut wurde*, 2 vols (Stuttgart, Berlin and Leipzig, 1925), I, 41; II, 35: 'il faut monter au plus hault pour contempler et le ciel et la terre et les choses qui y sont afin d'adorer dieu seul le père et le fils et le sainct esprit en esprit et vérité auquel soit seule gloire ès ciècles amen'.
Ascending the staircase of a tall building has always been a popular symbol for the ascent of the intellect. See Wolfram Prinz, *Schloss Chambord und die Villa Rotonda in Vicenza: Studien zur Ikonologie* (Berlin, 1980), p. 63; and Johann-Christian Klamt, 'Der Runde Turm in Kopenhagen als Kirchturm und Sternwarte: ein bauikonologische Studie', *Zeitschrift für Kunstgeschichte* 38 (1975), 153–70. Klamt mentions some interesting proto-cathedrals of learning, for example the English sixteenth-century 'Castle of Knowledge' (p. 158) and the round tower of the Church of Trinity, Copenhagen (pp. 153ff).

53. Bowman, op. cit., p. 7. Bowman added to this: 'The idea of force in action is attained somewhat in the way that Wagner carries us to the mountain top in the fire music of *Die Walküre*' (p. 9).

54. John Henry Cardinal Newman, *The Idea of a University, Defined and Illustrated* (1852) (London, New York and Toronto, 1935), p. 82.

55. Agnes Lynch Starrett, *Through One Hundred and Fifty Years: The University of Pittsburgh* (Pittsburgh, Penn., 1937), pp. 258ff.

A similar programme was incorporated into Jacques Perret's famous 'spiritual skyscraper' which he designed at the end of the sixteenth century (Fig. 17). It was accompanied by the following text: 'One has to climb to the top in order to contemplate the Heavens as well as the Earth and the other things which are there to Praise and Worshop the Lord, and the Son and the Holy Spirit, whose is the Glory in Eternity. Amen.'[52]

The significant difference between the Cathedral of Learning and its forerunners, and a characteristic of a great deal of American building culture, is that it was actually realized – the transcendence, once again, of materialism. From a practical point of view there was absolutely no need to build high; the University of Pittsburgh owned large expanses of land, and building in the horizontal direction would have been more useful and economical. Here the inherent contradictions of material transcendentalism are clearly illustrated. Naturally, appeals were made to efficiency and common sense, but only half-heartedly, as a necessary ritual performed for the benefit of the less imaginative investors. The weight of the argument was concentrated at the other extreme, in the almost religious fanaticism with which 'believers' were admonished to sacrifice their worldly goods to a work that was 'Forceful, unafraid, sublime, with a sense of upwardness; it starts our accustomed limits of thought and life to move farther away.'[53] The structure was to be 680 feet and 52 storeys high, and the style had to be Gothic. The ground floor was to be occupied by a vast hall in the guise of a Gothic cathedral, surrounded by a ring of so-called 'nationality rooms', classrooms decorated in the manner of the different ethnic groups of Pennsylvania – mythical reconstructions of a lost past, souvenirs of places never visited.

The significance of this impressive undertaking is, of course, its undiluted aspiration to express the 'Idea of Universal Learning'[54] by equating it with what had become the national means of expression: height. Once again, the dream of Jacob (Genesis 28: 12–16) had been recreated in skyscraper matter. The Jacob's ladder illustrated in Robert Fludd's *Utriusque Cosmi Majoris . . . II* of 1619 clearly shows the progressive stages of learning (as in Perret's and Filarete's models) which lead to such perfection that, by completing the final phase (in this case *verbum* – 'the word' – rather than Filarete's astronomy), one almost automatically enters into Heaven.

When the Crash finally came, in 1929, the Cathedral of Learning was not yet finished. The community had ruined itself and was left with empty pockets and half a tower. However, Bowman began, even in the deepest depths of the Depression, to collect funds to get the tower temporarily patched up with cloth and board, until finally, in 1937, he had gathered enough money together by exciting patriotic and religious sentiments – just as in medieval practice – to complete it to its proper splendour.[55]

*Fig. 18. Trinity Church eclipsed by the Irving Trust Building (from A.T. Leitich, New York, 1932).*

---

56. Ralph Adams Cram, *Church Building: A Study of the Principles of Architecture in Their Relation to the Church* (1899) (Boston, 1924), p. 71. The accusation was repeated in 1934, when the same fate befell St. Patrick's Cathedral: 'And almost in the shadow of Radio City will lurk the cathedral of the two thousand year old Catholic Church ... once its proud and confident towers dominated the low-lying town, now, like Wall Street Trinity, it will find itself abased and inconsiderable' (Ralph Adams Cram, 'Radio City Hall – And After', *Convictions and Controversies* (Boston, 1934), p. 41).

57. Expressions like 'to dwarf' and 'to eclipse' were frequently used in the competition among the builders of commercial skyscrapers. In the *Real Estate Record and Builders Guide*, 1 September 1888, p. 1064, the new building for *The World* newspaper on Newspaper Row, New York City, is announced in the following terms: 'When the *World* building is completed, the *Sun* [another newspaper] will be overshadowed by the other newspaper established nearby. It will never do for that bright paper to be eclipsed in any way.' In *Munsey's Magazine*, XII (February 1895), p. 526, George Holme wrote, 'Trinity's spire was for a long time the pride of New York, as its highest structure, but now it is being dwarfed by the huge office buildings.' The City Bank and Farmers' Trust published a booklet to inaugurate their new office tower at 22 William Street, New York City, in 1931 (Cross & Cross, architects), which included a section of Joshua Beal's panoramic photograph of Lower Manhattan in 1876 (featuring, by the way, the earliest skyscrapers: the Western Union Building of 1875 and the Tribune Building of the same year, which went unnoticed by the publishers), to which the following caption was added: 'New York in 1874 [sic] when Trinity Church tower had no skyscraper competition' ('The Oldest Trust',1931, p. 15). For Beal's photograph, see Mary Black, *Old New York in Early Photographs, 1853–1901* (New York, 1973), pp. vi–x.

## 'Restore the Cross to the Skyline!'

It is no surprise that the Church should react quite quickly to the intrusions of the worldly skyscrapers into its traditional domain, at first with a sense of injury and injustice, later with bitterness, and still later with publicly displayed vindictiveness. The objections were mainly to the way in which the skyscrapers loomed over and dominated existing church buildings, which had hitherto been the sole connections between heaven and earth. Ralph Adams Cram, an eminent church builder of stern authority, had begun his attacks on the skyscraper as early as 1899:

The church must adapt itself to new conditions, conform in measure to its environment ... We find churches with low walls, many little features, slender spires, and all other accessories of country design, set down in the immediate proximity of blocks of dwellings or mercantile buildings that lift absurdly above them, crushing them into ignominy, making towers that do not rise above the neighbouring cornices grotesque and laughable. [56]

First to be eclipsed by the commercial towers of New York was Trinity Church, at the junction of Broadway and Wall Street. Although the wealth of that parish was, and still is, enormous, it began to lose most of its parishioners, who moved uptown, until finally it was lost in the forest of tall buildings surrounding it (Fig. 18). In the end its sole *raison d'être* was to act as a yardstick against which the skyscrapers could be measured, and even to inspire boasts that they had 'dwarfed' or 'eclipsed that noble church of Trinity'. [57]

*Fig. 19. The Convocation Tower, by Bertram G. Goodhue, 1921 (from Hugh Ferriss,* The Metropolis of Tomorrow, *1929).*

58. Charles Harris Whitaker, editor, *Bertram Grosvenor Goodhue – Architect and Master of Many Arts* (New York, 1925), plates cxcvi and cxvii; Jean Ferriss Leich, *Architectural Visions: The Drawings of Hugh Ferriss* (New York, 1980), pp. 80–1, 135. Ferriss published the drawing in his *Metropolis of Tomorrow* (New York, 1929), p. 39, and wrote, 'This structure was proposed for a site adjoining Madison Square Garden; as may be guessed from its appearance, it was to house, on the main floor, a great auditorium [in fact a church] and above this, the huge shaft containing offices was to rise some thousand feet from the ground' (p. 40). The thousand-foot target had been, since the mid-nineteenth century, the recurring standard of the upward-reaching architectural imagination. It should be noted that the odd 304.8 metre height of the Eiffel Tower was merely the metric equivalent of 1,000 feet.

59. *The Western Architect*, 31 (April 1922), p. 50, plate 1. It is significant that those who kept apart from the trends of progressivism and modernism in American architectural history, G.H. Edgell for example, considered Goodhue to be the most original architect of his time. Edgell even gave the Convocation Tower the place of honour as the frontispiece of his *The American Architecture of Today* (New York and London, 1928) – a refreshing book indeed.

Cram's wrath was transmitted to his pupil Bertram Grosvenor Goodhue, who in 1921 designed the formidable Convocation Tower.[58] A rendering, for which it is renowned, was executed by Hugh Ferriss in his usual forbidding style: a total blackout of charcoal sweeps, broken here and there by patches of white, an explosion of light at the base that suggests a certain weightlessness, and a small but intense white light at the top, a cross exploding like a nova (Fig. 19). This was the Avenging Angel set loose to punish the worldly pretenders. Its location was to be Madison Square, a natural arena where it could crush both the Metropolitan Life Tower and that already ageing gladiator, the Flatiron (Fuller) Building.

The drawing was exhibited in Chicago (the city 'not a church entered into') at the Annual Architectural Exhibition of April 1922, and it was a smashing success. *The Western Architect* wrote, 'Bertram G. Goodhue's perspective of his proposed Convocation and Office Building, to house the centralized activities of the Protestant denominations, dominated the room in which it was hung, and, of course, was *the* wonderful drawing of the exhibition.'[59]

Here was the solution: a church and office tower in one! The idea was an immediate success and came to be known as the 'revenue church' (Fig. 20).[60] Although the Convocation Tower, alas, was never realized, it did produce a noble successor – the Chicago Temple, the First Methodist Church of Chicago, by Holabird and Roche, of 1924 (Fig. 21). The project was published in *Chicago Commerce* of 8 September 1923: 'Standing 556 feet from the street level to the tip of its spire, The Chicago Temple is the second highest building in the world ... It is the highest church in existence, being taller by a liberal margin than any European cathedral. It is also one foot higher than the Washington Monument.'[61] It was a foregone conclusion that the existing height-restricting ordinance of Chicago would have to be waived – after all, to be varied whenever it seems appropriate was the justification for its existence. And it seemed right, to many Chicagoans, and to its powerful Methodist congregation (we are in the middle of Prohibition, a battle successfully waged by Methodism), to call the New York skyscrapers of the twenties to order, so that the Church might re-establish its dominance in the sky. This was done in the most literal fashion imaginable. The building is shaped like an ambitious office tower, but on its 'shoulders' it carries a 'sky-chapel', a sort of miniature Sainte-Chapelle, accessible by an express elevator. The sky-chapel is, in essence, the ingeniously devised storeroom of the building's manifest conscience. It contains an unusual illuminated relief depicting Christ on the Mount of Olives, lamenting the destiny of Jerusalem. This tableau is the counterpart of a similar one in the street-level sanctuary, in which Christ is again shown brooding over Jerusalem, 'If thou hadst known' (Luke 19: 42) (Fig. 22). But here, in the 'sky-chapel', Jerusalem has been replaced by Chicago: Christ is looking down upon the Chicago Loop! Not hills and huts of clay, but the Union Carbide Building, the Lincoln Tower and the no doubt

*Fig. 20. 'Architect's Study for Revenue Type Building' (from M.W. Brabham,* Planning Modern Church Buildings, *1928).*

60. The idea of combining a church with other, secular, services was not an invention of the 1920s. Churches combined with shops had already existed in Europe, for example the church of S. Pietro di Banchi in Genoa, rebuilt in 1583, 'nella bizzarra mistione di architettura sacra e profana' (*Guida d'Italia: Liguria*, TCI Guide (Milan, 1967), p. 143), and in the United States, in New England, where several such churches were built in the 1830s (*Journal of the Society of Architectural Historians* (May 1980), p. 178–9). Indeed, American Methodism prided itself in having a considerable tradition in this field: 'To many an onlooker the combination of church and commercial buildings has the charm of novelty. One such enthusiast remarked the other day, 'Just see how the mind of John Wesley still energizes Christianity! he was the prince of innovators, and the church is nothing if not inventive.' ... Tremont Temple, in Boston, includes stores and offices. It was built thirty-two years ago ... The Old South, Congregational, in Boston, built stores on the land between parsonage and meeting house in 1800. The idea of building them originated in 1771' (*Finish the Broadway Temple* (New York, 1928), p. 23).

61. 'Chicago Temple: Wonder of Churches', *Chicago Commerce*, 8 September 1923, pp. 9–10. I am indebted to Robert Bruegman, who brought this rare article to my attention. To rise above the established height limit the city ordinance had to be broken. This was permitted by the City Council by unanimous vote. See *The Western Architect*, XXXII, 1, January 1923, p. 1.

*Fig. 21. The Chicago Temple, by Holabird & Roche, 1924 (postcard).*

*Fig. 22. Christ contemplates the City of Jerusalem – relief in the ground-floor sanctuary of the Chicago Temple.*

*Fig. 23. Christ contemplates the Chicago Loop – relief in the Sky-Chapel of the Chicago Temple.*

62. From a theological as well as mythological point of view, this is too wonderful a coincidence to be true, and in fact it is not. The Jewelers' Building (Thielbar and Fugard, architects, 1926) changed hands just after the building was put into operation, and by 1927 it had become the Pure Oil Building.

63. The Chicago Temple is not mentioned in Condit's main work on the architecture of Chicago, *The Chicago School of Architecture: A History of Commercial and Public Building in the Chicago Area 1875–1925* (Chicago and London, 1973), nor do the architectural guidebooks of the 1970s list it. In his *Chicago 1910–1929* (Chicago and London, 1973), Condit refers to it briefly as 'this curiosity' (p. 100).

64. Thomas Van Leeuwen, 'De commerciële stijl', in *Americana; Nederlandse architectuur 1880–1930* (Otterlo, 1975), p. 55.

65. A provisional list of 'sky-churches':
*New York City:* Convocation Tower, B. Goodhue, 1921 (project); Broadway Temple, D. Barber, 1924 (Broadway & 174 St., partly realized); A Combination Church, Store and Apartment Building in Brooklyn, Murray Klein, 1930 (project); Manhattan Congregational Church and Hotel Manhattan Towers, Tillion & Tillion, 1928 (2166 Broadway); Community Church and Apartment Building (10 Park Avenue); Second Presbyterian Church, 1929 (9 W. 96 St.); Calvary Baptist Church and Apartment Tower (W. 56 St.).
*Chicago:* Cathedral Building for the Protestant Episcopalian Diocese of Chicago, A. Granger, 1922 (project); Chicago Temple, Holabird & Roche, 1923 (77 W. Washington St.).
*Columbus, Ohio:* Central Methodist Church, R. Hood, Godley & Fouilhoux, 1931 (project).
*Pittsburgh, Pennsylvania:* Smithfield Church, 1926 (?) (project (?)).

hated Jewelers' Building, the most notable victim of the Temple's dominating height (Fig. 23). [62]

Although it was designed by a well-respected firm, the Chicago Temple remained relatively unknown, owing mainly to the disdain of the Modernists, who found it all in very bad taste. Thus it was ignored by post-Giedion American architectural historians, notably the local ideologist of the Chicago School, Carl W. Condit. [63] A visiting Modernist, Knut Lönberg-Holm (who became famous for his unsubmitted entry for the Chicago Tribune Competition), made a drawing of the Temple and sent it to his friend J.J.P.

*Fig. 24. Theomorphic architecture: The Broadway Temple, by Donn Barber, 1924 (from 'The Broadway Temple' album, 1924?).*

Oud in Holland. On the verso he wrote, 'Chicago DaDa Gotik'.[64]
The religious réveil began to invade all the big-city centres. The Methodist Church proved particularly aggressive in this. Sky churches were to be built, from 1924 onward, in Miami, Pittsburg, Minneapolis, Philadelphia and, in the heart of where it had all begun, New York City.[65] Here, as if having foreseen the deluge of 1929, the Methodist community of New York concentrated its efforts on a final, all-out attack. The Broadway Temple was to be the tallest building of all time — the Ultimate Avenging Angel — and it was to be built high upon the rocks of Upper Manhattan, in what is known as Washington Heights (Fig. 24). The aspirations of the builders were encapsulated in a single slogan: 'Restore the Cross to the Skyline!'[66]

**Theomorphism**

The rationale for this act was elucidated in the Broadway Temple album (Fig. 25):

For much too long a time, here in New York, secular architecture has dominated the scene. Manhattan boasts a 'Cathedral of Commerce', even a 'Cathedral of the Motion Pictures' — While office buildings, hotels and immense towering apartment houses dwarf (!) the tallest church spires, making the visible emblems of religion less and less conspicuous and planting in the young minds the idea that religion has ceased to be important. How far is the process to go? Build! Put the symbol of our saviour's dying love high above Manhattan, a sign and wonder, flashing back the sunlight by day and brilliantly luminous at night. Literally as well as figuratively: Let Your Light Shine![67]

It is apparent from this text that the chief object of attack was the Woolworth Building. Phrases like 'flashing back the sunlight' and 'brilliantly luminous at night' were actually lifted from Woolworth's dedication booklets. Suggestive drawings emphasizing the dominance and visibility of the Woolworth Building (Fig. 26) were paraphrased by the Broadway Temple's designers (Fig. 27) in order to make clear that the imposter was to be defeated by its own weapons.[68] For the sake of comparison, the Broadway Temple — in reality several

*Tulsa, Oklahoma:* Boston Avenue Methodist Church, Bruce Goff, 1926 (Boston Ave.).
*Los Angeles, California:* A Twentieth-Century Metropolitan Catholic Cathedral, Lloyd Wright, 1931 (project).
*Minneapolis, Minnesota:* Wesley Methodist Church and Office Building, 1926–1928, A.B. Boyer (partly realized (Figs. 28a&b). I thank Alan K. Lathrop, Minneapolis, who provided me with the necessary data.
*Miami, Florida:* First Baptist Church and Office Headquarters, after 1926 (projects).
See also: Mouzon William Brabham, *Planning Modern Church Buildings* (Nashville, Tennessee, 1928), p. 233; Alfred Granger, 'A Modern Cathedral for an Industrial City', *The American Architect – The Architectural Review*, CXXI (4 January 1922), pp. 5–10; G.H. Edgell, op. cit., pp. 369–72; *The Christian Advocate*, 9 September 1926, Part II, pp. 1245, 1247, 1255. I am grateful to Dennis Sharp, who recently unearthed an interesting contribution by the English skyscraper architect Alfred C. Bossom, a 'Proposed Church and Office Building, Dallas, Texas', illustrated in the *Journal of the Royal Society of Arts* (8 June 1928), p. 771. Raymond Hood's activities in this field have been described by Walter Kilham Jr, *Raymond Hood, Architect* (New York, 1973), p. 9, and by Rem Koolhaas, *Delirious New York* (New York, 1978), pp. 143–4.

*Fig. 25 (above). 'Let Your Light Shine!' (from 'The Broadway Temple' album).*

*Fig. 26 (right). 'The serried peaks made by the giant buildings, towers, church steeples, all seem to contend with each other for the distinction of "highest and greatest". But above them all rises the Woolworth Building, calm and unassailable.' (drawing and text from H.A. Bruce,* Above the Clouds & Old New York*, 1913).*

*Fig. 27. 'Restore the Cross to the Skyline! By day or by night — under the stars or through the storm clouds — the illuminated Cross will be a constant reminder of the rightful place of religion in the life of a teeming city. There was a time when the church spire was a familiar part of the Manhattan skyline. Now even the old Trinity is at the bottom of a wall of masonry. Hundreds of churches have been submerged. Out of sight, out of mind. Spiritual things must again be put first in the eye and thought of New York.' (original caption to the rendering, from 'The Broadway Temple' album).*

miles north of the business district — was drawn on a spot conveniently close to Madison Square and the Metropolitan Life Tower. The moon which hovered near the summit of the Woolworth Building had slipped squarely behind the Broadway Temple, as if to provide it with a natural halo, a halo that remained in all its representations — instead of being anthropomorphic, the building had become 'theomorphic'.

What the few sources which mention this ambitious project fail to tell us is that it was indeed executed, at least in part. Financial backing was generous and the best available designers were commissioned. Donn Barber, an outstanding and imaginative New York architect, drew up the original plans and it was Hugh Ferriss who made the presentation drawings (Fig. 24). Barber died shortly thereafter, in 1925, and the work was continued by the firm of Voorhees, Gmelin and Walker. Later still, after World War II, the building was brought to its present, unfinished, state by Shreve, Lamb and Harmon, the architects of the Empire State Building. What stands now are the two flanking apartment towers which were intended to bring in most of the revenues (Fig. 29). The central tower, with its colossal sanctuary, theatre, swim-

66. *The Broadway Temple*, album, 1924 (?), Broadway Temple Archives. I wish to thank the Reverend Richard S. Parker for giving me access to his material. Donn Barber and Hugh Ferriss's project for the Broadway Temple was first discussed by Herbert D. Croly, in 'The Skyscraper in the Service of Religion', *Architectural Record*, 55 (February 1924), pp. 203–4.

67. *The Broadway Temple*, 1924 (?).

68. *The Cathedral of Commerce*, op. cit., and H. Addington Bruce, *Above the Clouds & Old New York: An Historical Sketch of the Site and a Description of the Many Wonders of the Woolworth Building* (New York, 1913). Rem Koolhaas very generously lent me these books.

*Fig. 28a. Wesley Church, Minneapolis, A.B. Boyer, architect/engineer (project) (from:* The Christian Advocate, *September 9, 1926, part II, (167) 1255).*

*Fig. 28b. Wesley Church, Minneapolis, partly realized, on its present location on 115 East Grant Street (1926–1928).*

*Fig. 28a&b. 'A great down-town church where large crowds assemble morning and evening for the Sunday services and a "Seven-Days-a-Week" ministry continues the year round. A great advance has recently been made in the purchase of all the lots except two in block where church is located and a building programme adopted entailing an investment of approximately $4,000,000' (from* The Christian Advocate, *September 9, 1926, part II, (167) 1255).*

ming pools, basketball courts, Sunday schools and office quarters, never got off the ground. The war that Colonel Starrett had hinted at was fierce and destructive. The church spent all its money on a last attack, and the Crash of 1929 did the rest.

In the same year Hugh Ferriss published a collection of his drawings, *The Metropolis of Tomorrow* – but it certainly is not a view of 'tomorrow'. On the contrary, the dark, charcoal-drawn silhouettes of colossal but insubstantial

*Fig. 29. The Broadway Temple in its present state, at Broadway and 173 and 174 Streets, New York.*

buildings are a retrospective of pre-deluge architecture. The tallest figure by far is Religion, a sky-church, in which are housed Faith, Hope and Charity (Fig. 1). In its asthenic verticality, Religion, like its profane contemporaries, such as the extremely frail Mather (now Lincoln) Tower (1928) and 333 N. Michigan Tower (1928), in Chicago, and the Bank of Manhattan Building (now 40 Wall Street) (1929) and the Chrysler Building (1929), in New York, recalls the attenuated figures of Pontormo and Parmigianino. It seems that the aesthetic ideal of Mannerism haunted the desperate verticalism of the days of Prohibition, Fundamentalism and Black Wednesday, Thursday and Tuesday. In any case, Hugh Ferriss was sufficiently aware of the similarities between his city of doomed shadows and its grim biblical models. The final page of *The Metropolis of Tomorrow* is suggestively damaged on the lower right-hand corner, and the phrase 'who is made in the image of God' is violently interrupted, as if scorched by the approaching fire of His wrath (Fig. 30).

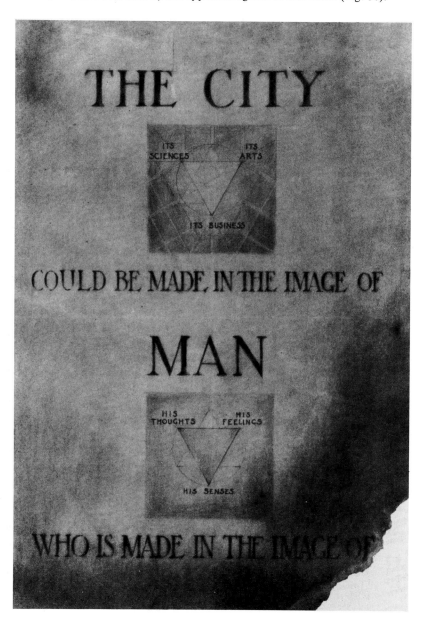

*Fig. 30. Scorched by the approaching fire of His wrath (from Hugh Ferriss,* The Metropolis of Tomorrow, *1929).*

# TUTTI

The following study concentrates on the emergence of the skyscraper in the down-town area of New York City about 1875.

'Growth comes naturally to New York.' – FLEMING AND KATES, New York, 1929.[1]

'Numberless crowded streets, high growths of iron, slender, strong, light, splendidly uprising toward clear skies.' – WALT WHITMAN, Mannahatta.[2]

## A Forest

'Every city is made and is as man makes it, but its growth is subject to the evolutionary processes of nature. It is an artificial growth in which art has to be allied with nature, and the supreme art in city building is to perfect that alliance.'

Thus were the opening lines of Thomas Adams' *The Building of The City* (1931), the monumental plan to re-create New York, the city that had already created itself.[3]

The 'laissez-faire' of the American economy could easily be translated into the 'laissez-pousser' of its big-city architecture. '... [I]n cities,' Claude Bragdon wrote in 1927, 'where for the most part the giant flora of architecture lifts its skyscraper heads,'[4] skyscrapers with the speed of well-cultivated plants shot up toward the sun.
Conditions for this rich growth were restricted to fantasy, capital and a simple, rectangular plant-bed in the shape of a giant gridiron (Fig. 1).[5]
It has often been said that the main characteristic of the American urban grid is its neutrality. It knows no hierarchy, it favours no special places, it disregards the topography of the site, and it allows no exceptions to the rule. Separation and division rather than centralization and symmetry were the ordering principles of the grid.[6] In the United States land existed to be sold, and the grid was a device for cutting it into handy portions, available to anyone who could meet the price. In the most generous interpretation the grid system has been described as America's democratic answer to the autocratic axiality of the European systems.
As Thomas Adams, chief author of the 1931 *Regional Plan* of New York City, summarized it, 'In the American city the disposal of the lots to individuals with liberty to make the best of them for their private purposes, was the governing factor in development, rather than architectural control in the interests of the community.'[7]
Since all plants in this nursery were granted quantities of soil, air and light, it might be expected that their growth rates would be similar. But, though conditions in the horizontal plane were equal, the vertical space was still free territory. And, because it was free, it was continuously disputed.
In their ambition for light and air all plants are engaged in a battle for the most advantageous exposure. Those with the misfortune of starting late have to content themselves with less favourable positions, and those which have grown tall create a new ecology in the air: the roof of the forest. Their crowns occupy the available space and no newcomers are allowed. They nevertheless have to share the terrestrial ecology with the short ones, which are doomed to continue their existence in ignoble and parasitic circumstances.

# THE MYTH OF NATURAL GROWTH I*

Fig. 1. 'A squared vegetable kitchen garden with light and air for everybody,' Kansas City in the 1930s (postcard).

92—Air View of Kansas City by Night, Kansas City, Mo.

*. 'The Myth of Natural Growth' was presented in part in a seminar given at the Art History Department of the University of Zürich, May 1985, and at the conference *L'Américanisme et la modernité*, organized by L'Institut Français d'Architecture and L'École Pratique des Hautes Études en Sciences Sociales, Paris, 23–25 October 1985. My gratitude goes to Prof. Stanislaus von Moos and Prof. Huber Damish, who encouraged me and offered me the opportunity to express my ideas in public.

1. 'Growth comes natural to New York; the topless towers of this modern Ilium soar beyond the wildest dreams of her founders.' Ethel Fleming & Herbert S. Kates, *New York*, London, 1929, p. 76.

2. Walt Whitman, *Leaves of Grass*, New York/ London (Norton), p. 475.

3. Thomas Adams, *Regional Plan of New York and Its Environs*, Vol. 2, *The Building of the City*, New York, 1931, p. 25.

4. Claude Bragdon, *Projective Ornament*, New York, 1927, p. 5.

5. References to the growth of New York and of its skyscrapers were very often made in terms of plants, particularly trees. The following samples give some idea of this: 'Every week ground is broken for new edifices, and a few months sees them rise into the blue, reaching, like the pine trees of the forest, ever upward' (Ethel Fleming and Herbert S. Kates, *New York*, London, 1929, p. 73); Eliel Saarinen spoke of '. . . the skyscraper forest springs starkly from the ground . . .' (*The City*, New York, 1943, p. 193); and: 'I procured a photograph of New York City, showing a forest of skyscrapers . . .' ('A New Architectural Language for America', *The Western Architect*, XXXII, February 2, 1923, p. 13). Dankmar Adler seems to have provided the earliest reference, when, in a contribution to *The Engineering Magazine*, IV, 1892, 'Light in Tall Office Buildings, p, 172, he compared the skyscrapers to 'the trees of the forest' (quoted by Donald Hoffmann, 'The Setback Skyscraper City of 1891: An Unknown Essay by Louis H. Sullivan', *J.S.A.H.*, 20, 1970, p. 103). The tropical rain forest is closely related to the idea of the big commercial city as a 'jungle'. 'Americans,' Henry Hope Reed wrote, 'embraced the idea of "bigness" as they embraced the ideas of free competition and the survival of the fittest — in the corporation, in wealth, in the labor force, in social problems and in their cities. Little wonder that they created hideous industrial towns and giant jungle cities, instruments at once of pride and despair.' Henry Hope Reed, *American Skyline*, Boston, 1956, pp. 118/119. The formation of the American grid is similar to the Romans' *centuratio*, a system by which land was parcelled into squares measuring twenty 'actus', containing one hundred little squares (*centuria*), and handed out to colonists. The grid is elaborately dealt with by John W. Reps, *The Making of Urban America*, Princeton, 1965. The grid as being analogous to plant-beds is examined in the poem *New York* by May Lewis:
'What are you, City, reared against the sky? Resounding city, mile on mile of stone!

With the assistance of a small refinement the comparison could be pushed a little further. Elevations of the skyscrapered city (Fig. 2) show two distinct levels: that of the skyscrapers and that of those beginning their rise where the others have ended. In the tropical rain forest these are called 'emergents'. Piercing the roof at certain places, they climb to heights more than 40 metres above the others. [8]

The set-back silhouette of the post-1916 skyscrapers is generally and uncritically accepted as the result of a public demand for air and light. [9] Nothing is farther from the truth. The general rule is that where business reigns business decides, and it is hardly imaginable that the civic authorities or even an army of pedestrians could have seriously impeded the ascent of the skyscraper. The real influence was business itself. In a tropical forest a limited number of positions are available for the tallest trees. No tree can fight its way up unless the other trees allow sufficient passage. Their leafy crowns recede and expand according to the mechanisms of a natural equilibrium. No such balance exists in the garden of business. Every little parcel can produce its own tower, whether it be a symbol of success, an advertisement or a speculative venture. But

Fig. 2. 'Sky-Line of New York – Old and New.' Pictures of the skyscrapered city show two levels of elevation: 'The old skyline is indicated by the darker shaded buildings in the foreground – the present sky-line by the lighter buildings beyond.' They represent the 'emergents' of the tropical rain forest. The picture dates from 1896 and was issued as a Supplement to Architects and Builders' Review, November 1896. It belonged to Cass Gilbert, the architect of the Woolworth Building. The darkly shaded tall building to the extreme right is one of America's earliest skyscrapers, the Washington Building, twelve storeys-plus-tower, 1882–1884, Edward Kendall, architect (demolished) (courtesy of the New York Historical Society, New York City).

THE EQUITABLE BUILDING, NEW YORK.

*Fig. 3. The (New) Equitable Building, New York, 1915, Ernest R. Graham, architect. 'The owners and tenants of these [other] buildings, who had looked down upon the roof of the old Equitable Building and up at the sky, didn't relish having to look out on a mammoth and towering new Equitable and no sky at all.'*[11] *(postcard).*

How was this towering, teeming harvest sown?
By little Man? not first floor window high!
What are the giant seeds that underlie
These checkered fields of granite, that have grown
Where Indian corn by river wind was blown?
What will the ultimate reaping signify?'
(Alice Hunt Bartlett, *The Anthology of Cities*, London, 1927, p. 163).
And Cecil Beaton, in his *Portrait of New York*, London/New York, etc., 1948 (1938[1]), p. 7, remembered 'a more realistic Chicago architect' who 'described Manhattan as an 'asparagus bed' with its sword-like shoots springing from the dense population and the fertile manure of wealth.'

6. See for the neutral, utopian and democratic aspects of the grid-iron, Ciucci, Dal Co, Manieri-Elia & Tafuri, *The American City, From the Civil War to the New Deal*, London, etc., 1980, 152; Dolores Hayden, *Seven American Utopias*, Cambridge, Mass., 1976, p. 118, n. 24; Rem Koolhaas, *Delirious New York*, New York, 1978, p. 15.

7. Thomas Adams, op. cit., p. 50.

8. See: Catherine Caulfield, *In the Rainforest*, London, 1985.

9. For example: Winston Weisman, 'A New View of Skyscraper History', *The Rise of an American Architecture*, Edgar Kaufmann, Jr., ed., New York, 1970, p. 149: '... N.Y. building code in 1916. Brought on by the ill effects these gigantic buildings were having on the city and the public ....'

around 1915, when towers (Fig. 3) of the elephantine proportions of the Equitable Building began to rise, real estate proprietors, old as well as new, were seized with fear. There were no regulating mechanisms to keep one skyscraper from suffocating another, and therefore it was agreed – businessman to businessman – to develop a scheme, the set-back system, that would enable skyscrapers to keep growing without having to sacrifice too much of the building lot. The essence of this system was to maintain the original area of the block at level, but to taper it upward into a pyramidal shape. This was done, not to admit light into the streets, but to ensure space for other skyscrapers. In order to keep the species alive, a synthetic law of nature had been instituted. [10]

An illustration is the uproar caused by the Equitable Building: 'When the owners of property adjacent to 120 Broadway learned that the Equitable planned to pile on one block of the city's surface the equivalent of 40 other blocks in what would be the world's biggest office building, a storm of protest arose. George T. Mortimer, vice-president of the U.S. Realty and Development Company, spearheaded the opposition. His firm owned two skyscrapers across Broadway – the Trinity and the U.S. Realty – and he rallied, in a sort of protective league, the other huge structures surrounding the Equitable block. ... They were willing to sacrifice a good deal to have this block covered by a low structure.'[11] The idea of erecting a gigantic tower had been a whim of General Coleman Du Pont of Delaware. Having conducted a brilliant business career manufacturing gun powder (at a time when it was as vital to the American society as gasoline is now), he now wanted, as he confided to his contractor, Louis Horowitz of the Starrett Company, 'a larger playground'.[12] Predictably, Du Pont was not interested in a 'low structure'. He wanted to spend as much money as possible, because for him, as Horowitz recalled, 'the second best in fun was making money; spending it was first, of course.'[13] The last, though certainly not the wisest manoeuvre the skyscraper-owners syndicate could think of was to buy Du Pont out: 'Later it was reported that the group offered Du Pont $2,500,000 if he would keep his building project down to eight stories. The case was hopeless, however, for the general had made up his mind.'[14]

This incident shows, once again, that the principle of 'laissez-faire' is all right as long as it does not interfere with the interests of those who are in power. Cartels, trusts and temporary interest groups such as the one which opposed Du Pont are regressive movements which come to life when the liberty that helped the individual entrepreneur to power threatens to destroy him by allowing others to do the same. The 1916 zoning regulations, though part of a much larger plan for eradicating 19th-century urban promiscuity, were a last resort, after bribery and the prospect of shady profits had proved ineffective. Unpopular and even 'un-democratic' as a coercive law might be, it had to keep up the appearance of being a regulating system of almost natural self-evidence. Although a product of pruning and manicuring, the stepped-back skyscraper looked just as if it had grown like that, all by itself. But, whereas down-town Manhattan still looked like a forest, it had by then become a garden.

10. The 1916 New York Zoning Ordinance consisted of a much larger body of restrictive legislation than the guidelines specifically intended to regulate the growth of buildings in the commercial district. My scepticism is merely directed toward this particular part of the law. See: Ciucci et al., op. cit., p. 207, n. 146. One of the drafters of the law, George B. Ford, explicitly stated that obviously compromises had to be made, dictated by 'the necessity of conserving real estate values.'

11. Earle Shultz and Walter Simmons, *Offices in the Sky*, Indianapolis/New York, 1959, pp. 78/79.

12. Louis J. Horowitz and Boyden Sparkes, *The Towers of New York*, New York, 1937, p. 134.

13. Ibid., p. 134.

14. Shultz and Simmons, op. cit., p. 79.

15. 'A comparison of the world's tallest structures', from *The Architectural Forum*, 140, 1, January–February 1974, p. 29. Gradually the skyscraper is taking on the form of a graphic representation of commercial growth.

16. Having exposed the land-scarcity theory, Corbett proceeded to present his own view, to be described as the 'efficiency rationale' or the 'proximity paradox' (see below: 'Hortus congestus' and 'Distance-corrective media'): 'The skyscraper,' Corbett continued, 'has developed in answer to a growing demand for maximum efficiency in the use of time, energy, and land [?]. And American architects, although of course not always successful, have already sometimes produced admirably fresh, striking, and unquestionably native building forms' (Harvey Wiley Corbett, '*America Builds Skyward*', *America As Americans See It*, Fred J. Ringel, ed., New York, 1932, pp. 44–52 (loc. cit., p. 46).

17. Thomas E. Tallmadge, *The Story of Architecture in Ameria*, New York, 1936, p. 180. The question of which city was first to erect a skyscraper has led to yet another New York–Chicago controversy. The criteria, based primarily on structure, were summarized by J. Carson Webster in 'The Skyscraper: Logical and Historical Considerations', *J.S.A.H.*, 18, 1959, pp. 126-139. Squabbles over the primacy of either city and over the exact origin of the skyscraper must have irritated even the architects themselves in the early phases – witness Cass Gilbert's remark that to him the matter was of no more importance than 'whether the hen or the egg came first' (Cass Gilbert, *Reminiscences and Addresses*, New York, 1935, p. 55).

## The hortus conclusus

This economic Garden of Eden took the form of a rectilinear garden with enough light and air for everyone. Basically, no one square was more privileged than the other; this element of fair competition was safeguarded. The ability to grow tall was a matter of individual merit and, thanks to the initial equality, the measure of success was the height of the column. Growth graphs and skyscraper silhouettes were physically identical (Fig. 4).[15]

But one question remains to be answered before the mechanisms of competition and vertical growth can be accepted as self-evident.

It has often been claimed that the vertical expansion of the American office block was the consequence of a shortage of space. Harvey Wiley Corbett, the noted skyscraper architect and urban planner, wrote in *America As Americans See It* (1932), a book expressly written 'for Europeans with the avowed purpose of making America more intelligible to them' (Foreword, p. vii):

The skyscraper with its steel skeleton and accented verticality, is America's outstanding contribution to the architecture of the world. It has not, as is frequently supposed, developed due to the topography of any specific area of land. It has not flourished in New York solely because the island of Manhattan ... is a long and narrow strip of land. One of the first skyscrapers was erected in Chicago, a city surrounded on three sides by vast tracts of level land. ... Cities of all sizes throughout America are erecting skyscrapers, cities with all the land horizontal expansion could require.'[16]

Indeed, it is also generally accepted that the first skyscraper (defined as a 'steel-framed tall building') originated in Chicago ('There never has been any serious contradiction of the fact that Chicago is the birthplace of the skyscraper,' Thomas Eddy Tallmadge used to say.[17]) Yet Chicago was also associated with the idea of unlimited space: 'situated, as Chicago is, on a broad expanse of Prairie, there is hardly a limit to her future potentiality,' spoke the Chicago *Inland Architect*, 1883.[18] Hence the paradox that an instrument designed to save space should be invented where space was proverbially abundant. Indeed, the grid on which Chicago was laid out was itself designed to exert control, at least administratively, over the immensity of the American continent. Therefore it was equipped with the capacity to be extended and multiplied ad infinitum. It was devised, not to save space, but, on the contrary, to control it and to channel it.

First to cast the grid, as a gigantic net, over the endless expanse of the prairie, and then to pretend that space had become limited was, of course, a contradictory assertion – though it was provided with a pinch of credibility, the claim that the growth of Chicago was restricted by the estuary of the Chicago River, so that its central business district, the 'Loop', could not expand with the rest of the city, making the land disproportionately expensive.[19] But in this case also the argument could hardly be more than a stratagem, for how could it possibly be believed that the same technological inventiveness, which was so celebrated as the apotheosis of Yankee ingenuity, could master the almost unprecedented vertical extension of buildings, yet could not find a way to neutralize that insignificant stream which Montgomery Schuyler, in one of his early articles on Chicago architecture, described as merely 'a ditch'?[20] The age-old crafts of tunneling, bridging and draining were hardly more challenging than erecting a steel-framed skyscraper. The truth is that the origin of the skyscraper was quite mysterious. Paul Starrett, the super-contractor who was responsible for, among other major undertakings, the Empire State Building (1930/31), claimed, however, that there was absolutely nothing mysterious about the origins of the skyscraper. 'It was merely,' he asserted, 'the application of common sense.'[21] This was Starrett's own contribution to the myth of self-reliance and Midwestern ingenuity. What cannot have escaped his

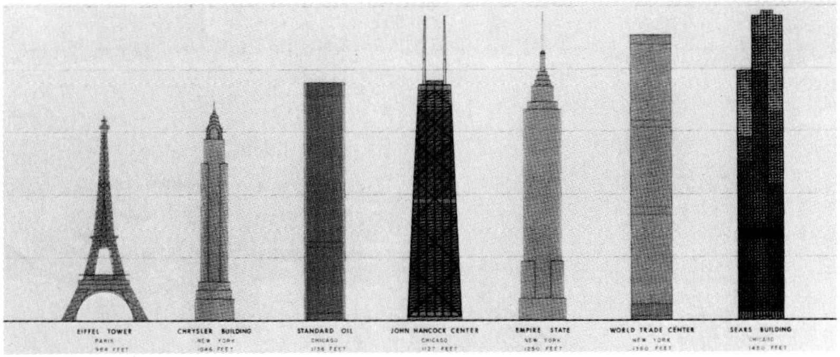

*Fig. 4. 'A Comparison of the World's Tallest Structures.' Gradually the skyscraper is taking on the shape of a graphic representation of commercial growth (from* The Architectural Forum, *140, 1, January/February 1974).*

18. Robert Prestiano, *R.C. McLean and The Inland Architect*, Unpublished Doctoral Dissertation, 1973, as quoted from *The Inland Architect, Review of Chicago Building for 1883*. Of a similar tenor is the statement of the Chicago city planners Daniel H. Burnham and Edward H. Bennett: 'Chicago has two dominant features: the expanse of Lake Michigan, which stretches, unbroken by islands or peninsulas, to the horizon; and a corresponding area of land extending north, west, and south without hills or any marked elevation. . . . Whatever man undertakes here should be either actually or seemingly without limit.' These lines, quoted by Henry Hope Reed, *American Skyline*, Boston, 1956, pp. 21/22, obviously compelled him to draw the only logical, though still odd, conclusion from this insuperable paradox: 'There you have it! Would the skyscrapers have risen in a country with limits?' (ibid., p. 22).

19. See above, note 16.

20. Montgomery Schuyler, 'Glimpses of Western Architecture: Chicago', originally in: *Harper's Magazine*, 83, 1891, reprinted in: *American Architecture and Other Writings*, William H. Jordy and Ralph Coe, eds., Cambridge, Mass., 1961, Vol. 1, p. 246.

21. Paul Starrett, *Changing the Skyline*, New York/London 1938, p. 34.

22. Superfluous perhaps, but nevertheless a useful reminder, is the first paragraph of the *Declaration of Independence*: 'When in the course of human events, it becomes necessary for one people to dissolve the political bands which have connected them with another, and to assume among the Powers of the Earth, the separate and equal station to which the *Laws of Nature and of Nature's God* entitle them, a decent respect to the opinions of mankind requires that they should declare the causes which impel them to the separation' (author's emphasis).

attention was that it looked very much like common sense, that the workings of the intricate mechanisms which had brought the skyscraper into existence gave the impression, on the surface, of being self-evident, but that the whole matter was in fact extremely complicated, especially in the sense of artistic and technological creation. After all, the title of Starrett's romantic autobiography, *Changing the Skyline*, refers to a conscious act of creation, with even a whiff of demiurgic arrogance.

Simple terms and simple explanations were used for complicated phenomena; for the skyscraper was a complicated undertaking even for those who built them. That the grid was a neutral system, of which the creation of equal opportunities was an essential aspect, cannot be contested.

The complicating factor is that, on this matrix of equality, another structure was superimposed, which acted in opposition to it. This was the force of competition. Instead of expanding, it contracted; whereas the other disclosed, this one restrained.

What looked, at first, like a neutral zone, had been transformed into a wilderness — an artificial wilderness, that is, with all sorts of obstacles being thrown up in a treacherous simulacrum.

In a similar way an innocent piece of nature is perverted into an artefact such as a golf course. Traps and hazards not normally found in nature have originated on the architect's draughting table with the intention of providing the player with a strongly condensed condition of savagery. At times this can be more savage than the real thing, suggestively contrasted as it is to the parklike meekness of the carefully manicured fairways and greens.

The objective of this improbable combination is to secure a fair and equal playground (fairway) for selective competition, the stimuli of which are presented as a neatly codified selection of superable insuperable hazards. The results of this competition can be measured objectively, thanks to the neutrality of its common basis.

To allow the operation of 'Man in Nature' was the object of the American commercial city. [22] The neutral grid guaranteed freedom of movement, and it knew no boundaries, nor did it have a centre or any special focus.

But man did not use these qualities to his benefit. Paralyzed by the urge to compete, not with nature, but with his companions, he confined himself instead to a fixed point within the grid. Commercial buildings huddled together and shot upward, demonstrating with a helpless gesture the workings of the law of a scarcity that did not exist.

The piling-up of towers in the epicentres of commercial activity had the character of stage sets, or of instruction models which demonstrated the principles of free trade, laissez-faire, competition and the like.

Fig. 5. 'The Ever Changing Sky-Line of New York,' or '"An Asparagus Bed" with its sword-like shoots springing from the dense population and the fertile manure of wealth' (from Above the Clouds & Old New York, An Historical Sketch . . . of the Woolworth Building, *Baltimore/New York, 1913*).

23. F. Scott Fitzgerald, *The Great Gatsby*, New York, 1953 (1925[1]), p. 69.

24. Montgomery Schuyler, 'The Sky-line of New York. 1881–1897', *Harper's Weekly*, March 20, p. 295. The passage was quoted by John A. Kouwenhoven, *The Columbia Historial Portrait of New York*, New York, etc., 1972, p. 394 and further elaborated by William Taylor, 'New York et l'origine du *skyline*: la cité moderne comme forme et symbole', *Urbi*, III, Mars 1980, pp. XII/XIII.

25. That the skyline 'changes' is the result of its intrinsic quality as an indicator of growth. Cass Gilbert, the architect of the Woolworth Building, wrote in the introduction to Vernon Howe Bailey's *Skyscrapers of New York*, New York, 1928: 'The changing skyline of New York is one of the marvels of a marvelous age. . . . The skyscraper is a creation unique to this epoch. In its aspiring lines we behold the very symbol of a bold, adventurous people; restless, eager and confident in their strength and power.'

26. Ethel Fleming, *New York*, with illustrations by Herbert S. Kates, London, 1929, p. 5.

27. *King's Views of New York, 1906*, New York, 1905 [sic!], p. 10. Moses King's guidebooks to the city of New York were generously illustrated mostly with business buildings. The information which was provided about these buildings was of an unusual indecency. As a rule, the names of architects and/or builders were not given; but the names of the occupants were spelled out and the annual profits of their respective firms are given in painful detail. For example, about the abovementioned, pre-1915, Equitable Life Insurance Co. Building, King enlightened his readers as follows: 'granite edifice, 120 Broadway, occupying block to Nassau Street, from Cedar to Pine Streets. Founded 1859 by Henry B. Hyde. One of the largest life-insurance companies in the world. Policies in force aggregate $1,495,542,892; surplus $80,494,861; assets $412,438,381. Reorganized 1905. Paul Morton, President' (ibid., p. 27). Earle Shultz, a 1920s building manager, wrote: 'The first tower buildings were concentrated on the southern end of Manhattan Island . . . . Immediately the towers took on prestige and glamor and became fantastically successful advertisements for their owners. The first towers actually were erected as super billboards . . .' (*Offices in the Sky*, Indianapolis/New York, 1959, p. 63). Earlier Shultz had stated: 'The character and quality of any city can be told from a great distance by its skyline, but these buildings do more than merely advertise a city. They show the faith of many men in its destiny, and they create a like faith in others' (idem, p. 12).

## The ever-changing skyline

'Over the great bridge, with the sunlight through the girders making a constant flicker upon the moving cars, with the city rising up across the river in white heaps and sugar lumps all built with a wish out of non-olfactory money. The city seen from the Queensboro Bridge is always the city seen for the first time, in its first wild promise of all the mystery and the beauty in the world.' – F. SCOTT FITZGERALD, The Great Gatsby.[23]

Montgomery Schuyler concluded in 1897 that the skyline of lower Manhattan was '. . . not an architectural vision, but it does, most tremendously, look like business.'[24]

The phrase 'ever-changing skyline' (Fig. 5)[25] was the standard code used to communicate prosperity and the accumulation of the city's collective wealth: 'That irregular outline which, in hazy weather, seems to rise enchanted from the Bay and to dissolve against the sky of a dream, represents more wealth, more power, more human energy than any mind can grasp.'[26]

What the European mind found difficult to grasp was the role of the office building as a growth graph — simply as a yardstick by which to measure wealth. The caption writer of *King's Views of New York* of 1906 described a full-page picture of the down town tip of Manhattan in the following terms: 'Eighteen downtown skyscrapers have an aggregate value of $26,290,000.'[27]

This peculiar tendency to translate qualities into quantities, preferably of dollars, was characteristic of the American habit of portraying the new Eden in objective, univalent terms. A similar means of describing the skylines of Paris or London is unimaginable. It is interesting to consider, by way of comparison, an early, perhaps the earliest, use of the expression 'skyline'. As a means of designating the silhouette of tall buildings against the horizon, the term, according to Burchard and Bush-Brown, was 'coined about 1897'.[28] Guessing at the source of their information, the probable truth behind this statement is that, in 1897, Montgomery Schuyler contributed an article with the title 'The Sky-line of New York' to *Harper's Weekly* (March 20, 1897). The same source also mentioned that the term had already been used in 1896 as the caption of a panoramic drawing — 'The Skyline of New York' — by Charles Graham for Hearst's New York *Journal* (May 3, 1896).[29]

*Fig. 6. Design for an Office Building on Battery Place, New York, 1883, Charles Atwood, architect. An early skyscraper of twelve storeys plus gabled clock-tower, conceived to be 'viewed from the Bay' (from* The American Architect & Building News, *April 21, 1883).*

28. John Burchard and Albert Bush-Brown, *The Architecture of America, A Social and Cultural History*, Boston/Toronto, 1961, p. 244.

29. John A. Kouwenhoven, op. cit., p. 394.

30. *The American Architect & Building News*, XIII, April 21, 1883, pp. 186-187.

31. *The American Architect & Building News*, I, July 29, 1876, p. 247.

32. Ralph Waldo Emerson, 'Stonehenge', in: *The Works of Ralph Waldo Emerson*, Vol. II, English Traits, London, 1913, p. 163.

33. Rem Koolhaas, op. cit., pp. 71/72.

But I believe that the word must have been in general use long before that date. The text accompanying a 'competitive design for an office building on Battery Place, New York, facing the Park and Bay, for Cyrus Field, Esq.' of 1883, by the well-known architect Charles Atwood (who, among other things, was responsible for the design of Burnham's Reliance Building, Chicago 1894/95), used the word 'skyline' in the following context: 'Naturally at this height the view of the Bay and distance would be magnificent, and the *ensemble* of terraces, gables and pitched roofs, was planned with reference to the effect of the "skyline" when the building was viewed from the Bay' (Fig. 6).[30]

Even earlier the *American Architect and Building News* of July 29, 1876 – one year after the completion of New York's first two skyscrapers – quoted an article published in the British magazine *The Architect*, titled 'Sky-line', which referred to a speech delivered in 1875 by a certain Mr. Beresford Hope, who had expressed the opinion that 'the proper study of sky-line is very commonly neglected,' which, 'in the composition of towers is, of course, most essential.' 'Yet,' *The Architect* continued, 'his good advice has not, apparently, been much taken to heart. ... In an important city like London, it is particularly essential that any building which has pretensions, and rears itself above its neighbors, should possess a decent profile.'[31]

Although both civilizations, the English and the American, were afflicted with the same coarse ambitions, it is nevertheless revealing to compare their respective attitudes toward the possibilities of the skyline: for one it was 'tremendously looking like business' or merely 'aggregate value of $26,290,000', whereas the other was mainly concerned with a 'decent profile'.[32]

Before the 1870s the word generally indicated 'the line where earth and sky meet,' as the *Oxford English Dictionary* defines it. Ralph Waldo Emerson must have meant it in this sense in his essay 'Stonehenge', in which he describes a visit to that place in the company of his friend Thomas Carlyle on July 7, 1848: 'I engaged the local antiquary, Mr. Brown, to go with us to Stonehenge, on our way, and show us what he knew of the "astronomical" and "sacrificial" stones. I stood on the last, and he pointed to the upright, or rather inclined stone, called the "astronomical" and bade me notice that its top ranged with the sky-line.'[32]

The skylines of the American commercial districts, rather than being the result of economic law, acted as the billboards of its simulated operations. It is strange, though, that such emphatic, almost archetypal centres should take shape in an ecosystem that was expressly designed *not* to have a centre.

### Hortus congestus

It was not an easy task to persuade people to concentrate their activities, their capital, and themselves on the smallest possible surface.

The paradox of the proverbial superabundance of space that was causing city centres to become congested can be resolved only by substituting gullibility for common sense. And, since common sense was unanimously acknowledged as the national characteristic *par excellence*, this topic has, with understandable circumspection, been avoided.[33]

When, if ever, the paradox has been dealt with seriously, without exception it has always been *after* the skyscraper has demonstrated its ability to multiply the commercial value of the plot and never before. [34] Rem Koolhaas was one of the first to recognize this paradox. His brilliant study of Manhattan is based on what he calls 'the culture of congestion', or the exploitation of synthetic density. He describes how the initial 'irrationality' of Manhattan's congestion was later to be 'rationalized' by Ferriss, Corbett and the authors of New York's Regional Plan of the early 1930s. [35] Voluntary clustering seems irrational indeed in the face of an abundance of space, but it is even more so if viewed in relation to another American myth, that of mobility. Was it not the essence of the spirit of the pioneer to consume available space with a voracity unique in the history of human migration? Was it not considered good practice to pick up one's possessions and move on to distant horizons, preferably the West? James Bryce was highly impressed in 1888 by what he called 'the extraordinary mobility of the population'. [36] It was Horace Greeley who condensed what in his time had already achieved mytical proportions into the exhortation 'Fly, scatter throughout the country — go to the great west — rather than remain here,' and 'Go west, young man, go west.' [37]

The notion of mobility and the magnetic attraction of vast expanses and unlimited opportunities were a commonplace but nevertheless dynamic part of the ideological baggage of the immigrant. Witness an extraordinary letter written by one Jan to his uncle and aunt in Vlaardingen (the Netherlands) on April 16, 1907 (Fig. 7) shortly after his arrival in the United States:

Daar stapte Jan in Amerika, daar stond hij, verlaten van God en alle menschen, zoo men wel eens zegt. Maar het is goed, niemand kende hij toch, goed Englisch kon hij ook niet, dus kon maar niet vragen wat hij wilde ook.

(The picturesque quality of Jan's use of the Dutch language is impossible to translate, nevertheless a rough translation is given in the note.) [38] Although Jan had just set foot on American soil, and spoke not a word of English, he instantly called himself 'the American'. ('Nogmaals, de beste zegen van de Amerikaan!'), a curious mannerism adopted by many others — visitors and immigrants alike — such as Le Corbusier, who in 1936, on a visit to New York, quite unnecessarily but apparently obeying an irresistible urge, exclaimed: 'I am an American!' [39] 'Ik ben op het ogenblik in Hoboken,' Jan continued, 'een stad met plusminus 10.000 man, het is vijf minuten van New York. Mijn plan is toch maar naar Chicago te gaan. Ik bekijk hier de boel maar eens, dan maar weer verder.' [40] Jan was but five minutes from the largest city in the world — indeed he paid it a brief visit — but he decided to do what everybody else did, to move westward. What Jan did after he arrived in Chicago is not known, but it is not inconceivable that he repeated the process and moved west once again. Every west, it seems, has its west.

The logic of mobility, apart from its ethical aspects, relies on the principle of following the line of least resistance. Commerce and industry are likely to settle where the costs of exploitation are lowest. Although the America of the era of abundance did not appear to pay much attention to the economic law of scarcity, in the way that Europe did, certain transfers were made in the 1920s, such as the jump from downtown Manhattan to Midtown. [41] Surprisingly, the same logic which had justified the congestion of early downtown was used to justify its dispersal. Already in 1893 William Birkmire, skyscraper propagator and author of *Skeleton Construction in Buildings*, pointed to this tendency: 'And where other cities have confined their high structures within narrow city limits, it is not so in New York; they are scattered along the principle thoroughfares from the Battery to Central Park, where high buildings are quite common.' [42]

34. See note 51.

35. Rem Koolhaas, op. cit., pp. 7, 103–105.

36. James Bryce, *The American Commonwealth*, New York, 1911, II, p. 887.

37. Stuart Berg Flexner, *I Hear America Talking, An Illustrated History of American Words and Phrases*, New York, 1976, p. 180.

38. Letter from 'Jan', on 'New York Sky Line' stationary, dated: Hoboken, 16 April 1907. 'There Jan set foot on America, there he stood, forsaken by God and men, alike as one sometimes says. But it is good, nobody he knew indeed, nor his English was any good, so he could not ask for what he wanted also.'

39. Le Corbusier, *Quand les cathédrales étaient blanches*, Paris, 1937, p. 55. 'Jan' wrote: 'Once again, best blessings from The American!

40. Letter from 'Jan' (see above, n. 38): 'At present I am in Hoboken, a city of about 10,000, it is five minutes from New York. It is my plan to go to Chicago, however, I'll look around for a while, then take the road again.'

41. See: Charles Lockwood, *Manhattan Moves Uptown*, Boston, 1976.

42. William Birkmire, *Skeleton Construction in Buildings*, New York, 1894, p. 9.

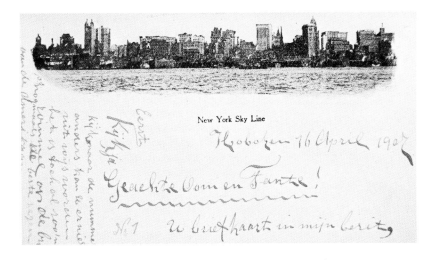

*Fig. 7. The 'New York Sky Line' as it had appeared to Jan from Vlaardingen in 1907 (stationary with decorative letter-head).*

### Distance-corrective media

Noise, bustle, excitement are the natural back-drop to business, [43] and there may have been a certain comfort in the congested concentration of its activities. One of America's chief characteristics has been its *display* of energy: '*The* feature of Chicago is its marvellous energy. America is energetic, but Chicago is in a fever. It does not rest one moment, but goes on, on − ever ceaselessly ahead − to buying, and selling, and getting gain.' [44]

A consequence of this energy is the stir and bustle of people and traffic, with its inevitable accompaniment of noise: 'Over a space of from one to two miles in each direction, every avenue is alive with the stir and bustle of an active, enterprising population.' [45]

Congestion has always been a popular yard-stick by which to measure a city's commercial success − the more successful, the more noisy: 'New York does not for a moment compare with Chicago in roar and bustle of its street life.' [46]

The proposition that cause and effect could be reversed, in the sense that noise and excitement could induce success, seems to hold some truth. When large companies have switched from the separate cell system to the open office plan, the result is bedlam and chaos, but also a most convincing display of energetic activity. Likewise, the appearance of haste was found to be an effective means of suggesting that important things were happening. Jacques Hermant noted this in 1893, while visiting Chicago on behalf of the Paris *Gazette des Beaux-Arts*. He witnessed the following conversation between two businessmen: 'Come in! Good day! − Entrez! Bonjour! − All right, quand c'est fini, en signe de conclusion et d'accord, le chapeau vissé sur la tête, on esquisse un petit salut, et c'est fini.' The extreme brevity of the session was emphasized by the hat remaining on the head of the visitor − this was recognized as a sign of great hurry, and of more important business waiting elsewhere. [47]

Baron de Hübner observed in 1880 that the Americans had developed an air of hurriedness which impressed him as being more a kind of unrest than a real symptom of activity: 'Ils ont l'air inquiet plus qu'affairé. On dirait que tout le monde craint de manquer son train.' [48]

Moreover, it should be noted that, although proximity of services was desirable from a practical viewpoint (just as the concentration of trades within a given era was a persistent medieval tradition), most transactions were conduct-

43. John Foster Fraser, *America at Work*, London, etc., 1904 (1903¹), pp. 14 ff.

44. C.B. Berry, *The Other Side; How it Struck Us*, London, 1880, quoted in: Harold M. Mayer & Richard C. Wade, *Chicago, Growth of a Metropolis*, Chicago, 1973, p. 134.

45. Mayer and Wade, op. cit., p. 36.

46. Ibid., p. 216.

47. Jacques Hermant, 'L'Art à l'exposition de Chicago', *Gazette des Beaux-Arts*, X, 3ième période, 1 septembre 1893, p. 248.

48. Le Baron de Hübner, *Promenade auteur du monde*, 2 Vols., Paris, 1881, p. 25. See also: John Foster Fraser, *America at Work*, op. cit., p. 15: 'Still, there is often more hustle than haste . . . .'

ed by proximity-insensitive or distance-corrective media such as the telegraph and the letter, and in particular the medium for which America had instantly developed a monumental fondness: the telephone. After about 1879 the telephone conquered the commercial scene. During a visit to America in that year W.G. Marshall noted that 'Everyone communicates by telephone in Chicago. Shops, hotels, private houses, factories – all are connected. The man who has not got a telephone is very much behind the age in Chicago, as indeed is the case, more or less throughout America.'[49] To illustrate his point this British observer described the unorthodox use of the telephone as a transmitter of liturgical activities: 'On Sunday, April 18, 1880, the sermons preached in Plymouth Church, Brooklyn, N.Y., were for the first time heard by telephone by certain members of the congregation in their own rooms at their homes stationed in six different cities and towns in the neighbourhood. ... Every sound was heard with distinctness, even the music of the choir and the organ accompaniment, even too, the thumping of the preacher on the Bible ....'[50]

## Hortus speculativus

The cause which, according to most authors, dictated the selection of the vertical direction was speculation in the ground. Charles Harris Whitaker was eloquent, in 1934, in his diagnosis as well as his disapproval: 'It is a curious commentary that America's most acclaimed contribution to architecture – the skyscraper – derives from steel mill, engineer, the law and frenzied finance, in which the architect is no more than a gambling society's errand boy.'[51] Whitaker nursed a puritanical aversion to anything that had to do with speculation, the creation of debts and inflation, which he had inherited from the days of the Great Crash of 1929, in the aftermath of which he had written *The Story of Architecture – From Rameses to Rockefeller*.

According to Whitaker, the building of skyscrapers had but one purpose, namely 'to enable the individual, or group, to cash in on land.'[52] Though this was indeed the case before and even after 1929, there is not much reason to believe that it applies to the period around 1873 when the first skyscrapers were erected.[53]

The New York *Real Estate Record and Building Guide* of 1887 wrote: 'The land speculation craze acts like a contagious disease. At first we hear of it in one part of the country and then again in another. It broke out in several distinct places in the Southern States, but was most particularly noticeable in Birmingham and the new iron regions in the South. ... This is but a sample of what is taking place in different parts of the country. There has been an abatement of the speculative fever near Birmingham, Alabama, but it looks as though this mania must run its course, and it is liable to make its appearance here East at any time. We are doing a great deal more building and trading in real estate than in former years, but, as yet *there has been no unwholesome boom in unimproved property, at least not in New York and its neighborhood*' (author's emphasis).[54]

Land speculation in America was as common as the amount of land available to speculate on, even in the most improbable backwaters. In 1883 *The Inland Architect and Builder* reported that 'Real estate rules very high in the city of Mexico. A building of the Cinoe de Mayo Street that was sold a few months since for $40,000 has just fetched $85,000.'[55]

Surprisingly, New York City remained free of it for a while. *The Record and Guide* of 1887 echoed the oft-repeated alibi of Manhattan's limited surface area: 'There would be some excuse for a speculative outbreak in New York real-estate, as the soil of the island is limited, being hemmed in on every side by water; but the cities in which the booms are raging have unlimited amounts

49. W.G. Marshall, *Through America; or Nine Months in the United States*, London, 1881, pp. 100/101. Quite puzzling is the conclusion Burchard and Bush-Brown drew from the widespread introduction of the telephone: 'together with the telegraph and the transportation systems, the telephone helped in *enlarging cities, pushing buildings up higher, decentralizing life*' (my italics) (Burchard & Bush-Brown, op. cit., p. 214.

50. Ibid., p. 101.

51. Charles Harris Whitaker, *The Story of Architecture: From Rameses to Rockefeller*, New York, 1934, p. 277.

52. Ibid., pp. 287/288.

53. H.-R. Hitchcock, *Architecture, Nineteenth and Twentieth Centuries*, Harmondsworth, 1958, p. 239: '*Despite* the Panic of 1873, the mid seventies saw the construction of what may properly be considered the first skyscrapers, the nine-story (260-foot) Tribune Building and the ten-story (230-foot) Western Union Building' (my italics).

54. *The Real Estate Record and Builders' Guide*, New York, September 3, 1887, p. 1123.

55. *The Inland Architect and Builder*, I, 1 February 1883, p. 12.

56. *The Real Estate Record and Builders' Guide*, New York, September 3, 1887, p. 1123.

57. *Michelin Guide to New York City*, New York, 1971, p. 16. To give the reader an indication of the size of Manhattan relative to another great metropolis, a small map is provided showing 'Manhattan and Paris on the same scale' (p. 27). It demonstrates, probably with unintended clarity, that the two cities have roughly the same usable surface area, thereby refuting all claims of a land shortage in a period in which the population of Paris was three times that of New York (more than three million for Paris compared to 1,206,000 for New York) (Jean-Pierre Rioux, *La révolution industrielle*, Paris, 1971, pp. 149/150; New York, 1880 census). Fanny Trollope made a similar observation in 1830, when she wrote: 'I think it [= Manhattan] covers nearly as much ground as Paris, but is much less thickly peopled' (Fanny Trollope, *Domestic Manners of the Americans*, Oxford/New York, 1984 (1832¹), p. 297).

58. Eliel Saarinen, *The City*, New York, 1943, pp. 191/192: 'Concentration of a large population does not of necessity create a need for vertical growth. London – to take the most enlightening example insofar as size is concerned – was larger than New York when the latter began its mass erection of tall buildings. Yet, while the ambitious New Yorkers believed it imperative to expand high into the air, the

well-balanced Londoners were satisfied with their horizontal stress. The Britishers, of course, had ample technical opportunity to go into the air, but such was not their inclination. Obviously the necessity of skyscrapers was not convincing to them. Nor are we convinced on our part. In those instances, however, where the skyscraper was wanted for ambitious reasons, its necessity was easy to explain.' Recently (1984) a *Stichting Hoogbouw* ('Foundation Highrise') was founded in order to sell the reluctant Dutchmen the idea of the skyscraper ('wolkenkrabber', being the ambitious variety of the generic 'hoogbouw' or high-rise) as the solution to their proverbial density problem. To no avail yet (*De fascinatie van hoogbouw*, Rotterdam, 1985).

59. Montgomery Schuyler, 'The Evolution of the Skyscraper', originally in: *Scribner's Magazine*, 46, September 1909, reprinted in Jordy and Coe, op. cit., pp. 425/426.

60. Of the Potter Building *King's Handbook of New York*, Boston, 1893, reported: 'The Potter Building possesses two unusual features, from a constructive point of view: first, it was the first building erected in this city ornamented elaborately with terra-cotta; second, it was the first in its locality which had its iron-work and stone-work covered with hollow brick, so that the iron and stone are not exposed to view or to heat from fire' (p. 824). It is apparent that the building, with its eleven stories, partial (?) iron framing, hollow-brick fireproofing and 'four large rapid passenger elevators' (ibid., p. 824) would easily qualify for a confrontation with the alleged 'first skyscraper', Jenney's Home Insurance Com-

*Fig. 8. The Potter Building, another neglected 'first' in the search for the origin of the skyscraper. Built on the former site of the New York World Building between 1883 and 1886 by N.G. Starkweather, architect (from* King's Handbook of New York, *Boston 1893). The new World Building is to be seen at the far left.*

of land near-by which are available for settlement.'[56] This is an interesting observation. The case of New York has always been used as the incontestable proof that skyscrapers were the result of an enormous influx of people to the relatively small area of Manhattan, which drove up real estate prices, which in turn led to the skyscraper. Even today the *Michelin Guide of New York City* tells us that 'At the beginning of the 20th century, New York's population grew very rapidly and the price of real estate rose accordingly. This inspired the promotors of that period to build higher and higher.'[57] Apart from the common misconception that skyscrapers were designed to absorb the growing population – they were built exclusively to house commercial activities – the major inaccuracy is the assumption that the price of real estate will rise the minute the population, for one reason or other, through mere quantity, makes a claim on the available land. If this were the case the prices of real estate would have been astronomical in contemporary Paris or London, but it was not the case, nor is it in Holland today which, though the second most densely populated country in the world, has the lowest real estate prices in western Europe. Furthermore, skyscrapers were not built in London or in Paris or in Holland, where the first skyscraping office-building has yet to be built.[58] Montgomery Schuyler, reflecting upon the skyscraper's beginnings, recalled that the New York *Tribune* and the *Western Union* Buildings were 'the most conspicuous objects on Manhattan Island,' yet one was also conspicuously slow to realize their commercial potential: 'A certain timidity accompanied these tentatives, bold as they looked ... The real-estate speculator who puts his 'premises' to their logical conclusions. When all the calls of the new honeycomb were found to be tenantable and rentable, the successors naturally bettered the instruction of the pioneer, and "built to the limit".'[59] However, it must be noted that *The Record and Guide* mentioned above was referring to 'speculation' and not 'investment'. In terms of investment New York real estate was, as always, sound business. Massive buildings like the 10-storey Mills Building, built in 1881 by George B. Post, the 13-storey Washington Building by Edward Kendall (1882), and the steel-framed, hollow-brick clad Potter Building of 1883 by N.G. Starkweather (Fig. 8) followed in the footsteps of the Tribune and Western Union Buildings by building big.[60] It might be expected that smart speculators would have drawn up their plans by that time, but apparently this was not yet the case in 1887. Exactly one year later, on September 1, 1888, *The Record and Guide* reported that building activity had increased considerably and that 'Important Buildings' were 'under way': 'The Market and Fulton Bank is another of the fiduciary institutions which has aspired to own and occupy an imposing modern structure.'[61] By then speculators and investors alike had found their way to quick profits and easy short-term returns on their investments. As *The Record and Guide* showed, it was only *after* the experimental skyscrapers had demonstrated their ability to multiply the original plot, and so to provide excellent opportunities for speculation, that there was an explosive growth in real estate activity. In his monograph of William Le Baron Jenney, Theodore Turak has argued that the rise of the Chicago skyscraper was the result of heavy speculation in ground: 'The price per square acre in the Loop area of Chicago stood at $130,000 in 1880. It had risen to $900,000 per square acre in 1890.'[62] But what does this prove? Jenney's first tall building was finished in 1885, exactly halfway through the designated period. Taller skyscrapers soon followed, and it is logical to assume that by 1890 most entrepreneurs knew where to get the fastest profits. Thomas Eddy Tallmadge rightly concluded in his *Architecture of Old Chicago* (1941) that in those years prices were pushed up because the more sophisticated skyscrapers which followed the example of the Home Insu-

pany Building, Chicago, 1884/5. The Potter Building, designed for the investor/ex-congressman Orlando B. Potter by N.G. Starkweather in 1883, had for some reason escaped the attention of architectural historians working in this particular field of 'who was first in what' (see 'Introduction', note 11, and above, note 17). The *AIA Guide to New York City*, Norval White and Elliot Willensky, eds., New York/London, 1978, listed the building as 'An elaborately ornate confection of cast and pressed terra cotta', but added that 'The invisibly used structural steel of this building is the first in New York to be fireproofed by terra cotta' (p. 31). Dr. Carl Condit, who is currently working on a study of the New York skyscraper, challenges the claim that this steel was in fact used structurally. An illustration of the Potter Building is on p. 825 of *King's Handbook etc.*. It might be useful to note that the Potter Building was erected on the old site of the *World* Building which was destroyed by fire but was to be rebuilt a few blocks to the north by its later owner Joseph Pulitzer. The new *World* Building appears in the photograph (Fig. 8) on the extreme left (Michael A. Mikkelsen, *A History of Real Estate and Architecture in New York City During the Last Quarter of a Century*, New York, 1898, p. 115).

61. *The Real Estate Record and Builders' Guide*, New York, September 1, 1888, p. 1065. The architect was William B. Tubby. The building shows a surprising similarity to the later work of the Dutch architect Hendrik P. Berlage. See: Manfred Bock, *Anfänge einer neuen Architektur*, Wiesbaden/The Hague, 1983, pp. 294-296.

62. Theodore Turak, *William Le Baron Jenney; A Nineteenth Century Architect*, Unpublished dissertation, University of Michigan at Ann Arbor, 1967, p. 240.

63. Thomas E. Tallmadge, *Architecture in Old Chicago*, Chicago, 1975 (1941[1]), p. 189.

64. *The Inland Architect*, IV, 2, September 1884, p. 24 plus ill., announced the planned Home Insurance Building was going to cost 'not less than $600,000', an enormous sum for a simple though luxuriously decorated office building. Normally office buildings in the Loop area were built for between $15,000 and $40,000. The difference in price was mainly due to the alarming inflation rate.

65. Hugh Ferriss, *The Metropolis of Tomorrow*, New York, 1929, p. 59.

66. Walt Whitman, 'Wicked Architecture', in: *Complete Poetry and Selected Prose and Letters*, London, 1938, p. 607. Quoted by Charles R. Metzger, 'Whitman on Architecture', *J.S.A.H.*, XVI, March 1957, p. 26.

67. Mircea Eliade, *Images et symboles, essais sur le symbolisme magico-religieux*, Paris, 1952, pp. 47, 49.

rance Building had shown the promise of handsome profits. With their internal steel framing, solid fire proofing and swifter elevators, the original lot seemed to be multipliable almost without technical limit.[63] On the other hand, statistics such as the ones quoted should be treated with circumspection. Too many variables are involved, and ordinary inflation is certainly the least reliable of them. For example, the price of an annual subscription to the Midwestern architectural magazine *The Inland Architect* jumped from $1 in 1883 to $1.75 the following year, to $2 in 1885.[64] This means the price doubled in only two years, which is far more dramatic an increase than that quoted for lot values!

The real-estate speculation theory, however slick and easily refutable, also has its attractive side. It provides a comprehensible alternative to the thoroughly unsound lack-of-space theories; thus it appeals to our sense of authenticity by using a means of persuasion which we can connect with our ideas of the American 'couleur locale', namely the power of money and easy ways of acquiring it ('an easy buck'), whereas the lack-of-space theory offends our sense of logic.

### The dearth attraction paradox and commercial agoraphobia

To many Americans, not least those who were directly involved with it, the piling up of skyscrapers in artificially created epi-centres of congestion remained a mystery. Hugh Ferriss, who made a living out of designing dream-towers in the air for no-nonsense businessmen and their architects, was very close to the truth when he said: 'Call it whatever you will: gregarious instinct or economic necessity: the primary trend, with which we must deal in any formulation of the future city, is the trend toward centralization.'[65] In defiance of rationality and common sense, man follows the dark call of gregariousness and pushes to the centre of the herd. But the urge to huddle together has its price: space becomes scarce and therefore expensive. Contrary to what one might expect, this does not cause a reaction resulting in a centrifugal movement; instead of deterring people it attracts them. The dearness of the spot begins to mediate its appeal. Walt Whitman wrote: 'In New York, closed in by rivers, pressing desperately toward the business center at its southern end, and characterized by an unparallelled fierceness in money chasing, land is dear. This of course makes the possession of it a basis for increased ostentation of it; for the dearer a thing is, the more pride in showing it.'[66]

The complement of this attraction is the neurotic notion that the surrounding open spaces harbour danger and discomfort. The world outside the city 'is unknown territory, redoubtable for demons, larvae, strangers and the dead,' Eliade wrote, 'briefly, the territory of chaos, death and night.'[67] Medieval walls, moats, labyrinths and ramparts had not only military but also magical functions, to keep out evil spirits as well as hostile humans. It seems that the modern commercial city was imagined as if encircled by protective walls, recalling the early capitalist Italian republics, such as Florence, Siena, Bologna and San Gimigniano, which defended themselves and their newly acquired wealth against the openly covetous landed nobility. Herbert Spencer drew this comparison in 1883, on the occasion of a visit to New York: 'After pondering over what I have seen of your vast manufacturing and trading establishments ... I was suddenly reminded of the Italian republics of the middle ages.'[68] Certainly the concentration of trades in certain areas was similar to that of the

68. Quoted in: Kenneth T. Gibbs, *Business Architectural Imagery: The Impact of Economic and Social Changes on Tall Office Buildings 1870–1930*, Unpublished dissertation, Cornell University, 1976, p. 29.
*The Architectural Annual Chicago 1930*, a book showing Chicago's architectural accomplishment for the years 1929–1930, wrote: 'Chicago has been referred to as the modern San Gimigniano, city of towers. These last two years have broken all records and have seen more commercial structures built than any previous decade' (p. 9).

69. Stanislaus von Moos, *Turm und Bollwerk; Beiträge zu einer politischen Ikonographie der italienischen Renaissancearchitektur*, Zürich, 1974, pp. 18–19.

70. Karl Lamprecht, *Americana*, Freiburg i.B., 1906, p. 81.

71. Francis S. Swales, 'The Architect and the Grand Plan', 1, *Pencil Points*, XII, March 1931, p. 167.

72. Richard A. Goldthwaite, *The Building of Renaissance Florence, An Economic and Social History*, Baltimore/London, 1976, p. 102.

*Fig. 9. 'View of Bologna at the Time of Dante – A City of Early Skyscrapers' (from* Pencil Points, *XII, March 1931).*

medieval guilds. Furthermore, the towers erected by the nobility after the notorious 'inurbanimento della nobilità' within the city walls, competed with each other for height and distinction. [69]

The image of towers simulating the aggressive displays of belligerent knights was to haunt some of those who were confronted with the skyscraper skyline of the American city. The German historian Karl Lamprecht, who visited New York in 1904, observed that 'New York is the San Gimignano of today. Its bankers and wholesalers playing Montecchi and Capuletti among each other.' [70] The architect Francis S. Swales, who was an active force in the urban reform movement of New York City in the 1930s, proudly pointed to the similarities between New York and 'Bologna at the time of Dante: A City of Early Skyscrapers' (Fig. 9). [71]

The comparisons were visually fitting and also, in their paradoxical nature, quite correct. The medieval towers were not, as one might expect, the showy headquarters of wealthy merchants, but compact, customized versions of the extramural castles of the landed nobility who, by the abovementioned act, were forced by the citizens to remain for part of the year within the city walls. The nobles were compelled to continue their habitual war mongering from specially adapted pencil-shaped castles. The Montecchi and Capuletti did not use their 'Torre Gentilizie' for banking, just as the New York bankers were not noblemen, but the skyscrapers could be seen as customized strongholds; once inside the city walls they had to compensate for lost horizontality and mass by exaggerating verticality and slenderness.

The fortress is pressed through the city grid and transmuted into a single tower in the same way that a bulky potato is reduced to slender french fries. Skyscrapers and Torre Gentilizie were playing Wajang games; silhouettes unable ever to get to grips with each other. Imaginary fights between buildings were staged to impress and frighten off competitors but, though restricted to the level of theatrical performances, they were nevertheless mercilessly destructive. Just how destructive the building of costly towers and luxurious city palaces could be was more than once demonstrated by the unfortunate calculations of some early-renaissance Florentine arrivés. Richard A. Goldthwaite, in his *The Building of Renaissance Florence, an Economic and Social History*, has concluded that: 'Palaces were obviously built to make a big impression, and the zeal with which men set about doing this is evidenced in what they were prepared to spend on construction. ... Some builders so strained their resources that they could not complete the job, or so burdened their estate that their heirs sold the building. A few went bankrupt.' [72]

VIEW OF BOLOGNA AT THE TIME OF DANTE A CITY OF EARLY SKYSCRAPERS

[ 167 ]

## The centripetal force

It is understandable that the old city of New York should have encouraged the medieval habit of clustering. The southern tip of Manhattan was, after all, but a continuation of the tradition of the European merchant city; it is conceivable that its tradesmen found a certain comfort in each other's presence and, before the advent of the telephone, it must have been more convenient as well. But in the case of Chicago and other new cities on the frontier, there was a difference. Even in a period when the telephone was generally in use, say 1881, a developer from Boston, Peter Brooks, was convinced that the desirability of real estate for commercial uses was determined not by objective factors such as accessibility, quality of the soil, etc., but by the naively acquiescent argument 'to be where everybody else is.' The legendary fate of the Monadnock Building proved Brooks's forebodings about its off-centre location. The nearness of the endless prairie drove even the coolest of speculators to huddle together like frightened sheep in the dark. Unintentionally, Donald Hoffmann has caricatured Brooks's agoraphobia by stating that 'The problem was that the lot was *dangerously* isolated, if only by a few blocks, from the concentration of office space'[73] (my italics). Nobody, however adventurous his undertakings, dared to take risks on his own. Charles Whitaker, in his diatribe against speculation and land debt, claimed that all misery had started with William Penn: 'Penn marked the city off in squares. He made the streets as narrow as he dared, for to him streets were hardly more than land that could not be sold. He then sold lots, keeping every other one in his own hands. As lots were bought, the price of neighbouring ones rose. Penn and his friends cashed in, although some held on for years. Generally that is the basis of what is called land-subdivision in the United States. The method is illustrated very simply by the tale of the man who asked for the price of a lot.

'Two hundred dollars,' said the realtor.
'I'll take two,' said the man.
'That will be five hundred dollars.
'How's that?' said the buyer.
'Well, you see, the moment you buy one lot,
the one next to it goes up fifty percent.'[74]

This implies that speculation and land debt were entirely relative and had little to do with absolute quantities. What counted was *proximity*. It was the amount of *available propinquity* that was scarce, and a propinquity shortage could be created anywhere: on Manhattan Island, on the plains of Chicago, or in Birmingham, Alabama. The will to settle in the same neighbourhoods must have been agreed in unspoken concordance, nourished by social loyalty, yet counteracted simultaneously by mutual distrust, suspicion, envy, and, as ever, competition.[75]

Competition and democracy could, in American nineteenth-century thinking, be seen as complementary. Emerson regarded democracy as a helpful antidote against tyrants and usurpers. 'Democracy,' he wrote, 'is morose and runs to anarchy. But in the state, and in the schools, it is indispensable to resist the consolidation of all man into a few men.'[76] Democracy, then, was conceived of as merely a means of protecting men from becoming subservient, of safeguarding their freedom and integrity.

It was a general framework which allowed many different mechanisms to operate within it, each one designed to safeguard the autonomy of the individual. One such tool is *competition*, another is *opportunity*. Opportunity allows a person to act freely, whereas competition is the motive for his actions. Com-

73. Donald Hoffmann, *The Architecture of John Wellborn Root*, Baltimore/London, 1973, p. 156.

74. Charles H. Whitaker, op. cit., pp. 281/282. See also above, note 5.

75. Earle Shultz and Walter Simmons, *Offices in the Sky*, Indianapolis/New York, 1959, p. 13: 'The great function of the office building is to make it possible for the businesses that deal with one another to be close together. . . . This need for nearness, which one writer (?) called 'the efficiency of proximity' is the reason for the central business district, the essential feature of the American city.' Shultz was a building manager during the 1920s but wrote this book in the late 1950s. It is hard to judge how far he is to be taken seriously, how much he believed himself and how much he wanted others to believe what he himself dismissed as part of the myth. To underpin the theory of proximity he claimed that 'doctors clan together in medical centers' (p. 12), which they do indeed, but not as a rule, and certainly not to make money. Shultz did his best to present the skyscraper purely as a business proposition, but he got so carried away that he could only describe them in terms of poetic transcendence. Skyscrapers, he wrote, '. . . show the faith of many men in its destiny, and they create a faith in others. They are the evidence of the community's spirit of life, the hallmark of progress . . . . They are a standing notice to the world that a particular city has arrived among the elect, . . . . Since man learned to build, he constantly has aspired to greater heights. Starting with the Hanging Gardens of Babylon, he reared the Pyramids of Egypt and the Gothic cathedrals of Europe. Finally he realized his ultimate ambition with the soaring skyscrapers of America' (ibid.). As for the commercial value of the very tall skyscrapers of the twentieth century, Shultz shared the opinion of other more critical minds that they were far from profitable: on the contrary, '. . . many of the skyscrapers of New York are monuments of uselessness' (Reginald P. Bolton at the 1913 national convention of Building Owners and Managers in Cleveland) (ibid., p. 74).

76. Ralph Waldo Emerson, 'Nominalist and Realist', *Essays*, London, 1906, p. 332.

77. Ralph Waldo Emerson, 'Fortune of the Republic', *Miscallaneous Pieces*, London, 1913, p. 417.

78. *The American Builder*, September 1873, 'Press Palaces', p. 202.

79. Michael A. Mikkelsen, A History of Real Estate and Architecture in New York City During the Last Quarter of a Century, New York, 1898, pp. 67/67. The old New York *Times* building was in fact erected in 1857, designed by Thomas R. Jackson, and by the 'present Romanesque structure' was meant the meanwhile razed building by George B. Post, 1888–89. See: Winston Weisman, 'The Commercial Architecture of George B. Post', *J.S.A.H.*, XXXI, 1972, no. 1, p. 192.

80. *King's Handbook*, op. cit., pp. 614, 624.

81. Ibid., pp. 612–614.

82. Ibid., pp. 611–612; Winston Weisman, 'New York and the Problem of the First Skyscraper', *J.S.A.H.*, XII, 1953, p. 18, fig. 10.

83. James D. McCabe, Jr., *Lights and Shadows of New York Life, Or the Sights and Sensations of the Great City*, Philadelphia, etc., 1872, XIV, pp. 244–255. On Greeley and his paper, see pp. 250–252. See further below, n. 84.

Fig. 10. 'Printing-House Square in 1868' (from King's Handbook of New York, Boston, 1893).

Fig. 11. 'Park Row, the Older Newspaper Row'. The Potter Building (Fig. 8) is visible at the extreme left (from King's Handbook of New York, Boston, 1893).

petitive behaviour is, above all, a test of comparative strength, and each competitor must rely entirely upon himself. Too much room though will almost certainly slacken the drive to compete, although Emerson's famous lines from 'Fortune of the Republic' emphatically contradict this: 'Let them compete, and success to the strongest, the wisest, and the best. The land is wide enough, the soil has bread for all.'[77]

Much more than the suggested centrifugal tendency the magic of the centripetal force has been made manifest in the growth of America's commercial cities, and most of all in one of its most colourful biotopos, the sado-masochistic concentration of newspaper activities: Printing House Square.

### Printing House Square — a sado-masochistic arena

'Probably in no direction is the progress and improvement of architecture in this country more obvious than in the magnificent buildings — veritable palaces — which are so rapidly taking the place of the old, dingy newspaper offices of our principal cities,' wrote *The American Builder* in September 1873.[78] Michael A. Mikkelsen observed in *A History of Real Estate, Building and Architecture* of 1898, that it was the New York newspapers which, from 1868 on, started to build 'modern, specialized structures'. He wrote: 'it is curious to note that the newspapers were among the first innovators in this movement as they have been more recently in the erection of the tower-like sky-scrapers. The *Times* as far back as 1859, had erected its once familiar headquarters, since replaced by the present Romanesque structure (Fig. 10), and in 1868 Oswald Ottendorfer purchased for $250,000 the corner on Chatham Street and Tyron Row, on which to build the new building on the corner of Ann Street and Broadway; and in 1874 the *Tribune* led the way to still higher altitudes than had been reached by any other building with the edifice in which it is at present housed.'[79]

Until about 1868 most of New York's newspapers were produced in an unexciting row of buildings at Park Row, just south of Beekman Street (Fig. 11). Between 1866 and 1868 a certain amount of unrest was caused by a new building for the New York *Herald*, which was put up at the corner of Ann Street and Broadway (apparently at the wrong time and in the wrong place, for the *Herald* soon moved again, into a site further north named Herald Square).[80] Then, quite suddenly, in 1868, *The Sun* as well as the *Staats-Zeitung* — two leading papers — picked themselves up and moved several blocks north. *The Sun* settled into the palatial Tammany Hall, whereas the *Staats-Zeitung* selected a site north of the projected Brooklyn Bridge approach, where it erected a large, imposing building which left little room for the bridge ramps to be extended.[81]

It had become clear that the migration was taking a north-easterly direction, along the lines of Park Row, Broadway's main branch-off, leading away from the downtown business district. The northward direction was also taken by the *Evening Post*, which commissioned Charles F. Mengelson to build a new office building at Broadway and Fulton Street in 1874. King's *Handbook of New York City* (1893) recognized the tall new building (ten storeys plus one extra floor in the mansard) as 'one of the first large office-buildings to be erected in New York'.[83] All this movement seemed to be activated by a force of which the centre of gravity was located somewhere in the block where *The Sun* had settled recently and where the New York *Tribune* had already been, even before Horace Greeley, its legendary founder and editor, acquired the lot in 1860.[83]

## 'A brick and mortar giraffe'

By 1873 the *Tribune* had also purchased the other lots in the block, enveloping the one owned by *The Sun*, and a competition, presumably closed, was held to provide it with a new building so splendid, so sublime, that it would hurl all newcomers back into the ignominy from whence they had come. Two of the designs are extant, one by Josiah Cleaveland Cady (Fig. 12) and the other, the one that was eventually built, by Richard Morris Hunt (Fig. 13). [84] Renderings were published in *The New-York Sketch-Book* of January 1874,

*Fig. 12. Competitive design for the New York Tribune, 1873, by Josiah Cleaveland Cady (from* The New-York Sketch-Book of Architecture, *1874).*

84. *The New-York Sketch-Book of Architecture*, Vol. 1, Boston/New York, 1874, under the editorial guidance of Henry Hobson Richardson, published 'The New Tribune Building' as the opening feature of its first issue. The description included the following: 'The general dimensions are as follows: Frontage on Printing-House Square, 93 feet; on Spruce Street, 100 feet; on Frankfort Street, 27 feet. The foundations start 25 feet below the curb. Height to top roof, 135 feet. Extreme height of tower 250 feet. There will be nine stories above basement .... The offices for the public will be on first floor above, with principal entrance on the Square; whilst the composing, stereotypist, and editorial rooms, etc., will occupy the entire stories in roof. Directly under the tower will be the main entrance to the building which will be occupied by offices to rent.' The building was to be equipped with two passenger elevators and the structure was, for fear of fire, entirely of masonry with the exception of floor beams ('not exposed') and the framing of the roof. 'The floor-beams throughout rest upon masonry, upright iron supports being cautiously avoided; experience having demonstrated that they cannot be relied upon when exposed to great heat' (p. 1). It could be concluded from this text that at least partial iron framing was used for commercial structures, but that it was given up in favour of fire-resistant materials such as brick and terracotta. That a tall structure like the *Tribune* had to be erected of brick alone was obviously not regarded as being disadvantageous.

The 'Competitive Design for the New York Tribune Building' by J. Cleaveland Cady was reproduced in the same volume, no. VII, July 1874, as plate XXV. Extensive information on the building history of the *Tribune* is provided by: *New York City Architecture; Selections from The Historic American Buildings Survey, Number Seven*, July 1969, HABS no. NY-5468 (typewritten pp. 30–43, prepared by Diana S. Waite, April 1968). The building was demolished on June 7, 1966. Paul R. Baker, *Richard Morris Hunt*, Cambridge, Mass./London, 1980, deals parsimoniously with the *Tribune* on pp. 221–223, and pp. 502/503, notes 23–28. On the question of whether or not the *Tribune* should be considered the first skyscraper, the relevant literature is given by Baker, op. cit., p. 503, n. 28. On the topic of the competition the author remains silent, and the name of J.C. Cady is not mentioned. For Cady, see: Dennis Steadman Francis, *Architects in Practice in New York City, 1840–1900, for the Committee for the Preservation of Architectural Records*, New York, 1979; and: Montgomery Schuyler, 'The Works of Cady, Berg & See', *Architectural Record*, 6, 1897, pp. 517–556. Cady lived in 1837–1919 and practised architecture in New York City.

J. CLEAVELAND CADY ARCHITECT N.Y.
N.Y. TRIBUNE COMPETITION

an ephemeral but highly valued publication, mainly because it counted among its contributors famous names such as Hunt, Richardson, McKim, Post, Upjohn and Vaux.[85]

Instinctively, subconsciously perhaps, both designs touched upon what could be acknowledged as the essence of a skyscraper: they were trying to reach much higher than they were able to. By extending one part, the tower, higher than the rest, the building seemed almost to be stretching itself out. Particularly the design of Richard Morris Hunt was making palpable efforts to over-

*Fig. 13. Competitive, and winning, design for the New York Tribune, 1873, by Richard Morris Hunt (from* The New-York Sketch-Book of Architecture, *1874).*

85. The *Sketch-Book*'s life span was limited to only two volumes for the years 1874 and 1875. See also: Jeffrey K. Ochsner, *H.H. Richardson – The Complete Architectural Works*, Cambridge, Mass./ London, 1984, p. 16, n. 23.

86. *Pictorial New York and Brooklyn, A Guide to the Same and Vicinity*, George F. Smith, ed., New York, 1890 and 1892, p. 40.

87. Ibid., p. 40. A similar way of designating what subsequently became known as the 'skyscraper' was apparently used by Charles Atwood in 1883. See above, p. 85, n. 30. For the origin of the term 'skyscraper' see: J. Carson Webster, op. cit., p. 4, n. 11 and Stanley P. Andersen, *American Ikon: Response to the Skyscraper, 1875–1934*, Unpublished dissertation, University of Minnesota, 1960, pp. 51 ff. The two authors differed considerably in their establishing of a terminus post-quem. Andersen opted for 1883, Webster for 1891. Arnold Dudley Lewis, *Evaluations of American Architecture by European Critics, 1875–1900*, Unpublished dissertation, University of Wisconsin, 1962, stated that: 'The Western Union Building and the Tribune Building, regarded today either as the original skyscrapers in the country or the direct antecedents to the structures which Chicago produced in the 1880's, were unnoticed by most European architectural writers for many years after they had been finished. ... When they were discussed in the seventies, visitors appeared to be disinterested in their respective heights, the aspect for which most historians find them important today' (p. 350). This, of course, cannot be sustained.
European visitors, on the contrary, were quite outspoken in their experiences of the tendency to build high. Ernst von Hesse-Wartegg, for example, in his four-volume study of America, showed himself to be very interested in the two early skyscrapers. In the first volume, of 1878, he wrote about the Western Union Building: 'Unser Auge kann den Gipfel dieser rothen Ziegel-Pyramide kaum erreichen; neun Stockwerke hoch, erhebt er sich über alle Gebäude der Nachbarschaft empor in die Lüfte, und als wollte er den Ausspruch wahr machen: "Coeli eripuit fulmen" ragt noch ein hoher Turm über das Gebäude in die Wolken hinein' (p. 15). About the Tribune Building he wrote: 'Zur Rechten des Cityhall-Parks finden wir den Park Row, die Residenz des Vertretungskörpers des ganzen Volkes von Amerika: Der Presse. Hier stehen sie Haus an Haus, die Zeitungsgebäude, alle noch um das doppelte überhöht von dem Riesenbau der Tribüne – des höchsten Gebäudes Amerikas' (ibid., p. 18). Ernst von Hesse-Wartegg, *Nord-Amerika, seine Städte und Naturwunder, sein Land und seine Leute*, mit Beiträgen von Udo Brachvogel, Bret Harte, Theodor Kirchhof, Henri de Lamothe, Charles Nordhoff, Bayard Taylor und Anderen, Leipzig, 1880 (1878 [1]), p. 15.).
Frank Moss, *The American Metropolis, from Knickerbocker Days to the Present Time – New York City Life in All Its Various Phases*, 3 Vols., New York, 1897, Vol. 1, pp. 198/199.

88. W.G. Marshall, op. cit., p. 12. Marshall travelled throughout the United States between 1878 and 1879. His account of the *Tribune* is a relatively early one. Stanley P. Andersen, op. cit., pp. 36/37, mentions M.C. Pictou, a writer for the Paris *Revue Générale de l'Architecture*, as an early case of a foreigner commenting on the Tribune in the *American Architect and Building News*, II, December 22, 1877, 'American Architecture from a French Standpoint', pp. 408/409.

89. Frank Moss, op. cit., I, pp. 198/199.

90. *The New-York Sketch-Book*, 1, 1874, p. 1. Pugin's theory of architectural idealism was reflected

reach itself. Unlike the smooth and even lengthening of, for example, Louis Sullivan's buildings some twenty years later, here the stretching caused protruberances, proud flesh, shaping cicatrices in the form of cornices and mezzanines.

The *Tribune*, by virtue of its height, immediately became the most conspicuous landmark of the city, and was nicknamed 'the Tall Tower'.[86] Buildings like the *Tribune* were not instantly classified as skyscrapers, but were often referred to as 'lofty buildings', or buildings 'which may be seen from the Bay'.[87] Because of its different-coloured 'cicatrices', the English observer W.G. Marshall described the *Tribune* in 1880 as a 'brick and mortar giraffe' which towered above the surrounding buildings.[88] 'The *Tribune* building,' Frank Moss wrote in his 1897 *The American Metropolis*, 'was the first of the many tower buildings in the lower part of the City, and when it was erected it was the wonder and the pride of Printing House Square. Many were the envious cuts at the editor of the *Tribune* by those less fortunate editors who could not compose their editorials on such a lofty plane.'[89]

To be tall and lofty was one thing, but to be respected to a degree of stern sublimity was another, and, for a newspaper with the ambitions of the *Tribune*, a highly desirable thing. It should therefore be simply clothed and with a minimum of ornament. The description of it in *The New York Sketch-Book* – 'The façades are purposely devoid of meretricious ornament' – suggested sturdiness and moral elevation.[90]

These qualities were recognized and translated into 'Neo-Grec' by a more artistically oriented guidebook, George F. Smith's *Pictorial New York and Brooklyn* of 1890.[91]

From its very beginnings the American press, unlike the European, had established itself, not merely as the provider of news, but as the ethical standard, commercial as well as political.[92] A case in point was Horace Greeley, a devoted Fourrierist whose main editorial passions were the anti-slavery movement and labour unions. If the American press was the conscience of the nation, Greeley's paper was the most conscientious of them all. His influence must have been almost boundless, for Henry Ward Beecher, who spoke at Greeley's funeral, declared that 'today, between the two oceans, there is hardly an intelligent man or child that does not feel the influence of Horace Greeley.'[93] His contemporary Ralph Waldo Emerson went as far as trying to explain the perhaps otherwise inexplicable growth of education in the Midwest: 'Greeley did all the thinking and theory for the Midwestern farmers at two dollars a year,' alluding to the far-flung popularity of the *Tribune*'s Sunday edition.[94] Because of its moral crusading and its hifalutin ethical standards, the *Tribune* was appropriately nicknamed 'The Great Moral Organ'.[95] In December 1872, a year before the cornerstone of the *Tribune* building was laid, Greeley, who had that year unsuccessfully run for the United States presidency, died. Whitelaw Reid, who had been foreign minister to France, succeeded him as editor and as the person responsible for the paper's subsequent building activities.[96]

### 'The Great Moral Organ'

Much ink has been spilled over the question of whether the *Tribune* was a 'real' skyscraper or merely an overgrown Second Empire-inspired five-storey mansard-roofed building.[97] In the modernist vision, tall buildings which did not display their steel frames, or worse, did not even have a frame, could not be seriously considered as skyscrapers. It was generally dismissed as an oddity which had little more to its credit than stylistic impurity. In 1964 Wayne Andrews wrote about the *Tribune*: 'The confusion of Richard Morris Hunt and of his pupil George Browne Post was typical. The nine-story *Tribune* Building

in an article in *The American Builder* VIII/IX, September 1873, p. 202, called 'Press Palaces', in which the recently erected newspaper headquarters were praised for their handsome appearance and their effect upon the moral standards of the population. 'In place of the old-time squalor and discomfort, we have now magnificent offices .... In fact, the architectural changes which have thus resulted in beautifying our cities with noble structures, have also encouraged a moral progress and more healthy atmosphere, whose influence cannot fail to be observed by all who come in contact with our newspaper press.' More particular praise went to the *Tribune*, '... now in progress of construction, and which will probably excell all the rest ....'
There were dissident voices, though, such as the New York architect A.J. Bloor who in an 'Annual Address at the Tenth Annual A[merican] I[nstitute] of A[rchitects] Convention', *American Architect and Building News*, II (Supplement to issue of March 24, 1877), thought the *Tribune* on the contrary too picturesque: 'Picturesqueness is not so much to be sought for a large structure — and especially in a high one — as that expression of repose which satisfies the public eye with an impression of stability and safety.' Bloor nevertheless was quite willing to praise the building's general performance as a big and tall building 'against the sky'. From: Stanley P. Andersen, op. cit., pp. 32—35.

91. *George F. Smith's Pictorial New York and Brooklyn*, New York, 1890, p. 40.

92. Alfred McClung Lee, *The Daily Newspaper in America; The Evolution of a Social Instrument*, New York, 1937, p. 62. Colonel McCormick, the publisher of the *Chicago Tribune*, asserted that the newspaper 'is an institution developed by modern civilization to present the news of the day, to foster commerce and industry ... and to furnish that check upon government which no constitution has ever been able to provide.' And: The newspaper should be 'like the parish priest, be guide, counsellor and friend' (ibid., p. 284).

93. Frank Luther Mott, *American Journalism — A History: 1690–1960*, New York, 1962, p. 276. Greeley must have concluded, after all, that, whether he embodied the public extra-constitutional conscience or not, he still had fostered strong desires to become president of the United States, for which he campaigned the year before he died in 1872. This must have been a natural tendency among newspaper moguls, for Warren Harding was a newspaper man, and the renowned Randolph Hearst seriously wanted to run for the presidency (ibid., p. 721).
*Progressive Architecture*, July 1966, pp. 57/58, directed in a small news report the attention of readers to the demolition of the *Tribune*. About the paper's former influence, it wrote: 'Such was the influence of the *Trib* that, with an 1860 circulation of 200,000, it was said to come "next to the Bible"' (p. 57).

94. Frank Luther Mott, op. cit., pp. 276/277.

95. Ibid., p. 271.

*Fig. 14. Hamden County Courthouse, Springfield, Massachusetts, 1874, by Henry Hobson Richardson. Originally submitted as a competitive design in 1871, it was finally realized three years later (from The New-York Sketch-Book of Architecture, 1874).*

designed by the former in 1873 was partly iron-framed behind its brick facade, but this was a secret from the public. The iron age was denied by this Old World Town Hall, stretched as in a nightmare beyond its intended dimensions.'[99] This was a profound insight. Both Cady and Hunt had been presented with a far more complicated problem than the so often mentioned one of 'designing the facade in concordance with its interior framing'; their task was to design a building which was to express its function, not as a structure, but as the headquarters of a very special newspaper, a 'Great Moral Organ'.

Sublime authority, subservience to the public, interest, and incorruptibility had to be emphasized and this they achieved by adopting the block-end-tower form which was, at the time, characteristic of important civic buildings. This model, of which the block represented power and the tower sublime authority, was familiar through the Palazzo Vecchio of Florence and the Palazzo Pubblico of Siena. Numerous and often frivolous derivatives were built in the United States; the worthiest of them was Henry Hobson Richardson's Hamden County Courthouse at Springfield, Massachusetts (Fig. 14).[100] Richardson's design preceded Hunt's by almost a year, which supports the suggestion that Hunt was influenced by it. Furthermore, in the 1874 *New-York Sketch-Book* the two buildings were published side by side.

Fig. 15. 'The Skyscraper – A Feudal Baron'. In their battle for supremacy, the anthropomorphic skyscrapers often created hierarchical mountains, in which the victorious building established the central axis, submitting the others to servile positions (from Claude Bragdon, The Frozen Fountain, New York, 1932).

96. Ibid., p. 721; Paul R. Baker, op. cit., p. 221; *King's Handbook*, op. cit., pp. 616/617. A necrology of Greeley was provided by *The American Builder*, January 1873, pp. 5/6.

97. H.-H. Hitchcock, op. cit., pp. 169, 239/240.

98. This moralistic-constructivist vision is still amazingly persistent. A recent book like Leland M. Roth, *A Concise History of American Architecture*, New York, etc., 1980 (1979 1), pp. 161–164, still insists on the 'frame expressive' nature of the wall.

99. Wayne Andrews, *Architecture, Ambition and Americans; A Social History of American Architecture*, New York/London, 1964, p. 207.

100. The most frivolous by far is the Emerson/Bromo-Seltzer Tower in Baltimore, built by Joseph E. Sperry in 1911 for Captain Isaac E. Emerson, developer of Bromo-Seltzer, 'who made a grand tour of Europe shortly after the turn of the century and was so fascinated with the Palazzo Vecchio in Florence that on his return he commissioned Sperry to design one like it' (*A Guide to Baltimore Architecture*, Baltimore, 1973, pp. 79/80). Other impressive specimens are: City of Boston Fire Department Headquarters, Boston, 1891, E.M. Wheelwright; Pilgrim Monument, Provincetown, Mass., and the Union Station of Waterbury, Conn., by McKim, Mead & White, 1909. On the European continent the block-and-tower model had a more serious following in the trend-setting Stockholm Town Hall by Ragnar Östberg of 1909 which influenced a good deal of town hall design of the 1930s and in the Copenhagen Town Hall by Martin Nyrop of 1892. The City Hall of Springfield, Mass., facing the Hamden County Courthouse across the square, also features an oversize 'torre gentilizie', distantly related to the Torre della Mangia of the Siena Town Hall. Richardson's Court House which was commissioned in a competition in 1871, was dedicated in 1874. It was published in the *New-York Sketch-Book* in its finished state as well as in a preliminary sketch (op. cit., p. 2, pl. I). The Tuscan character of the ensemble was noted by Mariana Griswold Van Rensselaer, *Henry Hobson Richardson and his Works*, New York, 1969 (1898 1), p. 54: '[it] speaks of the fortified palaces of Tuscan towns.' See also: Jeffrey Karl Ochsner, *H.H. Richardson; Complete Architectural Work*, Cambridge/London, 1984, pp. 90–91, 16, n. 23.

101. 'The skyscraper, a feudal baron, surrounded by his vassals,' was Claude Bragdon's interpretation of the skyscrapers' performance as a competitive fighting crowd, finally resulting in the dominance of one over the others. 'Silhouetted against the grey of dawn ... these campanili of the New Feudalism, however base-born and aesthetically uninspired, are none the less the planet's most august and significant symbol of proud-spirited man, flashing unquenched defiance to the stars' (Claude Bragdon, *The Frozen Fountain*, New York, 1932, p. 35 + illustration).

A tower shoots up from the roof of the main block of the *Tribune*, flanked by aggrandized lucarnes which are brought down to scale by the lower bays. The general outlines are those of the Palazzo Pubblico/Vecchio type, with its corbelled tower crowned, as usual, by a 'tempietto'. A striking feature of the *Tribune* tower was the typical town-hall clock fitted within the corner columns of the 'tempietto', thus filling in the openings.

As a tribute to Greeley's extraordinary position, both as an unusually influential editor and as an attempted president, the building was fitted with a speaker's rostrum which, presumably because Greeley had died recently, was left without visible access. His statue was placed in the entrance portico but was later moved to the square in front of the building.

A slight difference with respect to the position of the statue is revealed in the two competition designs: Cady positioned it 'in pontificio', over the gallery and under a baldacchino, whereas Hunt placed it outside, under an arcade to the right of the entrance.

### The skyscraper – a feudal baron [101] (Figs. 15 & 16)

Apart from being 'a check upon government' and 'a parish priest', as Colonel McCormick, publisher of that other *Tribune*, *The Chicago Tribune*, called it, the newspaper was an instrument of merciless competition. News was, above all, merchandise, and those who were selling it tried to sell more of it than the other manufacturer. The battles fought for the public's patronage were often fiercer than they were made to seem in the reports. Joseph Pulitzer's and William Randolph Heart's campaigns to stir up belligerence in the Spanish-American dispute over Cuba are a legendary example.

The newly annexed northern end of Park Row, known as Printing House Square, was selected by some atavistic consensus as the stage on which the press would fight its battles for supremacy. The newly built headquarters were to become the mercenaries, thus they had to look terrifying and invincible (in the same way that Francesco Sforza and Leon Battista Alberti advised their clients to clothe their fortresses). [102] Henry James, in *The American Scene*, called them 'those mercenary monsters', and Montgomery Schuyler compared their founders with Frankenstein: 'Like Frankenstein we stand appalled before the monsters of our own creation, literally – "monstrum horrendum, informe, ingens, cui lumen ademptum" – .' [103]

102. Stanislaus von Moos, op. cit., pp. 177, 55/56.

103. Henry James, *The American Scene*, London, 1907, p. 96; Montgomery Schuyler, 'The Skyscraper Problem', originally in: *Scribner's Magazine*, 34, August 1903, reproduced in Jordy & Coe, op. cit., II, pp. 445/446.

104. For the anthropomorphic simile, see for example Claude-Nicolas Ledoux's maxim: 'Toute puissance est faible si elle n'est pas couronnées qu'est-ce qu'un corps sans tête?', referring to the termination of the house of the director of the salt-works (*L'oeuvre et les rêves de Claude-Nicolas Ledoux*, Yvan Christ & Ionel Schein, eds., Edition Chêne, 1971, p. 60). See also, above, n. 89, and below, n. 110).

105. 'Sacred Skyscrapers and Profane Cathedrals', pp. 63, 65ff.

Fig. 16. The 'Monarchs of New York'. In the anthropomorphic analogy superior tallness is equated with a regal position (postcard).

Fig. 17. 'A Brick and Mortar Giraffe'. The Tribune Building as it was actually built: ten storeys instead of the projected nine. A mezzanine has been wedged in between the cornice and the lucarnes. The extra storey escaped most historians, probably because they had studied the print rather than the actual building. It was demolished in 1966. [84]

The buildings on Printing House Square were programmed to stand their ground until suffocated, in the fiercest possible battle of proximity. In their compulsive, neurotic determination not to move out, they had to rely on their ability to ascend along a vertical axis. From the very beginning the *Tribune* showed its capacity for telescopic growth. The earliest sketches show nine floors (Fig. 13), but by the time it was built a floor had been added. One floor slipped into a mezzanine zone between the cornice and the lucarnes (Fig. 17). The entire roof-line was jutted upward to reach just below the machicolation of the tower: the *Tribune* had straightened its shoulders.

Since the *Tribune* was exclusively interested in outward performance and thus had increased its material mass, the internal volume had increased also, beyond the actual need. It was decided to let the superfluous space to others. The less attractive floors, the lower ones, were let, whereas the brains of the paper settled where they belonged: at the top. [104]

### 'Toute valorisation est verticalisation'

An essential element in the history of the skyscraper is the recurrent theme of anthropomorphism. In 'Sacred Skyscrapers and Profane Cathedrals' (see pp. 63, 65ff.) it was introduced to illustrate the role of the skyscraper as an architectonic servant to its human master, shaped to his ideological likeness. [105] Instead of mixing with the competitive tumult, the proprietor equipped himself with an iron-and-brick stand-in (Fig. 18). [106]

The idea of upward movement and the image of verticality are certainly among the strongest and most persistent in history, and it is unlikely that any philosopher, historian of ideas, anthropologist or sociologist would dispute this. Yet in the history of the skyscraper the anthropomorphic theme has, with the exception of Louis Sullivan and of those who were spiritually akin, remained virtually untouched. [107]

Both Gaston Bachelard and Mircea Eliade have argued that the vertical axis, coinciding with the human form, has always been regarded as the bearer of the hierarchy of virtues and values. The higher the value, the nearer its position to the top, and vice versa. Images such as the Towers of Virtue and Learning, pagodas, or Jacob's Ladder are always conceived in tower-like form, and of course those images that are taken from the organic world such as tall growing plants and trees. [108] It follows that any architectural endeavour conceived on the vertical axis would necessarily express this hierarchy and, mutatis mutandis, would be experienced as such.

*Fig. 18. 'This stupendous form, towering like a lighthouse, commanding in its posture a wide horizon' (Horatio Greenough). The vertical axis makes the human and some architectural types, like towers, lighthouses and skyscrapers, interchangeable. The Singer Building, New York, 1906–1908, Ernest Flagg, architect, demonstrating the fusion of these two metaphors (postcard).*

106. See above, note 101. The vertical axis makes the human form and some architectural types, like towers, lighthouses and skyscrapers interchangeable. Horatio Greenough wrote: 'Let us now turn to the human frame, the most beautiful organization of earth, the exponent and minister of the highest being we immediately know. This stupendous form, this towering as a lighthouse, commanding by its posture a wide horizon, . . . , it tells of majesty and dominion by that upreared spine . . .' (*Form and Function, Remarks on Art, Design, and Architecture, by Horatio Greenough*, Harold Small, ed., Berkeley/Los Angeles, 1957, p. 120). It is hardly accidental that the skyscraper would be imagined casting a bright beam of light, impersonating a vigilant giant and a lighthouse in one metaphor (see Fig. 18). Picture postcards of skyscrapers were usually issued in pairs; one showing the building by day, the other at night, casting its beam of light (see, for example, Rem Koolhaas, op. cit., pp. 76, 135). References to skyscrapers as 'giants' and 'monarchs' are numerous on picture postcards.

107. Narciso Menocal, *Architecture as Nature – The Transcendentalist Idea of Louis Sullivan*, Madison, Wis., 1981, was the first to deal seriously with architectural anthropomorphism, mainly related to Sullivan, however (pp. 62–69). See also: Dolores Hayden, 'Skyscraper Seduction – Skyscraper Rape', *Heresies*, 1977, 2, pp. 108–115.

It has been said that the greatness of man is measured by the monuments he leaves behind. Napoleon summarized his theory of the inductive value of the monument thus: 'Les hommes ne sont grands que par les monuments qu'ils laissent.'[109] The erection of impressive monuments has been, and still is, an infallable means of ensuring fame and immortality. A direct way to achieve this is to have the desired connotative carriers of greatness converge on the vertical axis: the human form and the building are fused into one shape, the anthropomorphic tower.

This ideological shortcut was demonstrated by Gustave Eiffel's famous tower for the 1889 Paris World Fair. A contemporary print shows Eiffel casually posing between a pyramid and the tower of his own creation (Fig. 19). Leaning with his left hand on the pyramid and holding the tower with his right, he bridges, as it were, the connotative affinity of the two. On the pyramid is written: 'A la grandeur de l'oeuvre on mesure la grandeur de l'homme.' As if to emphasize the meaning of 'grandeur', Eiffel is depicted as having the same height as his tower, whereas the pyramid, being the proper carrier of the Napoleonic dictum, figures merely as a support to the great man's self-confident pose. Briefly, the image represents a triple equation, in which the man is drawn to the same height as the tower in order to make him, literally, 'great', in which the stature of the tower is equated with the stature of the man in order to invest it with his virtues, and in which the pyramid embodies historical proof of the correctness of the proposition, the words of which are inscribed on it.

In the process of identification of man with his building, it was only natural that those who held the highest office would settle on the highest floors of a skyscraper and that those who were inferior in rank, or merely tenants, would be restricted to the lower regions. Exceptions to this rule only emphasized its validity: powerful financial institutions, for example some aristocratic 'old money' banks, would sometimes take pleasure in drawing attention to the feudal overtones of horizontality by restricting their offices (and their buildings) to the ground level, even when soaring real estate prices were driving others to multiply the value of their lots by erecting tall buildings. A certain indifference to the level of profits and a regal prodigality suited their image of absolute independence.

Banks, observed Colonel W.A. Starrett, often settled on valuable corner lots with low, classical buildings, 'subordinating income to design,' no doubt to demonstrate that they were not in the least dependent on secondary sources of income. Another way of showing disregard for economy was, according to Starrett, to carry skyscrapers upward beyond their 'economic height'. The limits of this 'economic height' varied wildly, which he knew when he wrote it in 1928, but in the experimental times of the *Tribune* it must have been a term 'avant la lettre'.[110]

In any case, once the dominant verticality of the skyscraper had been established, it was accepted as the only way to communicate values of a higher order. 'La valorisation verticale,' Bachelard stated 'est si essentielle, si sûre, sa suprématie est si indiscutable que l'esprit ne peut s'en détourner quand il l'a une fois reconnue dans son sens immédiat et direct . . . : *toute valorisation est verticalisation.*'[111] In the arena of Newspaper Row most of the qualities connected with the vertical were desirable: dominance, superiority, etc.[112] The monolithic tower could also be interpreted as being representative of Darwinistic/Spencerian virtues such as self-reliance and individualism, which were highly esteemed in American popular ethics. The upright position was evolution's reward to its most ambitious creature. The vertical axis coincided with the erect stature of man, who has projected himself in the world observed and who has used himself as an orientation mark in amorphous space.

From the moment man discovered the need to have himself projected in architecture, he fulfilled it by giving it the only possible shape, the vertical.[113] The vertical was the mathematical symbol of man's great achievement, that of walking upright.

When we turn our attention once more to the field of competition, it seems fair to assume that the upright position is the basic requirement for survival. Since the notions of competition, survival and the like are related to the theory of evolution, it would be an interesting excursus to see how the other primates would react under competitive pressure. Would it, for instance, be

108. Mircea Eliade, *The Sacred and the Profane, The Nature of Religion*, New York, 1961, pp. 36ff., and *Images et symboles, essais sur le symbolisme magico-religieux*, Paris, 1952, pp. 33ff. Important also is Gaston Bachelard, *L'air et les songes, essai sur l'imagination du mouvement*, Paris, 1943, pp. 17ff., 71, 146ff.

109. 'Lettre à Champigny, 30 Mai 1807', in: Louis Hautecoeur, *Histoire de l'architecture classique en France*, Tome V, Paris, 1953, p. 148.

110. Col. W.A. Starrett, *Skyscrapers and the Men Who Build Them*, New York/London, 1928, p. 112. Whether skyscrapers were economically sound enterprises, or not, was a question that could be attacked from many angles. A positive answer could be obtained, naturally, from the American Institute of Steel Construction Inc., who were responsible for the publication of: W.C. Clark & J.L. Kingston, *The Skyscraper, A Study in the Economic Height of Modern Office Buildings*, New York/Cleveland, 1930. An economic height was defined as: 'The true economic height of a structure is that height which will secure the maximum ultimate return on total investment, within the reasonable useful life of the structure ...' (p. 9). The authors conceded, however, that extremely tall buildings, such as were under construction at the time (for example the *Empire State* Building), were almost certain to produce considerable losses. As a rule, very tall buildings required investments too large to yield profits, even for a longer term than normally is taken into consideration. Some investors thought it better business to sell buildings than to own them (see also: 'Sacred Skyscrapers and Profane Cathedrals', p. 69, note 50). It should be remembered, however, that not all owners of skyscrapers considered the idea of letting space to others in their building an appealing one. The early newspaper skyscrapers did have spare office space to let, but they did so reluctantly, or not at all. George C. Booth, president of the *Detroit News*, for example, '... vetoed the original plans to build office space over the new home of the paper,' on the grounds that 'the institutional character of the newspaper ought not to be obscured; that the designing of a building to serve two purposes must result in the sacrifice of one.' It was evident that Booth feared that letting space to others would have a negative effect on the newspaper's public image. (Lee A. White, *The Detroit News, 1873–1917*, Detroit, 1918, p. 25).

111. Gaston Bachelard, *L'air et les songes*, op. cit., pp. 17/18.

112. See: 'Sacred Skyscrapers and Profane Cathedrals', p. 74, n. 65.

113. Cornelis Verhoeven, *Symboliek van de voet*, Assen, 1956, p. 16.

Fig. 19. 'A la grandeur de l'oeuvre on mesure la grandeur de l'homme.' A triple equation, in which man is drawn to the same height as the tower; the tower is shaped to the stature of man and the pyramid is representing the historic proof of the justness of the proposition whose text it carries (from Le Central, I, 4, 1889, facsimile edition).

GUSTAVE EIFFEL (1855)

18

*Fig. 20. 'Cats, when terrified, stand at full height, and arch their backs in a well-known and ridiculous fashion' (Charles Darwin,* The Expression of the Emotions in Man and Animals, *London, 1904 (1872¹)). In a social climate generally characterized as 'Darwinistic', it should not be surprising that the behaviour of animals was regarded analogous to that of buildings representing their clients as anthropomorphic 'mercenaries'.*

114. Charles Darwin, *The Expression of the Emotions in Man and Animals*, London, 1904 (1872¹), p. 144.

115. Ibid., p. 130.

116. Ibid., pp. 113, 105–113.

117. Ibid., p. 130.

118. Winston Weisman, 'The Commercial Architecture of George B. Post', *J.S.A.H.*, XXXI, March 1972, no. 1, p. 192; *Moses King's Handbook of New York*, Boston, 1893, p. 618. Russell Sturges, 'The Works of George B. Post', *The Architectural Record, Great American Architects Series*, June 1898, pp. 11–18.

119. *The World, its History & its New Home* (New York?, 189. (?)), p. 2. The daily circulation in 1890 was 320,130 as opposed to 33,521 in 1883 (see *King's Handbook*, 1893, pp. 620–622). When Pulitzer bought the *World* in 1883, architectural critic Montgomery Schuyler 'abandoned the *World* for the *Times*' (Jordy & Coe, op. cit., I, p. 159, no. 62).

reasonable to assume that the chimpanzee would change from a stooped to an erect position, were it challenged into competition? Charles Darwin, in his 1872 *The Expression of the Emotions in Man and Animals*, described several experiments with monkeys, which were intended to induce fear: 'Their faces seemed somewhat lengthened. They occasionally raised themselves on their hind-legs to get a better view.'[114] And another observation: 'Cats, when terrified, stand at full height, and arch their backs in a well-known and ridiculous fashion.'[115] (See fig. 20.)

In the chapter 'The Inflation of the Body, and Other Means of Exciting Fear in an Enemy', Darwin elaborated on the subject, giving examples of experiments with toads, frogs, snakes (the cobra!), horses (who stand on their hind-legs when frightening off an opponent, while, on the contrary, they throw up their hind-legs when frolicking, etc.).[116] 'I am inclined to believe,' he went on, 'that, in the same manner as many birds, while they ruffle their feathers, spread out their wings and tail, to make themselves look as big as possible, so cats stand upright at their full length, arch their backs, often raise the basal part of the tail, and erect their hair, for the same purpose.' It was observed that the larger feline animals, such as the tiger and the lion, had no such tendencies, and Darwin concluded that this was because they had no serious competition to fear.[117]

## Two dreams

By the time the *Tribune* had established its dominant position, the others had lost their nerve and kept to a respectful distance. The *New York Times* replaced its old five-storey block with a new and distinguished-looking twelve-storey building by George B. Post in 1888–1889. The paper remained on its original triangular lot at the confluence of Park Row and Nassau Street, looking askance at the *Tribune* building (Fig. 31).[118] Although the *Times* building boasted more floors than the *Tribune*, its total height remained well below that of the latter.

But then Joseph Pulitzer upset this uneasy equilibrium. Having moved from the Midwest to New York, he set himself the goal of conquering the East. He did exactly what history expects of a conquerer. In 1883 he bought the *World*, a paper with modest circulation which he had boosted by ten times a mere seven years later.[119] In 1889 Pulitzer decided that the time had come to crush his opponents, which he did most dramatically by erecting a building so tall that it literally took the light away from the *Tribune*. To this end, he took the trouble to build the tallest building in the world (Fig. 21).[120] But in the battle of proximity tallness is effective only if it is related to a nearby opponent, and so Pulitzer wanted to move his new headquarters as close as possible to the *Tribune* building. The site he chose was adjacent, but it also was an extremely uncomfortable one. It was situated on Park Row at the northwest corner of Frankfort Street, about where Brooklyn Bridge was to have its southern ramps – in fact, traffic heading for Brooklyn had to pass alarmingly close to the windows of the third and fourth floors. This only shows how

Park Row, New York

*Fig. 21. Joseph Pulitzer's new headquarters for* The World, *New York, 1889–1890, George B. Post, architect. Pulitzer had moved* The World *from the old site (see Fig. 8) to the new one, more to the north, immediately adjoining the New York* Sun *and the* Tribune *buildings. From his executive offices, situated in the Michelangelo-inspired dome, Pulitzer could look down on his less prominent competitors. (demolished) (postcard).*

120. *History of Architecture and the Building Trades of Greater New York*, Vols. 1 & 2, New York, 1899, p. 218.
*The World*, op. cit., p. 6: 'It is the highest office building in existence' and *King's Handbook*, op. cit., p. 622: '. . . the tallest office-building in the world'. The cautiously added specification of 'office' in 'office building' was obviously prompted in order to stay clear of the Eiffel Tower's claim of being the tallest tower until the advent of the over-1000 feet skyscrapers such as the Empire State Building and the Chrysler Building from the early 1930s. The existence of the (roughly) 543 feet tall Mole Antonelliana (1863) in Turin was, without exception, lightheartedly overlooked.

121. Allen Churchill, *Park Row*, New York, 1958, p. 43 and John L. Heaton, *The Story of a Page, Thirty Years of Public Service and Public Discussion in the Editorial Columns of the New York* World, New York/London, 1923, p. 70.

122. 'The imposing dome, which distinguishes the building from every other in the metropolis, was originally and entirely Mr. Pulitzer's conception. The same may be said of the splendid three-storied entrance-arch, an equally notable and effective architectural feature' (*The World*, op. cit., p. 8). Winston Weisman, 'George B. Post', op. cit., p. 191, fig. 31. The common reproaches made in respect of its design are that it showed no coherence and that 'The unsuccessful skyline and general massing of this building are purely matters of accident which the architect had no obvious means of controlling' (Sturgis, op. cit., p. 15), shortcomings that can easily be explained by the client's own enthusiastic interference.

desperately the *World* wanted to close in on the *Tribune*: arguments of a practical or economic nature had to give way to motives emanating from a fevered imagination. Pulitzer was indeed obsessed by his building. Being the proverbial romantic – frail constitution combined with diabolical ambition and capacity for work – he devoted his entire life to this one desire: 'Yet even as his nerves commanded him to stop, Pulitzer conceived his most grandiose idea,' to build 'the highest building in New York as a proper home for *The World*.'[121] It was claimed that he had a hand in the design, particularly in the idea for the dome, which after all was as much Pulitzer's as it was Michelangelo's.[122] In this Pulitzer was a trend-setter, since both the San Francisco *Call*

Building (1896) and the Vancouver *World* Building (1911) gratefully borrowed the idea (Figs. 22 & 23). [123] In any case, the personal intervention of rich clients with lively and, above all, boyish imaginations is more than likely, Frank W. Woolworth, Randolph Hearst and now Pulitzer being cases in point.

Nevertheless, the design for the *World* was the result of a limited competition, of which only two entries are known: one by R.H. Robertson, which was not unlike Cady's successful design for the *Tribune*, and the other by George B. Post, which was eventually executed in 1889–1891. [124]

The new building was a massive and downright anthropomorphic presence on the skyline, resembling one of the knights of iron which grew out of the dragon's teeth sown by Cadmus, or the colossus which appeared to Nebuchadnezzar in one of his dreams. [125] This colossus was conceived of in the vertical dimension and consisted of different materials, which were arranged in hierarchical order, so that the low-ranking materials, such as clay and stone, formed the base for more durable metals like iron and brass, whereas the most precious ones like silver and, finally, gold, rested on the top. Nebuchadnezzar's colossus was a representation of a vertical order of values, which his court analyst, Daniel, explained as the king's own career arranged along a vertically positioned axis of time. Amazingly, this parallel was noted by the *New York Times* of April 3, 1875, on the occasion of their moving to the new headquarters at the intersection of Park Row and Nassau Street: 'New York has outgrown the period of clay, though its feet are literally in the mud, ... but it is rapidly becoming a city of marble, iron and plate glass.... The commercial metropolis at the New World will be very nearly a fulfillment of the vision of Nebuchadnezzar.' [126]

*Two followers of Pulitzer's concept of a prestigious newspaper building:*
*Fig. 22 (below). The San Francisco Call Building, San Francisco, 1896, James M. Reid, architect (demolished) (from San Francisco and Vicinity, M. Rieder, Los Angeles, 1904). At the time it was the tallest office building of San Francisco.*
*Fig. 23 (right). The Vancouver World Building, Vancouver, 1911–1913, W.T. Whiteway, architect. The building is now the home of the Vancouver Sun. It was for three years the tallest building in the British Empire.*

*Fig. 24. Also the New York* Tribune *had set a fasion which was occasionally followed; this time by the Oakland* Tribune, *Oakland, California, 1923, Edmund T. Foulkes, architect (photo Thomas Gordon Smith, Richmond, California).*

123. It is to be expected that the headquarters of the great New York papers set the fashion in the design of newspaper headquarters elsewhere. The Vancouver *Sun Tower*, 1911–1913, W.T. Whiteway, architect, was originally the home of the Vancouver *World*, for which it was built (*Exploring Vancouver*, 2, Harold Kalman, ed., Vancouver, 1978, p. 40). The San Francisco *Call Building*, 1896, James M. Reid, remained most faithful to its model. It survived the 1906 earthquake but was nevertheless destroyed (*1868–1968, California Architecture*, an exhibition organized by David Gebhard and Harriette von Breton, Santa Barbara, 1968, pp. 13, 43). Interesting as a vague reflection of the New York *Tribune* is the Oakland *Tribune* in Oakland, California, 1923, by Edmund T. Foulkes (Fig. 24). I am grateful to Thomas Gordon Smith who provided me with the photograph.

124. Winston Weisman, 'George B. Post', op. cit., p. 191. Robertson's design is illustrated as figure 31, 'Competition drawing for the *World* Building, New York, R.H. Robertson, 1889.'

125. *Daniel*, 2: 30–45.

126. *History of Architecture and the Building Trades of Greater New York*, Vols. I & II, New York, 1899, p. 184.

127. *The World*, op. cit., p. 86.

128. 'Sacred Skyscrapers', etc., p. 68, n. 46.

129. At night the dome's ribs and lantern were illuminated. The gallery of the lantern was open to visitors 'at all times during the day, [and] a wonderful view may be obtained of the metropolis and environs for miles around' (*Pictorial New York*, op. cit., p. 40).

Pulitzer made a point of presenting his newspaper and its building as part of the public domain – 'it well deserves to be known as the People's Palace,' he wrote. [127] Accordingly, he stressed the fact – just as Frank W. Woolworth would do twenty years later – that there was no mortgage on the project and that he, the 'benevolent ruler', had paid for it all from his own pocket. [128] The result was majestic indeed. The self-supporting walls are built of a wide variety of different-coloured materials, ranging from the darker shades of the ground-floor zone to the lighter tones near the top, culminating in the shining gold of the dome. [129] Following the pattern of hierarchic ascension and the anthropomorphic analogy, Pulitzer claimed the second floor of the drum for his executive offices,[130] corresponding more or less to the place where the eyes are located on the human body. He took possession, so to speak, of his own creation by moving into the part of it where the two heads, the human and the architectural, could converge. Both personalities, his own and that of the building, were inflated to the point that their respective greatness could be measured in the way that Gustave Eiffel and his celebrated tower were balanced against each other, as in the Napoleonic dictum: 'A la grandeur de l'oeuvre on mesure la grandeur de l'homme' (Fig. 19).[131]

A contemporary illustration of this analogy was provided by the author of *The American Metropolis*, Frank Moss. Elaborating on New York's origin, and praising its 'spirit of tolerance', Moss stated that '. . . the great and almost unmatched benevolent enterprises of the City have reached a magnificent growth, and are stretching their heads to heights unmeasured.'[132] The conjecture that the author was using an anthropomorphic analogy is supported by the passage which follows, in which, boasting of his Dutch ancestry, he claimed that the Dutch had 'built their ships on the model of their women' (Fig. 25).[133]

Another of Nebuchadnezzar's visions could be regarded as the complement of the abovementioned one, sharing as it does the same symbolic composition, which Mircea Eliade once defined as 'le symbolisme du centre'.[134] The king saw a gigantic tree standing in the middle of his kingdom, with its top reaching into the heavens. When he demanded that this vision be analyzed, Daniel explained that the tree represented the king himself, conceived as the convergence of the two dimensions of absolute dominance: *verticality and centrality*. The archetypal tree of which the king had dreamt was probably a familiar image in the heyday of the Babylonian empire. As an iconic 'axis mundi' it represented the cosmic centre of the world in the same way that the ziggurat represented the cosmic mountain.[135] An interesting aspect of this latter vision is the emphasis upon its anthropomorphic form. The axis mundi is traditionally visualized in the form of a tree, a mountain or a similar iconic representation. But if a ruler assumes the shape of either one it instantly becomes the centre of the world. Thus, with the help of his limitless ambition and his natural erect posture, man can easily assume a variety of vertical shapes – tree, mountain, ziggurat or skyscraper (Fig. 26).

'L'arbre seul, dans la nature, pour une raison typifique, est vertical, avec l'homme,' wrote Paul Claudel. Bachelard proposed that, since the tree is a symbol of heroic uprightness, particularly in its solitude and its opposition to the flatness of the earth, a dialectic could be discerned between the tree and the grass, a forest and existence in a higher sphere.[136] Nietzsche's *Thus Spoke Zarathustra*, particularly the tale of the *Tree on the Mountainside*, is the classic study of the analogy between the tree, which aspires to the heights, yet digs its roots deep into the earth, and the difficult coexistence of spiritual ecstasy on the one hand and the attraction of the earth on the other; of the dialectic of ascent, with its promise of freedom as well as danger, and descent, with its temptations of the charms, but also impurity, of earthly life.[137] This combined with the Nietzschean passionate temper, the joyous range of energy, illustrates the tyrannical dominance of the will over matter in the case of Joseph Pulitzer. The drive to erect his *World* headquarters as an obscenely obtrusive neighbour to the *Tribune* resulted in a monstrous perversion of the tale of Philemon and Baucis. The suggestion being put forward here is that the centre of gravity in this field is defined by a process in which structures move franti-

Ship and Woman.

Fig. 25. 'The Dutch,' Frank Moss wrote in 1897, 'built their ships on the model of their women' (*Frank Moss*, The American Metropolis, *New York, 1897*). *A profound, and for the question of anthropomorphic design, enlightening observation.*

"I like it. It has authority."

*Fig. 26. 'I like it. It has authority.' Man, with the help of his limitless ambition and his natural erect posture easily can slip into the shapes of centrality and verticality and can become tree, mountain, ziggurat or skyscraper (from* The New Yorker, *March 31, 1986; cartoon by Ed Fisher).*

cally, and maybe also helplessly, where they start piling up on the smallest possible surface. It must be emphasized that movements which constitute this action happen *simultaneously*, and not, as is generally understood, in a sequence of cause and effect. In their moving towards the magic spot, the buildings are being condensed and stretched out at the same time. [138] In other words, when all the newspaper headquarters were flocking to the same place, they were gradually growing, rising up to the tallest possible heights, while moving to that spot. The buildings which settled closest to the magic spot necessarily had to be the tallest, and the top of the mountainous pile which resulted was formed by the most ambitious, most successful of the lot. Consequently, as soon as another competitor had successfully challenged the leader in growing taller, the mountain would change its silhouette and shift to another centre of gravity. Claude Bragdon (who will be introduced later) held the theory that 'The raison d'être of the skyscraper is therefore not physical but psychical: it arose in answer to the desire of the herd to become a super herd. ... Skyscrapers appear only and always on those sacred acres which for some mysterious reason have become the blue heaven of the business man.' [139]

## Acromegaly [140]

After the *World* had out-topped the *Tribune*, an artifical abyss was created, in the dark depths of which sat the old *Sun*, helplessly sandwiched between the two peaks (Fig. 21). The New York *Real Estate Record and Builders' Guide* of 1887 wrote: 'When the *World* building is completed, the *Sun* will be overshadowed ... it will never do for that *bright* paper to be eclipsed.' [141]
Frank Moss reported in *The American Metropolis* of 1897 on the subsequent events: 'The *Sun* building is strangely out of place among the towering newspaper buildings that surround it, and it seems a pity that the corner cannot be thrown into the incomplete *Tribune* building [Moss was referring to the odd L-shaped lot that the *Tribune* occupied], but the hostility that has existed between those two newspapers for many years prevents any such arrangement.

130. *The World*, op. cit., p. 31.

131. See above, note 109.

132. Frank Moss, op. cit., I, p. 3.

133. Ibid., I, p. 4.

134. Mircea Eliade, *Images*, op. cit., pp. 33ff.

135. Ibid., p. 52; Cornelis Verhoeven, op. cit., p. 15.

136. Gaston Bachelard, op. cit., p. 237; see also p. 236.

137. Friedrich Nietzsche, *Thus Spoke Zarathustra*, Harmondsworth, 1969, pp. 69–70.

138. See Mircea Eliade, *Images*, op. cit., p. 51.

139. Claude Bragdon, *The Frozen Fountain*, op. cit., p. 26.

140. Acromegaly: A disease caused by abnormal activity of the pituitary gland, which permanently enlarges the bones of the extremities. An abnormal growth of the skeleton.

141. *Real Estate Record and Builders' Guide*, New York, 1887, September 1, p. 1064.

... If the plans of the *Sun* owners have been truly announced, some day there will stand upon the site of the little red building a towering edifice that will look down even on the *World*'s dome' (Fig. 27). [142]

*Fig. 27. The proposed new building for the New York* Sun, *New York, 1890, Bruce Price, architect (from William Birkmire,* Skeleton Construction in Buildings, *New York, 1894). 'If the plans of the* Sun *owners have been truly announced, some day there will stand upon the site of the little red building a towering edifice that will look down even on the* World's *dome' (compare Fig. 21; the 'little red building' sits between the* World *and the* Tribune*). Competitive height had of course top priority, but a battle for sublime beauty was also waged at the same time. Whereas the* World *had selected a colossal single arch as its entrance, the* Sun *had thrown in a complete triumphal arch; and instead of St. Peter's Dome, the emblem of the* Sun *was carried by King Mausolos' monument at Halikarnassos. The world's ancient wonders had become arguments in an aesthetic polemic.*

*Fig. 28. The Mail and Express Building, New York, 1891, Carrère & Hastings, architects. A not much respected paper at the time, which nevertheless tried to attract attention with respectable but badly composed architectural means. The un-promising L-shaped lot produced at the narrow outlet on Fulton Street enough architectural decoration to furnish a whole block. Noteworthy is the steeple which is stretched to almost unbearable extremes (from* King's Handbook of New York, *Boston, 1893) (demolished).*

684      *A HISTORY OF REAL ESTATE.*

DESIGN FOR PROPOSED "SUN" BUILDING.
City Hall Square, New York City.      Bruce Price, Architect.

The plans of the *Sun* were 'truly announced' indeed, in 1890, but alas, the design, by the celebrated architect Bruce Price, was never executed. William Birkmire included it in his book of 1894 on skeleton construction, with the following comment: 'the *Sun* . . . contemplates a building twenty-two storeys in height, and if carried out as the architect intends, will, no doubt, take its place as one of the handsomest office structures in existence.[143]

It was of course a formidable building, featuring a solid, unadorned body tapering towards a peristyled shoulder-block, carrying a proud head crowned by a radiating solar emblem. Full of classical and mythological allusions (triumphal arch as entrance; Artemisia's Mausoleum on the top), it was very much the predictable materialization of frustrated dreams of absolute hegemony, shaped into this condensed pile of world wonders.

Then, in brisk succession, the other papers began to add their tall and often loud contributions to the pile. *The Mail and Express*, a recently amalgamated and not much respected paper, moved into its new ten-storey headquarters at Broadway and Fulton Street, which was crowned by an extremely slender, high-reaching and certainly impractical tower, designed by the firm of Carrère and Hastings in 1891 (Fig. 28).[144] In 1895/6 *The American Tract Society Building* made an arresting appearance on the corner of Spruce Street, hovering over both the *Times* and the *Tribune* buildings (Fig. 29). Built by the firm of R.H. Robertson for the world's largest publisher of biblical and other edifying literature, it was the tallest tower on Newspaper Row − 23 storeys reaching to a height of 288 feet (c. 99 metres). Its crowning feature was an arcaded pergola, which acted as an observatory for visitors who, in the spirit of the firm's ideology and in the terms of Jacques Perret (see p. 70, fig. 17; p. 70, note 52), could contemplate the wondrous works of the Creator. Certainly the *Tract Society* did not ignore this possibility, and it encouraged visits to the building's upper regions, affording: 'a glorious opportunity to those inclined to meet in the upper stories or on the observatory roof and sing most effectively: "Nearer My God to Thee"' (Fig. 30).[145]

142. Frank Moss, op. cit., I, p. 198.

143. William Birkmire, op. cit., pp. 10, 13, fig. 5.

144. *King's Handbook*, op. cit., pp. 614–616 + illustration.

145. Moses King, *New York; The American Cosmopolis, The Foremost City of the World*, Boston, 1894, p. 27. On the *Tract Society Building*, see also: *History of Architecture and the Building Trades*, op. cit., Vol. I, p. 98; Montgomery Schuyler, 'The Works of R.H. Robertson,' *The Architectural Record*, VI, 1896, September/December, pp. 217–219; *The American Architect and Building News*, XLIV, 1894, May 26, p. 92 + illustration.

*Fig. 29 (above). The American Tract Society Building, New York, 1895–1896, R.H. Robertson, architect. Erected by the largest publisher of biblical and other edifying literature of the world, it was the tallest building on Newspaper Row (from* The American Architect and Building News, *XLIV, 1894, March 26).*

*Fig. 30 (right). Observatory of the American Tract Society Building, affording 'a glorious opportunity to those inclined to meet . . . and to sing most effectively: "Nearer my God to Thee"' (from* The Architectural Record, *VI, 1896, September/December).*

City Hall and Newspaper Row, N. Y. City

No. 9. National Art Views Co. N. Y. City.

*Hinke*

16 CITY HALL PARK AND NEWSPAPER ROW, NEW YORK.

TIMES BUILDING, NEW YORK

1919. ILL. POST. CARD CO., N.Y.

*Fig. 31. (opposite above) Newspaper Row as it was about 1900. Five newspapers and publishing firms were lined up for their unusual act. From right to left: The New York Times Building (George B. Post, 1888/1889); The American Tract Society Building (R.H. Robertson, 1895/1896); The New York Tribune Building (Richard M. Hunt, 1873/ 1875); The New York Sun Building (the existing building into which the paper moved in 1868); The World Building (George B. Post, 1889/1890) (postcard).*

*Fig. 32 (opposite below). The same site, a little after 1903. The Times and the Tribune Buildings have grown miraculously, as if they had been struck by acromegaly, an abnormal growth of the skeleton. To the extreme right: the 1883 Potter Building (compare Fig. 8) (postcard).*

*Fig. 33 (right). The New York Times Building of Cyrus Eidlitz, 1904, on its present location on what later became known as Times Square. It was shaped in the Newspaper Row tradition: tall (22 storeys) and following a model of unbeatable aesthetic authority (Giotto's Campanile of Florence Cathedral). To bestow it with even more irresistible beauty the picture was dusted with gold (postcard).*

146. To grow in order not to be overtopped by other buildings was regarded as a logical reaction, as early as 1899 when the *History of Architecture and the Building Trades*, op. cit., reported that several three-storey buildings in the neighbourhood of Newspaper Row extended their fronts to four stories, 'because the tendency to high building in the neighbourhood and the near coming time when the fronts on Broadway and on Park Row would dominate and dwarf by contrast a three story structure made it essential to reach a greater vertical height. *This was actually urged as a reason for building what we now have*' (p. 59) (my italics). An enlightening explanation.

By now an untenable situation had developed in which both the *Tribune* and the *Times* were drastically overtopped by newcomers. Their reaction was unusual but, given the circumstances, quite logical: In 1903 it was decided that they would extend their buildings by a telescoping action (Fig. 32). [146] Roofs and towers were temporarily removed and upper structures were placed on the existing substructures. Comparing photographs of before and after the operation, it must have looked as if the buildings had grown spontaneously (Figs. 31 & 32).

The *Times*'s facelift seemed halfheartedly done in comparison with that of the *Tribune*, but that might have had its own reasons. About that time the paper announced its withdrawal from the old *corrida*, and its intention of moving to a quieter part of town, further northward, to what later became known as

Times Square. Cyrus Eidlitz's design for the new building was perfectly in line with the *Tribune—World* tradition: a building in the shape of Giotto's Campanile in Florence (Fig. 33). But the Tribune still refused to give up the battle in Park Row. In 1903 it filed plans for an addition of nine (!) floors. The New York *Times* wrote: 'The *Tribune* Association is to add a skyscraper to the Printing House Square neighbourhood by increasing the height of its building from ten to nineteen stories. The *Tribune*'s home was known from the first as the 'Tall Tower', and when it is more than 100 feet higher than it is now it will have the distinction of being not only a landmark visible within a radius of twenty five miles from City Hall, but the only skyscraper with solid masonry walls, and not having a skeleton core of steel.'[147] Its newly accredited distinctions were certainly not as glorious as the old ones, nor were they entirely accurate, for the addition was to be built with the assistance of partial steel framing, encased in the existing masonry work. The construction was carried out in 1905 and the result was certainly impressive. By means of its tower, an old success formula to which it had remained faithful, the building had lifted itself − with admittedly the last of its strength − over its competitors. It was a pyrrhic victory, but an inescapable part of the ritual of building cosmic mountains by exhaustive battle (Fig. 34). When the mountain was finally finished, new mountains had sprung up, other centres of gravity had originated; those who had remained did so in loyalty to their original vow of competitive wed-lock until death by exhaustion (Fig. 35).

*Fig. 34. The same site as in Figs. 31 and 32, but now (1904) looking south, along Broadway. While the Times Building (left) is being deprived of its roof in order to make place for the five added stories, other,much taller structures have already taken their positions behind the old post office, such as the Park Row Building (1899, R.H. Robertson), which was the tallest commercial building in the world until the advent of the Singer Tower in 1908, and the St. Paul Building (1897–1899, George B. Post) (from* King's View of New York, *Boston, 1905). The picture shows the tragic side of the newspapers' suicidal battle for supremacy: in their obsessive fixation on pyrrhic victories, they have had no eye for the world around them.*

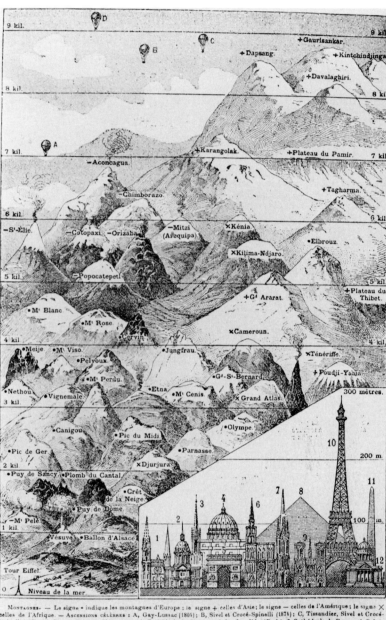

Montagnes. — Le signe • indique les montagnes d'Europe ; le signe + celles d'Asie ; le signe — celles de l'Amérique ; le signe ×
celles de l'Afrique. — Ascensions célèbres : A, Gay-Lussac (1804) ; B, Sivel et Crocé-Spinelli (1874) ; C, Tissandier, Sivel et Crocé-
Spinelli (1875) ; D, Berson (1894). — Monuments : 1. Cathédrale de Chartres ; 2. Les Invalides (Paris) ; 3. Cathédrale de Rouen ; 4. Saint-
Pierre de Rome ; 5. L'Arc de triomphe de l'Étoile ; 6. La cathédrale de Strasbourg ; 7. La cathédrale de Cologne ; 8. La grande
pyramide d'Égypte ; 9. Notre-Dame de Paris ; 10. La tour Eiffel ; 11. L'obélisque de Washington ; 12. Le Panthéon (Paris).

*Fig. 35. The striving for pyrrhic victories was part
of the ritual of building cosmic mountains by
exhaustive battle. And since the nearest equivalent
of building mountains is to construct skyscrapers,
the result was not unlike the picture from the 1925*
Petit Larousse Illustré, *in which famous architectural endeavours of mankind are uncompromisingly
juxtaposed to analogous works of nature.*

147. *H.A.B.S. report 1969*, op. cit., p. 8.

148. *The World*, op. cit., p. 12.

But around 1900 most of the papers departed. The *Herald* moved to Mid-
Town in 1893/4, the *Times* in 1905 and the *News* in 1919. Within a quarter of
a century, in almost laboratory conditions, the New York press had demonstrated the workings of the law of vertical-centralization, with no attempt to
provide rationales for its actions. That 'growth came natural to New York'
was accepted as a matter of course. Pulitzer himself described the phenomenon in the following terms: 'The massive edifice sprung like magic from the
ground, to the never ending wonderment of the multitude that passed it every
day.'[148]

**THE MYTH OF NATURAL GROWTH II**

*SOLO*

'I am a small brunette. What shall I eat and what exercises shall I take to make me appear a large blonde?' – JOHN MEAD HOWELLS[1]

'Very early I perceived that the object of life is to grow.' – MARGARET FULLER[2]

### Wild work

'The skyscraper is a natural growth, and a symbol of the American spirit.'
CLAUDE BRAGDON[3]

The collective performance of the early New York skyscraper has been experienced as impressive and convincing in its communication of the notions of growth, energy and progress. The skyline of the commercial metropolis has been subjected to a variety of analogies with nature, ranging from tropical forests to mountain peaks (the latter one was pushed to its limits on the 1935 *Magical City – Intimate Sketches of New York* by Vernon Howe Bailey, in which all distinctive silhouettes on the skyline are renamed Mount so-and-so: 'In the view to the south rise the adjacent peaks of Mount Empire State, the Everest of all the Himalayas, and, to the left in the foreground, Mount Chrysler, Mount New York Central, Mount Lincoln, Mount 500 Fifth Avenue, Mount 10 East 40th Street, and Mount Chanin. A glance to the east shows Mount Waldorf-Astoria, Mount General Electric' – and so on, for a whole page).[4] As was observed by nineteenth-century, mainly European, writers, the emphasis on natural growth as an instrument of comparative analysis was to indicate the presence of mysterious forces, of powers that were beyond the control of man. 'The Ever Changing Sky Line of New York' (Fig. I, 5) was to be read as an iconic growth-graph, indicating the effect of these forces in the way a geiger-counter measures radioactivity or the Richter Scale registers terrestrial shock waves (Figs. 1 & 2). The often quoted words of Paul Bourget, that the commercial buildings of Chicago '... seem to be the work of some impersonal power, irresistible, unconscious, like a force of nature, in the service of which man has been but a docile instrument,' clearly reflected his belief in these forces.[5] The degree of credence the notion gained was shown in Sigfried Giedion's acceptance of the anonymity of American design as a paragon of modernity.[6]

If Americans were considerably more like 'docile instruments' in the service of nature than the countrymen of Bourget or Giedion, of all Americans it was the man of business who was supposed to be most finely tuned to 'the force of nature'. The businessman's distrust of the intellect and of science, and his preference for 'Fingerspitzengefühl', or the 'wisdom of intuition',[7] was proverbial. The antithesis between academic training and native genius was understood by men like Andrew Carnegie and Charles Dana, who had divided society into two classes: those who worked in exchange for a salary and those who pursued 'fortunes' (meaning luck or chance, but also wealth). The first class was dependent and thus not free; the second, independent and free.

1. Quoted by John Mead Howells, 'Vertical or Horizontal Design?', *The Architectural Forum*, 1930 Special issue, p. 782: 'How fortunate to leave behind us the belief that a vertical skyscraper must somehow be made to look like a horizontal Farnese Palace! It is as impossible as the problem of that charming woman in Miss Hyatt's book, who wrote to the paper: "I am a small brunette. What shall I eat, and what exercises shall I take to make me appear a large blonde?"'

2. Orison Swett Marden, *Success, A Book of Ideals, Helps, and Examples for All Desiring to Make the Best of Life*, Boston, 1897, p. 318.

3. Claude Bragdon, *The Frozen Fountain*, New York, 1932, p. 25.

4. *Magical City — Intimate Sketches of New York*, Pictures by Vernon Howe Bailey, Notes by Arthur Bartlett Maurice, New York/London, 1935, p. 232. About this book Le Corbusier remarked: 'L'éditeur Scribner a publié pour le Noël, un album exposé dans les devantures: "The Magical City". Je réfléchis, je discute avec moi-même. Je corrige: "La catastrophe féerique"' (*Quand les cathédrales étaient blanches*, Paris, 1937, p. 129). The title — *Magical City* — was explained by the author as a reference to the amazing speed at which skyscrapers were erected: 'Yesterday there was the spectacle of an open space with gnomes toiling below. Today on the site a great tower rises to the sky as if wrought overnight by jinns summoned by some Alladin rubbing his Wonderful Lamp. It is this suggestion of magical transformation that makes New York the Magical City' (ibid., p. 13).
References to mountains, and their logical reverse image — the canyon — are too numerous to mention. Suffice it here to point to some randomly selected loci: Ethel Fleming and Herbert S. Kates, *New York*, London, 1929, p. 6: '... one penetrates into the canyon of cliff-like buildings that overshadows Broadway'; Danish diplomat and compiler of a picture book on America Roger Nielsen could not resist including the amazing juxtaposition of the Smith Tower of Seattle and the snow-capped Mount Rainier in the background and to call it: 'Zwei Wolkenkratzer' (Roger Nielsen, *Amerika in Bildern*, Leipzig, 1924, p. 204). See also: Manfredo Tafuri, 'The Disenchanted Mountain: The Skyscraper and the City', *The American City*, London, etc., 1980 (1979 and 1973[1]), pp. 389–529.

5. Paul Bourget, *Outre-mer, Notes sur l'Amérique*, Paris, 1895, p. 161.

6. Sigfried Giedion, *Space, Time and Architecture*, Cambridge, 1941, p. 303.

7. See: 'Sacred Skyscrapers and Profane Cathedrals', pp. 63ff.

8. Andrew Carnegie, *The Empire of Business*, London, 1902, pp. 137/138.

9. Hugo Münsterberg, *The Americans*, New York, 1905, p. 229.

10. Thorstein Veblen, *The Theory of the Leisure Class*, Harmondsworth, 1979 (1899[1]), pp. 276ff. Veblen is referring to the 'hamingia', or the guidance of an unseen hand, from the Icelandic sagas and German folk-legends (pp. 280/281).

Fig. 1. *American history depicted as being analogous to the growth-rings of a Californian redwood tree (postcard, 1930).*

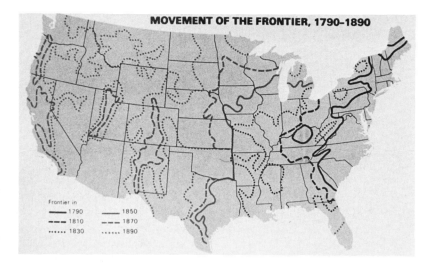

Fig. 2. *The growth-rings of the American nation: The Movement of the Frontier (from Allen Weinstein & R. Jackson Wilson,* Freedom and Crisis — An American History, *New York, 1974).*

Dana, editor of the New York *Sun*, once wrote: 'That is one class of man that I refer to, the thinkers, the men of science, the inventors; and the other class is that of those whom God has endowed with a genius for saving, for getting rich, for bringing wealth together.'[8] Whether this mysterious force was identified as God or Nature is irrelevant; what is important is that it was incessantly invoked. Hugo Münsterberg, the German Harvard psychologist, stressing the opposition between the intellectual's dependence on *words* and the commercial man's preference for *deeds*, exclaimed in the words of Goethe's *Faust:* 'The spirit aids! From anxious scruples freed, I write, "In the beginning was the deed!".'[9] The urge to gamble and a strong faith in luck were, according to another economist, the renowned Thorstein Veblen, the major incentives of American economic life.[10]

Speed acquired an almost sacred dimension. To be in a perpetual state of hurry was the only way to stay in tune with the forces of change.[11] Whether the haste was genuine or assumed was irrelevant.[12]

117

*Fig. 3. The Singer Building (1906/1908, Ernest Flagg, architect), the tallest building of the world, shown in the company of other skyscrapers in an artfully composed group portrait, from which the Eiffel Tower for reasons of convenience was excluded (it was a little less than 400 feet taller) (from O.F. Semsch, ed.,* A History of the Singer Building, *New York, 1908).*

Once seized by the desire to build, the businessman's rhythm was translated into a feverish swiftness of construction. Builders would boast of the short time it had taken to put up a skyscraper. Speed of construction vied with the aesthetic value of the result. The author of the *History of the Singer Building Construction* (1908) described in the idiom of the time the newly finished tower as a marvel which had 'become as distinctive a feature of the sky line of New York as the Egyptian pyramids are of the Valley of the River Nile.'[13] Repeating the same analogy, but this time alluding to the speed of construction, he drew the following odd conclusion: 'The building was practically completed on May 1, 1908, or only one year and eight months after the start. Compare this with the time it took to erect the Cologne Cathedral the twin towers of which the Singer Building surpassed in height. The Cathedral was begun in 1248 and finished 641 years later − in 1889. A comparison might also be made with the great pyramid of Cheops, on which 100,000 men were employed for 30 years, which would be equivalent to 3,000,000 men working every day for one year − as against 1,200 men employed for one year and eight months on the Singer Building' (Fig. 3).[14]

The aggressive growth of Newspaper Row was, on the whole, a life-or-death game in which the owners and not their architects decided upon the shape, ornament and general behaviour of their buildings. Montgomery Schuyler had already noted, to remain within the idiom, that it was the clients who followed the course of nature, whereas the architects followed the dictates of art. The two were not yet able to combine, and this resulted in what Schuyler called so much 'wild work', by which he meant work that was stylistically indecisive. As was customary in this sort of criticism, Schuyler left it to the ubiquitous 'British observer' to pass judgment: 'New York from either side is hideous and magnificent for that it cries aloud of savage and unregulated energy.' Whereupon Schuyler, combining this modern equivalent of the 18th-century

11. De Tocqueville suggested that in times of disbelief the end is not, as it was in times of belief, after death, but before. And, since time is short, people are compelled to hurry, change places, keep moving, before death makes an end of it all. '... l'idée d'une fortune subite et facile, des grands biens aisément acquis et perdus, l'image du hasard, sous toutes ses formes, se présente à l'esprit humain. L'instabilité de l'état social vient favoriser l'instabilité des désirs. Au milieu de ces fluctuations perpétuelles du sort, le présent grandit; il cache l'avenir qui s'efface, et les hommes ne veulent songer qu'au lendemain' (Alexis de Tocqueville, *De la démocratie en Amérique*, Paris, 1864, III, p. 244).

12. Le Baron de Hübner, *Promenade autour du monde*, 2 Vols., Paris, 1881. See above, 'Myth' I, note 48.

13. *A History of the Singer Building Construction, Its Progress from Foundation to Flag Pole*, edited by O.F. Semsch, New York, 1908, p. 9.

14. Ibid., p. 11.

sense of the sublime with the inability of the architects to channel that unregulated energy into a consistent architectural form, concluded: 'There was a great deal of wild work, and some interesting work, but there was no entirely successful work. There was no convention … ; designers were not agreed with each other, and a designer often appeared to be at odds with himself, upon the very data of his problem.'[15]

It might be that clients were pleased with their creations; certainly the charming booklets commemorating the dedications of their buildings never hit a lower note than that of exalted jubilation; but to critics and architects the state of affairs was downright deplorable.[16] Lewis Mumford, in both *Sticks and Stones* (1924) and *The Brown Decades* (1931), although generally championing close collaboration between architect and client, now suddenly developed second thoughts about it and ventilated his criticism on these insults to good taste. This sudden skyward growth, Mumford wrote, had shown us 'all our characteristic American weaknesses, our love of abstract magnitude, our interest in land-gambling, our desire for conspicuous waste.'[17] The collective performance of the early skyscrapers was satisfactory from a general, almost abstract viewpoint, but the individual members made, aesthetically speaking, a poor show. They looked too diverse, too dilettantish, too clumsily designed. The problem which Montgomery Schuyler and critics after him referred to as 'the sky-scraper problem' was therefore to be reduced to the question of how to shape the individual skyscraper according to the general traits of its genus.

### 'The skyscraper problem'

The 'problem' was expounded in two articles written by Schuyler: 'The "Sky-scraper" Up To Date', for *The Architectural Record* of 1899 and 'The Sky-scraper Problem', for *Scribner's Magazine* of 1903 (his concern was limited to aesthetics and had nothing to do with the legal and social discord the sky-scraper caused later on).[18] By the time these critiques were published the sky-scraper had achieved the status of a distinct architectural type, and had even been acknowledged as characteristic of American civilization.[19] Its height had stabilized somewhere between twenty and forty stories and its construction was invariably of the steel cage or skeleton type.[20]

Attempts to provide the skyscraper with some respectable and aesthetically satisfying order developed along the lines of the Aristotelian 'taxis', the tripartite system (also called 'the columnar analogy') by which the three elements of the classical column – base, shaft, and capital – were transferred to the façade. This principle was applied with considerable success by men like George B. Post in the design of his Union Trust Building (1889/90) and his New York *Times* Building (1888/89) and Bruce Price in his unexecuted design for the New York *Sun* (1890) and his American Surety Building (1894/95), both mentioned earlier (Myth I, Figs. 27 & 31).[21]

Another suggestion was put forward by Louis Sullivan in his Midwestern 'tall buildings' such as the Wainwright Building (1891), the Chicago Stock Exchange Building (1893/94), the Guaranty Building (1895) at Buffalo, N.Y., and the New York Bayard Building (1898). In Sullivan's design of the façade the tripartite organization was maintained throughout, but he treated the 'shaft' in strict classical terms, by giving it fluting similar to that of the Doric columns of the Parthenon (as Adolf Loos was later to shape the 'shaft' of celebrated design of 1922 for the Chicago *Tribune*). Schuyler admired Sullivan's solution greatly, although he interpreted it differently. About the Bayard Building he wrote: 'There is nothing capricious in the general treatment of this structure. It is an attempt, and a very serious attempt, to found the architecture of a tall building upon the facts of the case. The actual structure is left, or rather, is helped to tell its own story, this is the thing itself.'[22]

15. Montgomery Schuyler, 'The "Sky-scraper" Up to Date', *The Architectural Record*, VIII, January–March 1899, 3, p. 232.

16. These brochures are unique. Without them no study of the skyscraper could be properly documented. Best known are the above-quoted brochures of the Woolworth Building, of the World Building, of the Metropolitan Life Building and the luxuriously executed Singer Building History (above, n. 13). But, assuming that most prestigious undertakings yield at least one prestigious brochure, there are many more to be found. An inventory of these invaluable documents should be encouraged.

17. Louis Mumford, *Sticks and Stones; A Study of American Architecture and Civilization*, New York, 1955 (1924¹), pp. 91/92; and *The Brown Decades, A Study of the Arts in America, 1865–1895*, New York, 1971 (1931¹), p. 63.

18. Montgomery Schuyler, 'The Skyscraper Problem', originally in *Scribner's Magazine*, 34, August 1903, pp. 253–256, reproduced in: William H. Jordy & Ralph Coe, eds., *American Architecture and Other Writings by Montgomery Schuyler*, Cambridge, Mass., 1961, II, pp. 442–449.

19. Montgomery Schuyler, 'The "Sky-scraper" Up to Date', op. cit., p. 231.

20. Loc. cit. By 1899 the average height of the tall buildings was 21 stories. Bruce Price and George B. Post designed, in 1890 and 1899 respectively, a thirty-storey tower for the New York *Sun* (see above, Fig. 27, p. 108) and for the Prudential Life Insurance Co. a tower of more than forty storeys (see Winston Weisman, 'A New View of Skyscraper History', *The Rise of an American Architecture*, Edgar Kaufmann, Jr., ed., New York/Washington/London, 1970, p. 145). The tallest office tower in the world, till the advent of the 47-storey Singer Building in 1908, was the 30-storey Park Row Building built in 1899 by R.H. Robertson, both in New York.

21. Winston Weisman, 'A New View', op. cit., p. 115, fig. 3–1 and p. 116, fig. 3–2.

22. Montgomery Schuyler, 'The "Sky-scraper" Up to Date', op. cit., p. 255.

Schuyler's praise is remarkable for insisting upon the organic analogy. A comparison with the Doric column is avoided; instead there is a direct reference to the skeleton construction – 'the actual structure' – upon which 'the case' is to be based. It is typical of the rhetorical power of the organic analogy that it blends the moral and aesthetic components of the argument; because of its similarity to the human skeleton, the structure of the frame is elevated to a higher status. Moreover, to exhibit the structure is regarded as an act of honesty in the moral sense, as it is, in the scientific sense, a revelation of the truth. Every now and then architectural theory is enlivened by a proclamation of the necessity to strip architecture of its superfluous dress and to emphasize the structure. As a corollary, structure is equated with truth, and truth, in turn ('Le beau c'est le vrai'), is equated with beauty.

To Schuyler and his contemporaries the conviction that Nature is never 'capricious', always truthful and therefore always 'beautiful', must have seemed self-evident; nor did they ever question the assumption that architectural structure can be equated with that of natural organisms. Thus Schuyler's conclusion that architecture is beautiful as long as it is allowed 'to tell its own [providing structural] story', could count on enthusiastic support from American progressivist, and even patriotic, thinking. [23]

This theory, which has been 'de rigueur' for about a century, is generally associated with Louis Sullivan, but its full scope and deeper consequences were in fact realized by Claude Bragdon and translated into architectural form by Eliel Saarinen. The three men were contemporaries but, owing to Sullivan's lack of commissions and his untimely death, it was left to the two survivors to bring the raw idea to perfection.

### Sullivan's problem

In his 'Tall Office Building Artistically Considered' (1896), Sullivan started off with this dramatic question:

Problem: How shall we impart to this sterile pile, this crude, harsh, brutal agglomeration, this stark exclamation of eternal strife, the graciousness of those higher forms of sensibility and culture that rest on the lower and fiercer passions.' [24]

How Sullivan dealt with this problem is well known, and even better known is his famous maxim 'form follows function.' It has been said that this maxim was abused by many, mostly the proponents of modernism, whose interpretation of *function* was dangerously close to that of Sullivan. So close even, that Sullivan was designated 'the father of modern architecture'. [25] This, however, led to an increasing number of other misunderstandings, of which Giedion's emerging realization that the father of his own ideology was suffering from an artistic 'split personality' was certainly the most tragic. [26]

For modernists, Sullivan's life-long interest in the metaphysics of architecture and artistic creation was, though slightly off the track, mildly acceptable. The boxy shapes of his Chicago-style tall buildings and the neutral treatment of their fenestration were hailed as clear prophecies of modernity, but the naturalistic ornament he applied to the surface caused the deepest estrangement. [27] The reasons for this confusion were complex, a complexity due to differences in theoretical training, religion, and attitudes towards the question of Creation; and to a fundamentally antagonistic notion of the term 'function'.

In European modernism the term 'function' pertained to socially determined activities, such as they are – to have a place to live, to work, to recreate, to move. Function in this sense is understood as an externally organized activity, performed by the members of society as well as by their respective tools. The CIAM manifestoes often interpreted in the sociological sense, and the corollaries for architectural and urban planning were essentially of an economizing

23. See above, 'Introduction', pp. 3/4.

24. Louis Sullivan, 'The Tall Office Building Artistically Considered', originally in: *Lippincott's Magazine*, 57, March 1896, pp. 403–409; reproduced in: *Kindergarten Chats and Other Writings*, Isabella Athey, ed., New York, (1947 [1]) 1976, pp. 202–213. Ibid., p. 202.

25. Hugh Morrison, *Louis Sullivan, Prophet of Modern Architecture*, New York, 1935; Philip Johnson, 'Is Sullivan the Father of Functionalism?', *Writings*, New York, 1979, pp. 183–186; Leland McRoth, *A Concise History of American Architecture*, New York, etc., 1979, pp. 183/184: 'Sullivan was both creator and prophet of the modern commercial skyscraper, and is rightly lauded as the father of modern architecture'. See above, 'The Skyward Trend of Thought', pp. 20ff.

26. Sigfried Giedion, op. cit., p. 312. 'The Skyward Trend of Thought', p. 25.

27. 'The Skyward Trend of Thought', pp. 25ff.

and ergonomic nature. A functional house, for example, was interpreted as a house that enabled the maximum number of actions to be performed in the minimum number of movements. The kitchen of such a house was above all a study in ergonomics. [28]

If Sullivan's maxim 'form follows function' is applied to this frame of thinking, the 'form' of the kitchen must be determined by the 'functions' performed in it, in other words, the ergonomics of that kitchen. No such thing is to be found in Sullivan's writings; on the contrary, he was not in the least interested in the technical requirements nor in the economics of movement. His fascination with motion was entirely directed at its expression, not its economics.

### The function of function

Having summarized the main conditions of the tall office building, Sullivan went on to say that,

As to the necessary arrangements for light courts, these are not germane to the problem, and as will become soon evident, I trust need not be considered here. These things and such others as the arrangements of elevators, for example, have to do strictly with the economics of the building, and I assume them to have been fully considered and disposed of to the satisfaction of purely utilitarian and pecuniary demands. [29]

That Sullivan regarded 'the arrangements of elevators' as 'not germane to the problem' only goes to show how profoundly the two approaches differed. For Sullivan the problem was not the social or external function, but the biological-internal, or organic, function. Architectural form was dependent not on external influences, as it was in European functionalism, but on a process of internal evolution. A building is like an organism, and it should grow as if coming from a seed planted in the ground. Sullivan wrote, in his *System of Architectural Ornament* (1924): 'The germ is the real thing. Within its delicate mechanism lies the will to power: the function is to seek and eventually to find its expression in form.' [30] In other words, the qualities of the plant are contained in the germ; the form of the plant is but the realization of those qualities. Or, as Sullivan put it, 'The pressure we call Function; the resultant, Form.' [31]

The transition from organic to inorganic was a matter of conviction. Sullivan explained:

By the word inorganic is commonly understood that which is lifeless, or appears to be so; as stone, the metals, and seasoned wood, clay, or the like. But nothing is really inorganic to the will of man. His spiritual power masters the inorganic and causes it to live in forms which his imagination brings forth from the lifeless, the amorphous. . . . For man is power, and this power is native in nature with the power of the germ of the seed. Thus he commands at will the realm of the organic or living, and therein again he creates as he wills; for he has the power to will . . . . Hence, for the germ of the typical plantseed with its resident powers, he may substitute, in thought, his own will as the seat of vital power.' [32]

It is quite evident that Sullivan's organic theory went far beyond the scope of European Functionalism, and recent research by Narciso Menocal and Philip Steadman, for example, has made this clear enough. [33] What has not been sufficiently acknowledged, though, is that Sullivan's interest in traditional biological analogies was not as profound as it might seem, particularly compared to his quest for demiurgical creation and the imparting of life to lifeless matter.

28. See Reyner Banham, *Theory and Design in the First Machine Age*, London, 1972, pp. 320ff. Jürgen Joedicke, 'Anmerkungen zur Theorie des Funktionalismus in der modernen Architektur', *Jahrbuch für Ästhetik und allgemeine Kunstwissenschaft*, X, 1965, pp. 14–24.

29. Louis Sullivan, 'The Tall Office Building', op. cit., p. 203.

30. Louis Sullivan, *A System of Architectural Ornament*, New York (?), 1967 (1924[1]), n. p.

31. Louis Sullivan, *Kindergarten Chats*, op. cit., p. 48. See also Donald Drew Egbert, 'The Idea of Organic Expression and American Architecture', *Evolutionary Thought in America*, Stow Persons, ed., New Haven, 1950, pp. 344–366.

32. Louis Sullivan, *A System*, op. cit., n.p.

33. Narciso Menocal, *Architecture as Nature – The Transcendentalist Idea of Louis Sullivan*, Madison, Wis., 1981; Philip Steadman, *The Evolution of Designs, Biological Analogy in Architecture and the Applied Arts*, Cambridge, etc., 1979.

Claude Bragdon singled out this particular aspect of his intellectual and spiritual curiosity: 'The core of his philosophy was his belief in the essential divinity of man: "For man is godlike enough did he but know it, did he but choose, did he but remove his wrappings and his blunders, and say good-bye to his superstitions and his fears". These quotations from *The Autobiography of an Idea*,' Bragdon continued, 'may aid in an understanding of the following letter, written after the reading of my manuscript [of an article Bragdon had written for *House and Garden*] in its finally recast form' [from December 1903 which he had submitted to Sullivan for approval]. Upon which followed, on 2 January 1904, a letter from Sullivan to Bragdon (reproduced in full on page 159), in which he wrote: 'These principles have as their prototype the Great-God of the Universe. This divinely-human and humanly-divine creative element and power it was my purpose to show forth, to the receptive mind, in "Kindergarten Chats".'[34] Sullivan's conception of the 'divinely-human' creator is directly dependent on the idea of the demiurge as revealed in the book *Pimander* of the *Corpus Hermeticum*.[35]

A reconstruction of the possible sources of Sullivan's thinking has yielded a rather mixed bag. French and Anglo-American evolutionism predominates, blended with mostly German nineteenth-century idealism. The influence of Herbert Spencer as well as that of Hegel, Schelling and, as may be deduced from the above, Schopenhauer, has been proposed.[36] Menocal has pointed to Emanuel Swedenborg's cosmology and the theory of opposite forces as a possible source for Sullivan's ideas on ornament and decoration, as well as the theories of the Prague-born American architect Leopold Eidlitz concerning artistic creation and the notion of anthropomorphism.[37] Eidlitz must have been a major source indeed. After all it was he who first expounded the form-follows-function formula – not in the same succinct form, but nevertheless with the same purport: 'In nature forms are the outcome of environment. Environment determines function, and forms are the result of function.'[38] In the passage which follows the tendency toward evolutionism is strongly present, as is the Hegelian notion of artistic creation:

This energy of function is expressed in nature in visible form. As art is re-creation, and the forms of architecture are entirely ideal, the problem to be solved may be stated thus: We know the methods by which nature arrives at her forms: shall the architect presume to create his forms at once full-fledged, complete as it were, in their final shape; or, in other words, shall he attempt to tell a story before he has analyzed the facts to be related? Can this be done? No; what he must do is to study the conditions, analyze the environment, yield to it everywhere, respond to it always, until the functions resulting from all this are fully expressed in the organism; and while he is thinking of all this, forms will grow under his hands . . . .[39]

The solution Eidlitz suggested must have held a strong appeal for Sullivan, and it may have inspired his definitive statement in *A System of Architectural Ornament*. 'A work of Art, like a work of nature, is a realized idea,' Eidlitz wrote echoing the words of Hegel, 'and the ideal is the essence of architecture. It is the godlike attempt to create a new organism, which because it is new, cannot be an imitation of any work of nature, and, because it is an organism, must be developed according to the methods of nature.'[40] Eidlitz's thoughts on anthropomorphism, architectural empathy and the animation of the artefact were, apparently, quite compatible with American transcendentalism, or at least with Sullivan's thinking, which eventually developed into a unique and interesting bricolage enabling him to penetrate the question of cre-

34. Claude Bragdon, *The Secret Springs, An Autobiography*, London, 1938, pp. 158/159.

35. *Corpus Hermeticum*, A.D. Nock, ed., Paris, 1945. The books 'Pimander' and 'Asclepios', attributed to Hermes Trismegistos, represent the story of creation in the dualistic-gnostic sense, in which man, as a fallen angel, is gifted with the same powers of creation as his original creator. The demiurge is the god that God created after himself. The demiurge is known from Plato's *Timaeus* in which he is represented as the agent who brings order to the physical world. I am grateful to Dr. Oosterbaan, who introduced me to hermetic thought.

36. Narciso Menocal, *Architecture as Nature*, op. cit., pp. 10ff. and passim.

37. Ibid., pp. 24/25. Leopold Eidlitz, *The Nature and Function of Art, More Especially of Architecture*, New York, 1881.

38. Leopold Eidlitz, *The Nature and Function of Art*, op. cit., p. 358.

39. Ibid., p. 358.

40. Ibid., p. 57.

41. See above, n. 35.

42. Louis Sullivan, 'The Tall Office Building', op. cit., p. 206.

43. Vivian C. Hopkins, *Spires of Form, A Study of Emerson's Aesthetic Theory*, Cambridge, Mass., 1951, p. 83. The source is: Manuscript Journal B., 1835/36, II, Comments on aesthetic form, etc.

44. Louis Sullivan, *The Autobiography of an Idea*, New York, 1956 (1924[1]), pp. 313/314.

45. The Aristotelian, or tri-partite columnar principle of ordering architectonic elevations was proposed by Montgomery Schuyler, 'The "Sky-scraper" Up to Date', op. cit., pp. 232ff. Sullivan referred to it in 'The Tall Office Building', op. cit., p. 206. See also Philip Steadman, *The Evolution of Designs*, op. cit., pp. 9ff.

46. Louis Sullivan, 'The Tall Office Building', op. cit., p. 208. In his essay 'Ornament in Architecture', for the *Engineering Magazine*, August 1892, reproduced in: Louis Sullivan, *Kindergarten Chats*, op. cit., p. 18, Sullivan wrote: 'That is to say, a building which is truly a work of art (and I consider none other) is in its nature, essence and being an emotional expression. This being so ... , it must have, almost literally, a life.' This is a paraphrase of Eidlitz's dictum that 'every structure, like the human body, that assumes to be a work of art, must also be possessed of a soul' (*The Nature and Function of Art*, op. cit., p. 92).

47. 'The Tall Office Building' was published in 1896, whereas the Guaranty (later: Prudential) Building was begun in 1894 and finished in 1895.

48. James Marston Fitch, *American Building and the Historical Forces*, op. cit.: '... in the Wainwright and Guaranty buildings he [Sullivan] produced the prototype, which ... was materially not to be improved upon for half a century' (p. 201). Claude Bragdon, on the other hand, being unconvinced that the line of evolution would run straight to the post-World War II steel-and-glass slabs, pointed to the interregnum of the Woolworth Building type: 'In Sullivan's day the skyscraper as a sky-piercing obelisk, like the Woolworth Tower and the Empire State Building, did not exist, and Sullivan's buildings must look stunted and old-fashioned by comparison.' Bragdon, however, admitted: 'but he nevertheless gave vertical building its true dramatic expression' (Claude Bragdon, *The Secret Springs*, op. cit., p. 149). In the modernist vision, however, the Sullivan model remained sacrosanct, his tall buildings 'a milestone in the evolution of the Modern Movement' (Nikolaus Pevsner, *Pioneers of Modern Design* [formerly: *Pioneers of the Modern Movement*, 1936], Harmondsworth, 1975, p. 141.

49. Alfred C. Bossom, *Building to the Skies, The Romance of the Skyscraper*, London/New York, 1934, p. 62. For Bossom see also *Alfred C. Bossom's American Architecture, 1903–1926*, Dennis Sharp, ed., London, 1984.

50. Louis Sullivan, 'The Tall Office Building', op. cit., p. 205.

ation. From 'The Tall Office Building' to *A System of Architectural Ornament*, a progression towards a radical Hermetic belief in the demiurgical powers of man becomes apparent.[41] In 'The Tall Office Building Artistically Considered', Sullivan expounded the idea of the 'active' skyscraper:

'We must now heed the imperative voice of emotion. It demands of us, what is the chief characteristic of the tall office building? And at once we answer, it is lofty. This loftiness is to the artist-nature its thrilling aspect. It is the very organ-tone in its appeal. It must be in turn the dominant chord in his expression of it, the true excitant of his imagination. It must be tall, every inch of it tall. The force and power of altitude must be in it, the glory and pride of exaltation must be in it. It must be every inch a proud and soaring thing, rising in sheer exultation ....'[42]

There is something of Emerson here, in the combination of loftiness and movement, or rather in his description of the relation between architecture and the law of gravity. Emerson wrote:

'In architecture, height and mass have a wonderful effect because they suggest immediately a relation to the sphere on which the structure stands, and so to the gravitating system. The tower which with such painful solidity soars like an arrow to heaven apprizes us in an unusual manner of that law of gravitation ....'[43]

### Architectural alchemy

In his *Autobiography of an Idea* of 1924 (an enigmatic title which becomes less enigmatic if read with Hegel's terminology in mind), Sullivan again takes up this image, referring to it as 'the element of loftiness, in the suggestion of slenderness and aspiration, the soaring quality of a thing rising from the earth as a unitary utterance.'[44] If there be a dominant idea that could be distilled from Sullivan's writings on the form of skyscrapers, it should be his insistence upon movement and life: the skyscraper should look like its action. Since this action was originally integrated in a collective performance, the task of the designer, following the Aristotelian principles of organic entity, was to find a form for the part that would harmonize with the whole and would reflect its quality.[45]

The tragedy of Sullivan was that his theories were not followed by a successful application, and that, despite what most of the critics thought, he did not find an adequate way 'to impart life to the sterile pile.' Nevertheless, there were others who were adept in this bizarre branch of architectural alchemy, and they came amazingly close, both in theory and practice, to fulfilling Sullivan's ideal.

'Life and the form,' Sullivan wrote, 'were absolutely one and inseparable,' 'whether it be the sweeping eagle in his flight, or the open apple blossom, the toiling work horse, the blithe swan, the branching oak, the winding stream at its base, the drifting clouds, over all the coursing sun.'[46] For Sullivan the essence of life resided more in their *doings* than in their *being*, thus it was the 'sweeping' that made the eagle an eagle, distinct from, say, the sparrow, which would merely flutter. Correspondingly, a skyscraper was a skyscraper by virtue of its 'soaring' quality and not the number of its storeys, elevators or steel beams. But how might this quality be imparted to the sterility of the steel cage? The steel frame of a tall building is essentially built of horizontal units – the beams must be longer than the columns are tall. Sullivan's solution was to subdivide the distance between the two verticals by means of intermediate, non-load-bearing columns, and he used it successfully in the Bayard Building, the Wainwright, the Chicago Stock Exchange and, best of all, in the Guaranty (Prudential) Building in Buffalo (Figs. 4 & 5), which was erected almost simultaneously with the publication of 'The Tall Office Building'.[47] By eliminating horizontal divisions and by articulating the vertical elements, Sullivan created a calm, uninterupted, up-rising quality which was new to the sky-scraper. For this he was rightly praised, but it would be unwise to believe that the problem had been solved for good. [48] 'Lofty' and 'proud' his buildings were, but their ability to 'soar' was severely limited. The Guaranty Building (shown here, Fig. 5, in an early picture postcard of 1904, the title of which — *St. Paul's Church, Buffalo, New York* — displays a delightful innocence not yet afflicted by history's arrogant correction of the topographic priorities), clearly illustrates this: darkly looming over the church, it has an effect of depressing rather than of rising upward. The vertical movement of the piers, which Sullivan has so diligently achieved, is abruptly curtailed by a heavy cornice and darkly shaded attic. With its cantilevered roof it resembles the flattened top of a pile driven down by a steamhammer, sinking deeper into the ground with every other blow. It looks like the Palazzo Strozzi, jammed by some freak accident into the heart of Buffalo, New York (see also John Mead Howell's comment in note 1). Sullivan no doubt perceived the obvious contradiction, but this is perhaps the best he could do with the type of Chicago office building ('the packing case type of building', as the English-born skyscraper architect Alfred C. Bossom called it), in the structural shape of which he had no say (Fig. 6). [49] Sullivan made the following comment in 'The Tall Office Building':

This brings us to the attic which ... gives us the power to show by means of its broad expanse of wall, and its dominating weight and character, that which is the fact — namely, that the series of office tiers has come definitely to an end. This may perhaps seem a bald result and a heartless, pessimistic way of stating it, but even so we certainly have advanced a most characteristic stage beyond the imagined sinister building of the speculator-engineer-builder combination. [50]

*Fig. 4 (below). The Guaranty (Prudential) Building, Buffalo, N.Y., 1894/1895, Louis H. Sullivan, architect. The building was almost contemporary with the publication of Sullivan's important credo 'The Tall Office Building Artistically Considered',* Lippincott's Magazine, *1896 (from John Szarkowski,* The Idea of Louis Sullivan, *Minneapolis, 1960, p. 107).*

*Fig. 5 (right). The Guaranty Building as it is not yet afflicted by art history's arrogant correction of topographic priority: 'St. Paul's Church, Buffalo, New York' (postcard, 1904). Darkly looming over the church's picturesque silhouette, it demonstrates a general effect of depression rather than of up-rising.*

*Fig. 6. 'The Packing Case Type of Building' (from Alfred C. Bossom, Building to the Skies, the Romance of the Skyscraper, London/New York, 1934).*

51. See William H. Jordy, *American Buildings and their Architects*, III, Garden City, N.Y., 1976, p. 174, n. 76.

52. Claude Bragdon, *Merely Players*, New York, 1929, p. 92.

53. See above, n. 26.

54. Menocal, *Architecture as Nature*, op. cit., refers to Bragdon as Sullivan's 'friend' (p. 46), or 'his friend and apologist' (p. 101). Bragdon himself always kept a respectful distance in his published writings. Their correspondence on the publication of the *Kindergarten Chats* was conducted in terms of 'Mr. Sullivan' and 'Mr. Bragdon' (see *Secret Springs*, op. cit., pp. 154–159). As to whether Bragdon is to be seen as a disciple of Sullivan, Jordy stated that Bragdon was 'a closer disciple of Sullivan ... whose writings on architectural symbolism were eventually inspired as much by theosophical beliefs as by Sullivanian mystique' (*American Buildings*, op. cit., III, p. 259). Deborah F. Pokinski, *The Development of the American Modern Style*, Ann Arbor, Mich., 1984, p. 132, n. 81, spoke about '... protégées [sic] and self-appointed disciples, as Wright and Bragdon.' Bragdon himself recalled: 'My formal education was of the scantest but I have had the inestimable privilege of being inspired and instructed in the arts I practiced by two masters of them: Harvey Ellis and Louis Sullivan' (*Secret Springs*, op. cit., p. 41).

The architect-artist had no choice but to cooperate with this 'speculator-engineer-builder' alliance – and he grudgingly acquiesced. On the other hand, he was dominated by Hegel's conviction that architecture is essentially a system of post-and-lintel, and he must have found it impossible to think in any other forms than the block. The Guaranty and Bayard Buildings were his last skyscraper commissions. Unable to exert any influence on the shape of the building, and stranded in the periphery of the architectural profession as 'a mere decorator' (which in all honesty he was), Sullivan had, by 1900, reached the end of his career, and he died in 1924. The few charming commissions that he realized in the Midwest were but proof of his lack of success, and therefore not charming at all but merely tragic.[51] This tragedy was summed up by Claude Bragdon, who wrote: 'Sullivan failed to write himself in an arresting way on the skyline of any of our cities.'[52]

To call Sullivan 'the prophet of modern architecture', as so many historians have, is not only a flagrant misjudgement of modernity, but also a merciless denial of a great man's right to choose his own company.[53]

55. Sheldon Cheney, *The New York Architecture*, New York, 1935 (1930[1]), p. 308.

56. G.H. Edgell, *The American Architecture of To-Day*, New York/London, 1928, pp. 82, 83, 381.

57. Lewis Mumford, *The Brown Decades*, op. cit., p. 69.

58. Lewis Mumford, *Roots of Contemporary American Architecture*, New York, 1972 (1952[1]), pp. 422/423: 'Perhaps Bragdon's own philosophy would have had a greater impact on his contemporaries had not his architectural theories been intermingled with Theosophy – the central interest of his life – and a four dimensional theory of ornament.'

59. For example: Eugenio Battisti, 'Claude Bragdon: Teosofia e Architettura', *Psicon*, 2/3, Gennaio-Giugnio, 1975, pp. 147–151; Daniele Baroni, *Grattacieli Architettura Americana tra Mito e Realtà, 1910–1939*, Milano, 1979, pp. 23, 64/65.

60. Claude Bragdon, *The Secret Springs*, op. cit., pp. 169-182.

61. Bragdon credited Henry Parker Manning, *Geometry of Four Dimensions*, New York, 1914, among others, as a source for his ideas on geometric ornament (Claude Bragdon, *The Frozen Fountain*, New York, 1932, p. 2). The fourth dimension was *the* subject of the time. 'In January 1909 a friend of the *Scientific American*, who desired to remain unknown, paid into the hands of the publishers the sum of Five Hundred Dollars, which was to be awarded as a prize for the best popular explanation of the Fourth Dimension, .... The essays, 245 in number, were submitted under pseudonyms, in accordance with the rules .... Despite the character of the subject, extraordinary interest was manifested in the contest. Competitive essays were received not only from the United States, but from Turkey, Austria, Holland, India, Australia, France, and Germany. In fact almost every civilized country was represented' (Henry P. Manning, *The Fourth Dimension Simply Explained*, a collection of essays selected from those submitted in the *Scientific American*'s Prize Competition, London, 1921, p. 3). Bragdon himself had entered the competition and his contribution was included in the volume under his pseudonym 'Tesseract': 'Space and Hyperspace', pp. 91–99. Linda D. Henderson, *The Fourth Dimension and Non-Euclidian Geometry in Modern Art*, Princeton, 1983, pp. 193–201, provides a detailed account of Bragdon's contribution. The book was recently brought to my attention by Saskia ter Kuile.

62. See below, note 69.

## Claude Bragdon

A friend of the great man Claude Fayette Bragdon (1866–1946) probably was not, but as a congenial spirit, perhaps a disciple, he could not have been closer.[54] Bragdon was a prolific writer and an architectural theorist; but he never made a name for himself in the history of art. Although a general book on architecture such as Sheldon Cheney's *The New World Architecture* of 1935 could mention him in the same breath as Frank Lloyd Wright ('Architects like Wright and Bragdon, who never fail to see the spiritual significance behind material architecture, have remarked on the appropriateness of the increased utilization of glass in this hour when man is between ancient darkness and a new enlightenment'),[55] and G.H. Edgell, in *The American Architecture of Today* (1928), referred to his writings,[56] and Lewis Mumford, in *The Brown Decades* (1931), described him as an 'excellent critic'.[57] By the time modernist historiography established its dominance, Bragdon had been written out of the plot. Giedion's *Space Time and Architecture* (1941) does not mention him, nor does Carl W. Condit's *The Chicago School of Architecture* of 1964 (originally called *The Rise of the Skyscraper* (1952)). This is strange, because, apart from his achievements both as a theorist and as an architect, Bragdon was largely responsible for the survival of the ideas of the man whom those very writers unanimously considered to be the greatest American architect, as well as the Father, Prophet or whatever, of modernism: Louis H. Sullivan. For the sake of this argument, it might even be said that without Bragdon there would have been no Sullivan. Had it not been for Bragdon, the *Kindergarten Chats* would not have been made public, and it was at his instigation that Charles Whitaker, author of the aforementioned *The Story of Architecture; From Rameses to Rockefeller* and the then editor of the *Journal of the American Institute of Architects*, undertook the publication of *The Autobiography of an Idea*, for which Bragdon wrote the introduction. Although Hugh Morrison, Sullivan's biographer, paid due attention to this fact, later authors for the most part disregarded it. A possible explanation for this is, as Lewis Mumford hinted in his *Roots of Contemporary American Architecture* (1972 (1952[1])), Bragdon's lifelong relation with theosophy.[58] Mumford nevertheless acknowledged that Bragdon,

by reason of his contact with Louis Sullivan and his natural sympathy with all that pertained to the life of our democracy ... became the chief link in writing, apart from Sullivan and Wright, with the architectural critics of an earlier period. Because he took the work seriously and published a series of books on architecture, Bragdon's influence was greater than that of ... Irving Pond ... and he was a sounder critic than Geoffrey Scott.[59]

Bragdon was also a more than capable designer of architectural ornament, which brought him contemporary renown and even a slight interest among present-day historians.[60] His system of ornament, expounded in *A Primer of Higher Space* (1913), *Man the Square* (1912) and *Projective Ornament* (1915), was based upon his conviction that there is a universal canon of proportion, which is mathematical in nature and to which the natural world conforms.[61] His intention was to provide modern architecture with a modern system of ornament that incorporated the most recent discoveries in mathematics, particularly the newly opened territories of space and time. The system, composed of simple geometrical forms, a bit like Moorish pattern work but less curved, was couched in the fourth dimension. This four-dimensional geometrical ornament was illustrated in Bragdon's *Projective Ornament* and his last important book on architecture, *The Frozen Fountain* of 1932.[62]

63. Narciso Menocal, *Architecture as Nature*, op. cit., p. 208; Claude Bragdon, 'The Whitman of American Architecture', *New York Herald Tribune Books*, 12 (22 December 1935), p. 4.

64. Hugh Morrison, *Louis Sullivan*, op. cit., p. 226.

65. Claude Bragdon, 'Architecture in the United States, III, The Skyscraper', *The Architectural Record*, XXVI, July–December 1909, pp. 84-96.

66. See above, notes 15 and 18.

67. Bragdon, op. cit., n. 65, pp. 92/93.

68. Ibid., p. 96.

69. This list of printed works by Claude Bragdon is intended to be complete, but I fear it probably is not. Undated publications or publications of which a date is not known to me are listed at the end. I am much indebted to Barbara Lister-Sink, who drew up a list of Bragdon's works as they are catalogued in the Rochester City Library.

C.B., *The Golden Person in the Heart*, New York, 1898.
—, 'An American Architect, Being an Appreciation of Louis H. Sullivan', *House and Garden*, 7, January 1905, pp. 47–55.
—, *Theosophy*, Rochester, 1909.
—, 'Architecture in the United States, I. The Birth of Taste; II. The Growth of Taste; III. The Skyscraper', *The Architectural Record*, 25, June–August 1909, pp. 426–433; 26, July–December 1909, pp. 38–45; 85–96.
—, *A Brief Life of Annie Besant*, Rochester, 1909.
—, *Self-Education – An Address Given Before the Boston Architectural Club, April 3, 1909*, Rochester, 1910.
—, *Episodes from an Unwritten History*, Rochester, 1910.
—, *The Beautiful Necessity, Seven Essays on Theosophy and Architecture*, George Routledge & Sons, London, 1910.
—, *The Small Old Path*, Rochester, 1911.
—, *Man The Square; A Higher Space Parable*, Rochester, 1912.
—, *A Primer of Higher Space; The Fourth Dimension*, Alfred A. Knopf, New York, 1913.
—, *The Message of the Buddha*, Rochester, 1914.
—, 'Organic Architecture' and 'The Language of Form', in: *Six Lectures on Architecture by Ralph Adams Cram, Thomas Hastings and Claude Bragdon*, Chicago, 1915.
—, *Projective Ornament*, Rochester, 1915.
—, *Four Dimensional Vistas*, George Routledge & Sons, London, 1916.
—, *More Lives Than One*, New York, 1917–1938. Most probably identical with:
—, *The Secret Springs; An Autobiography*, London, 1917–1938.
—, *Architecture and Democracy*, Alfred A. Knopff, New York, 1918.

Bragdon's most conspicuous quality, however, and probably the reason for the disfavour in modern times, was that he completely abandoned himself to architectural esotericism.

He recorded his early involvement with the Theosophical Society in America in *Episodes from an Unwritten History* (1910), translated and wrote the introduction to Peter D. Ouspensky's influential *Tertium Organum* (1920). [62] Theosophy had a considerable popularity in America, especially during the first quarter of the century, which was due to its spontaneous reception by indigenous esotericism and its ability to blend smoothly with the existing brands of natural theology. Bragdon's familiarity with the naturalist poets Thoreau and Whitman (it was Bragdon who called Sullivan 'the Whitman of American Architecture' in a *New York Herald Tribune* article of 1935) [63] and his sympathy for Emerson's thinking made him not only receptive to theosophy, but also an excellent link between its European sources and the American public. His abilities as an architect and as a theatrical designer, combined with his familiarity with the various kinds of esotericism and his ability as a writer, made him the ideal interpreter of the often mysterious ways of Louis Sullivan.

Sullivan had a wonderful style of writing, muscular and melodious, and contrary to common belief he was a popular and much appreciated presence at architectural conferences throughout the Midwest. Yet appreciation of his undeniably interesting ideas was hampered by a penchant for polemics and an abnormal inclination to repeat his point. Most of his minor writings were deformed to the point of unreadability owing to his tragic resistance to sympathetic understanding. From his first article onward ('An American Architect; Being an Appreciation of Louis Sullivan', *House and Garden*, January 1905), Bragdon devoted himself to liberating Sullivan from his philosophical occlusion and helping him to get the best of his thoughts published. This resulted in their collaboration on the publication of *Kindergarten Chats* in 1918. [64]

Bragdon began to formulate his own ideas on the skyscraper in 'Architecture in the United States – The Skyscraper', the last of a series of three articles he wrote for *The Architectural Record* of 1909. [65] The main ingredients were similar to the ones Schuyler had used in his skyscraper critiques of 1899, 1903 and 1909. [66]

Both authors agreed upon the unique position of Louis Sullivan as the harbinger of a national style of architecture in writing the 'facts' of the structure with the practical requirements of the business building to produce a smoothly shaped piece of architecture incorporating no known style from the past. This is the argument that, repeated over and over by later generations of critics and historians, raised the Tall Buildings of Sullivan to the level of canon. But suddenly Bragdon took a tangential course and launched into an attack on the paradigm of all of Sullivan's skyscrapers: the Guaranty Building, arguing that, although it was a sound piece of work and looked every inch 'the tall building' Sullivan had wanted it to be, it had none of the qualities of a real skyscraper: 'Though it represents perhaps the highest logical and aesthetic development of the steel-frame office building, it is scarcely deserving, in the light of recent developments, of the name of skyscraper. It is an insignificant pile of twelve stories.' [67] Instead, Bragdon suggested, we should look at the work of the New York architect Cass Gilbert, whose West Street Building of 1905 (Fig. 7) was 'the work of a master mind, the last work in New York skyscraper architecture; in it, the Caliban has become – if not yet Ariel – human at all events.' The main quality of the building resided in its full use of Gothic principles, so that it resembled a cathedral 'so delicately adjusted, so almost perilously poised, thrust against counterthrust, that like the overstrained organism of an ascetic it seems ever about to overcome that centripetal force which is nevertheless the law of its being.' [68]

*Fig. 7. Sketch of the West Street Building, New York, 1905, by Cass Gilbert ('Mr. Gilbert's sketch May 7th 1905'). This is the first version of the building, admiringly described by Bragdon as 'the work of a master mind' (courtesy of the New York Historical Society, New York City). The tower was abandoned later.*

Ouspensky, Peter D., *Tertium Organum: The Third Canon of Thought, A Key to the Enigmas of the World*, translated from the Russian by Nicholas Bessaraboff and Claude Bragdon, with an introduction by Claude Bragdon, Rochester, 1920/ Alfred A. Knopf, New York, 1922.

C.B., *Oracle*, Rochester, 1921.

—, 'Towards a New Theatre', *The Architectural Record*, LII, 1922, pp. 170–182.

—, 'Abstract Thoughts on Concrete Bridges', *The Architectural Record*, LIII, Jan. 1923, pp. 3–10.

—, 'A Theatre Transformed; A Description of the Permanent Setting by Norman Bel Geddes for Max Reinhardt's Spectacle "The Miracle"', *The Architectural Record*, LV, April 1924, pp. 388–397.

—, 'Louis H. Sullivan', *Journal of the American Institute of Architects*, XII, May 1924, p. 241.

Sullivan, Louis H., *The Autobiography of an Idea*, New York, 1924, with an introduction by Claude Bragdon.

C.B., 'Letters from Louis Sullivan', *Architecture*, 64, July 1931, pp. 7–10.

—, 'The Frozen Fountain', *Pencil Points*, XII, 6, October 1931, pp. 721–724.

—, *The Frozen Fountain, Being Essays on Architecture and the Art of Design in Space*, Alfred A. Knopf, New York, 1932.

—, *An Introduction to Yoga*, New York, 1933.

—, 'The Whitman of American Architecture', *New York Herald Tribune Books*, 12, 22 December 1935, p. 5.

—, *The Architectural Lectures*, New York, 1942.

—, *Yoga for You*, New York, 1943.

Sprague, Alice, *Sensitive Horizons*, edited and introduced by Claude Bragdon, Rochester, 1946.

—, *Delphic Woman*, ?.

—, *The Eternal Poles*, ?.

This was an unexpected turn for the man who was traditionally Sullivan's 'disciple', but an interesting one, for it reveals a fundamental disagreement on the subject of skyscraper design, and raises the perhaps less urgent question of intellectual dependence – who influenced whom?

I shall begin with the latter question. Although Sullivan started to publish his writings at a time when Bragdon seemed to be relatively unproductive, things changed in 1908, when Bragdon began a prolific output of more than thirty books.[69] Judging from the number of editions of his best known works, the popularity of his writings must have been considerable (also interesting in this respect is the fact that his publishers, Alfred A. Knopf in New York and George Routledge & Sons in London, were among the most prestigious). Among Bragdon's books which might have been read by anyone interested in esotericism as applied to architectural theory – Sullivan, for example – the ones most likely to have been influential were, in chronological order, *The Beautiful Necessity* (London, 1910), *A Primer of Higher Space: The Fourth Dimension* (New York, 1913), *Projective Ornament* (New York, 1915), *Four Dimensional Vistas* (London, 1916), *Architecture and Democracy* (New York, 1918), and *The Frozen Fountain, Being Essays on Architecture and the Art of Design in Space* (New York, 1932).

Important also were his 1915 Scammon Lectures on 'Organic Architecture' and 'The Language of Form', published, together with contributions by Ralph Adams Cram and Thomas Hastings, as *Six Lectures on Architecture* (University of Chicago Press, Chicago, 1915).[70] In the former Bragdon expressed the oppositions 'organic' and 'arranged' in the well-known aphorism 'Gothic architecture is organic; Renaissance architecture is arranged.'[71] Leaning comfortably upon Sullivan's theories (which he was about to collate in the *Kindergarten Chats*), he continued: 'Arranged and organic architecture correspond to the two hemispheres of thought and feeling into which mankind is divided, the one pre-eminently intellectual, the other psychic.'[72] This division was elementary in the thought of both writers. Feeling and intuition were judged superior to reason and logic. Consequently, science and common sense were condemned for belonging to the territory of lifeless, inanimate things, whereas intuition was thought to deal directly with life – 'it is related to reason, as flame is related to heat.'[73] In *Four-Dimensional Vistas* (1916) Bragdon unfolded his ideas, the origin of which he duly attributed to Ouspensky, Einstein's theory of relativity, and a great many other sources ranging from 'Eastern Teachings' to Nietzsche, Schopenhauer and Bergson. The book has proven extremely helpful in tracing the origins of Sullivan's thinking. What seemed initially a mere supposition on my part, that Sullivan borrowed his ideas about demiurgical creation from the *Corpus Hermeticum*, now proves to be a realistic suggestion, since Bragdon, in the *Vistas*, devoted substantial attention to Hermes Trismegistos, more particularly the highly relevant book *Asclepios*.[74] The philosopher and mystic Emanuel Swedenborg also played an important part in Bragdon's as well as in Sullivan's ideological development, though this is less surprising, since Emerson, to whom both men were strongly indebted, wrote a monograph on him.[75] Moreover, as Menocal has noted, Sullivan's friend John Wellborn Root was a member of the Swedenborgian Church.[76]

**Frozen Music**

With the publication of *The Beautiful Necessity* in 1922 (a largely improved version of the rather incomplete first edition of 1910), Bragdon began to establish a direct link with architecture. The book was intended for a public with an architectural interest and Bragdon, himself an architect, set out to facilitate the transition from theory to practice with the help of many nicely executed drawings illustrating the principles of 'changeless change', 'latent geometry', 'the arithmetic of beauty' and, in the concluding chapter, the beginnings of what was to become his theory of arrested motion in design, 'frozen music'. (Now I come to think of it, isn't it odd that Sullivan never illustrated his books, apart from *A System of Architectural Ornament*?)

70. See above, note 69.

71. Claude Bragdon, 'Organic Architecture', op. cit., p. 128.

72. Louis Sullivan, *Kindergarten Chats*, op. cit., pp. 46ff. Bragdon, 'Organic Architecture', op. cit., p. 128.

73. Claude Bragdon, *Four-Dimensional Vistas*, op. cit., p. 22.

74. Ibid., pp. 113ff.

75. Ibid., pp. 124ff.; Ralph Waldo Emerson, 'Swedenborg', in: *Representative Men* (1850). See Vivian C. Hopkins, *Spires of Form*, op. cit., p. 124 and passim; Narciso Menocal, *Architecture and Nature*, op. cit., p. 25.

76. Narciso Menocal, *Architecture and Nature*, op. cit., pp. 24/25.

Set against the background of a long history of the use uf musical proportions in architecture, this idea of architecture as 'frozen music' was, of course, not new. Goethe's notion of architecture as '*erstarrte* Musik' has been noted by Eckermann:

Montag, den 23. März 1829.
'Ich habe unter meinen Papieren ein Blatt gefunden,' sagte Goethe heute, 'wo ich die Baukunst eine erstarrte Musik nenne. Und wirklich es hat etwas; die Stimmung, die von der Baukunst ausgeht, kommt dem Effekt der Musik nahe.'

It was taken up by Schelling in his *Philosophie der Kunst* and it was Friedrich Schlegel who had provided the transitional step by comparing architecture to '*gefrorene* Musik': 'es steigt der hohen Säulen Pracht, und der gefrornen Musik Schall ist ganz harmonisch überall' (Johann Peter Hebel after Friedrich Schlegel) (Fig. 8). [77] In fact, Bragdon's resuscitation of the musical analogy

*Fig. 8. 'Es steigt der hohen Säulen Pracht, und der gefrornen Musik Schall ist ganz harmonisch überall' (Johann Peter Hebel after Friedrich Schlegel). The Empire State Building as the inevitable embodiment of organ music (cartoon by Millns, TAM, 37, 1985).* [79]

77. Johann Peter Eckermann, *Gesprache mit Goethe in den letzten Jahren seines Lebens*, Leipzig, 1913, p. 305. The Schlegel quote was found by Dr. Jeannot Simmen, Berlin/Zürich. Grimm, *Deutsches Wörterbuch*, VI, pp. 2739/2740 ('nach einem Ausspruch Fr. Schlegels'). Stravinsky wrote: 'Goethe thoroughly understood that when he called architecture "frozen music"' (*Composers on Music, An Anthology of Composers' Writings*, Sam Morgenstern, ed., New York, 1956, p. 442).

8 — CHRYSLER BUILDING, NEW YORK CITY

*Fig. 9. The Chrysler Building, New York, 1929/1930, William Van Alen, architect. 'The needle pointed flèche of the Chrysler tower catches the sunlight like a fountain's highest expiring jet' (postcard).*

78. See Menocal, *Architecture and Nature*, op. cit., p. 25. Daniel Burnham and John Wellborn Root belonged to the Swedenborgian Church. Louis Sullivan's lectures were always well attended. See Deborah F. Pokinski, *The Development*, op. cit., pp. 33–35.

79. I thank Simone Rümmele, Zollikon, Switzerland, for sending me the highly appropriate cartoon.

80. Claude Bragdon, *The Frozen Fountain*, op. cit., p. 11; Idem, 'The Frozen Fountain', *Pencil Points*, XII, October 1931, 10, p. 722.

81. See above, note 80.

82. Sullivan's fascination with the architecture of arrested motion was emphasized by Robert Craick McLean, editor of *The Western Architect*, in his necrology of Sullivan, 'An Appreciation', *The Western Architect*, XXXI, May 1924, 5, p. 54: 'Mr. Sullivan's theory of design, if it can be reduced to an equation, is natural growth. As a tree, sturdy of stem, reaches upward and outward, ever extending shoots of lesser girth and weight, branches that reach up into the terminal filigree ....'

83. Claude Bragdon, *The Frozen Fountain*, op. cit., p. 17; Idem, 'The Frozen Fountain', op. cit., p. 724.

would not deserve special attention, had it not served as the prelude to a broader conception that was to develop during the next ten years, that of 'architecture as a frozen fountain'. This enticing image, drawn from the originally Swedenborgian concept of the 'ascending and declensing forces', an analogy Sullivan had used frequently, provided the answer to Sullivan's quest, which ended, to Bragdon's and possibly also to his own discontent, with the Guaranty Building in Buffalo. *The Frozen Fountain*, preceded by the homonymous article of October 1931, appeared in 1932, eight years after Sullivan's death. It was the last book Bragdon wrote on the subject of architecture.

To return to the earlier question, it is still hard to establish who influenced whom, nor is it a very important question. Their circle of congenial souls, however, was larger than one would think. Architects, particularly Midwestern architects, have always been inclined towards different sorts of metaphysics, and though the Sullivan/Bragdon axis was an important one, it was not the only one.[78] Nevertheless the remarkable aspect of this spiritual axis is, to make a ruthless generalization, that it was Sullivan — notwithstanding the commanding tone of his rhetoric — who asked the questions and it was Bragdon who answered them.

### The Frozen Fountain

Late in Bragdon's career — too late, in any case, for Sullivan to have read it — came the publication of this book of self-revelation: 1931 and 1932, the years in which a long evolutionary line was crowned by three of the most beautiful and tallest skyscrapers of all times, the Chrysler, Empire State, and R.C.A. Buildings (see I, Fig. 16). Bragdon saw in these 'monarchs' of the skyscraper era the embodiment of the idea of arrested motion. Finally his long-cherished ideal had been realized in the form of buildings which resembled frozen fountains: 'The needle pointed flèche of the Chrysler tower catches the sunlight like a fountain's highest expiring jet' (Fig. 9).[80]. 'The white vertical masses of the Waldorf-Astoria, topped with silver, seem a plexus of upward rushing, upward gushing fountains, most powerful and therefore *highest at the center*, descending by ordered stages to the broad Park Avenue river' (Fig. 10).[81]

The conception of the fountain was as simple as its image was effective, Bragdon concluded: 'In the skyscraper, both for structural truth and symbolic significance, there should be upward sweeping lines to dramatize the engineering fact of vertical continuity and the poetic fancy of an ascending force in resistance to gravity — a fountain.' So far not much progress has been made since Sullivan's demands for a visualization of 'the force and power of altitude' and the 'rising in sheer exultation',[82] but the silhouette now sketched, of a building whose center should be drawn up high in order to show the fountain's strongest gushing in the centre, is a new and powerful image: 'what goes up must come down: gravity reasserts itself after the initial impulse is exhausted; every building however lofty must terminate'; and '... the force seeming to have faltered and failed at those mathematically related stages where the diminishments occur and most powerful at the center the upthrust terminal parallelepipedon finishes in jetlike tracery against the sky. ... The building "dies" on the white counterpane of the sky.'[83]

The transitions the type of the skyscraper had undergone are evident: the heavy architecture was broken, the central part shot upward to seemingly infinite heights, and the top was conceived of as dissolving into the sky. More interestingly, though, is that Sullivan's germ-plant image was supplanted by a more general and certainly more dynamic analogy. Architecture thus represented appeals strongly to our ideas of the arch-architecture. Bragdon stated that architecture 'should portray not only a world aspect, but the world *order*:

through and by means of the concrete and particular it should suggest the abstract and the generic — it must not only be typical but *archetypical*.'[84] The archetypical should be seen as the 'unit form' of nature, in which all its principles, such as gravitation, tension, or suspension, are represented. It should both contain the elements of life and express the process of life. How this could be achieved is now clearly revealed: 'Is it not an ascension and a declension — in brief a fountain: a welling up of a force from some mysterious source, a faltering of the initial impulse by reason of some counter-aspect of that force, a subsidence, a return all imagined in the upward rush and downward fall of the waters of a fountain, a skyrocket, a stone flung from the hand into the air?'[85] Architecture, Bragdon insists, must symbolize the 'struggle upward': 'What happens in a fountain and in its every drop happens also in a building and in all its parts, where stress and strain, compression and ten-

WALDORF-ASTORIA HOTEL — Park Avenue, New York City

*Fig. 10. The Waldorf-Astoria Hotel, New York, 1931, Schultze & Weaver, architects. 'The white vertical masses of the Waldorf-Astoria, topped with silver, seems a plexus of upward rushing, upward gushing fountains, most powerful and therefore highest at the center, descending by ordered stages to the broad Park Avenue river' (postcard).*

84. Claude Bragdon, *The Frozen Fountain*, op. cit. p. 8; Idem, 'The Frozen Fountain', op. cit., p. 721

85. Claude Bragdon, *The Frozen Fountain*, op. cit. p. 10; Idem, 'The Frozen Fountain', op. cit., p. 72

132

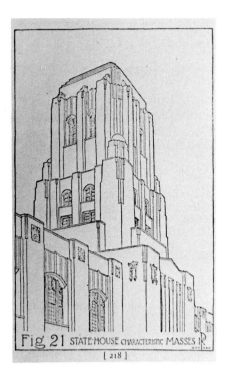

Fig. 11. 'When the aspiring spirit has been diverted
from its upward course by an obstacle, it will seek
immediately and indeed throughout the conflict to
assert its upward tendency.' 'State House – Characteristic Masses' (from Irving K. Pond, The Meaning of Architecture, Boston, 1918).

86. Claude Bragdon, The Frozen Fountain, op. cit.,
p. 10; Idem, 'The Frozen Fountain', op. cit., p. 721.

87. Irving K. Pond, The Meaning of Architecture,
An Essay in Constructive Criticism, Boston, 1918.
Pond's thinking is not unlike Sullivan's and Bragdon's. There is a strong emphasis on the organic
principles of design and the presence of an 'animat-
ing spirit', such as central in Eidlitz's work
(pp. 11ff.). The philosophical approach to art tends,
as it did with Sullivan and Bragdon, to an all embracing religious experience. ('Philosophy is the
child of intellect,' Pond says, '... Religion is the
child of the emotions and its field is action .... I
am using religion here in the sense in which it was
understood and employed by the contemporary disciples of Him, who gave His name to our Era and
imposed Himself upon our civilization. ... The religion of which I speak may be summed up in the
phrase: He went about doing good. Religion, then,
is feeling and doing in terms of goodness; art is
thinking and feeling in terms of beauty.' Etc.; pp.
15/16). Irving K(ane) Pond, The Meaning of Architecture, An Essay in Constructive Criticism, Boston,
1918. The copy I consulted and one of the very few
I ever saw of this rare book is in the Avery Library,
New York, and belonged formerly to architect Wallace K. Harrison. The 1918 edition was reprinted in
1937. Other publications by Pond were: 'High
Buildings and Beauty', I & II, Architectural Forum,
38, February 1923, p. 42ff.; April 1923, pp. 181ff.;
'Zoning and the Architecture of High Buildings',
The Architectural Forum, 35, October 1921,
p. 211ff.; 'Toward an American Architecture', in:

sion, thrust and counter-thrust are ceaselessly operative.'[86] Again, the idea of
architecture as a representation of its static determinants is not new, but the
Hegel-Sullivan post-and-lintel paradigm has been dramatically superseded by a
more primitive, mythical image of arch-power and life: a fountain, a geyser, a
volcano. The quiet analogy of gradual growth has been rendered obsolete by
the momentary eruption. Time has been condensed into moment.

The appeal of the fountain analogy lies in its ability to reconcile angular
shapes and to evolve patterns of line and mass that were situated between the
square and the circle. Bragdon referred to the architect-author Irving K. Pond
who, in his 'admirable book' The Meaning of Architecture (1918)[87], had already worked out a system of curving, undulating lines, in which the angular-
ity of the cubic shape was reconciled with the fluidity of the undulating line.
Pond wrote: 'The cube is the most refractory form in art. ... Nothing would
seem to be more inherently ugly, nothing would seem to fit less readily into
any scheme of beauty. The cube in itself makes no imaginative appeal. The
spirit rises to meet this object, this fact of life; a field of force is developed
and a line of beauty results from the conflict. ... When the aspiring spirit has
been diverted from its upward course by an obstacle it will seek immediately
and indeed throughout the conflict to assert its upward tendency' (Fig. 11).[88]
The idea of the upwardly gushing fountain of lines of force, overcoming obstacles, is inversely proportional to the lines of least resistance as sketched by
Bragdon, in which the upward-gushing waters of the fountain meet their death
at the summit of their powers and then return to the earth.

### Sinbad

The skyscraper and the frozen fountain meet in the self-evidence of their similarity, a natural coincidence by which each one explains the other. 'In the skyscraper,' Bragdon wrote, 'both for structural truth and symbolical significance, there should be upward sweeping lines to dramatize the engineering
fact of vertical continuity and the poetic fancy of an ascending force in resistance to gravity – a fountain.'[89]

Looking over Sinbad's shoulders (Fig. 12), we see a picture that is in more
than one respect familiar. The little figure of the Arabian voyager, 'summoned from the ink-bottle and sent forth on his voyage' through the world of
the frozen fountains, as a guiding element similar to the 'idea' of Sullivan's
Autobiography, is seen contemplating 'megopolis' [sic!], a cross between Fritz
Lang's Metropolis, as Bragdon suggests, and 'an' Eternal City seen from the
parapet of the Villa Borghese. The city's frozen fountains are of a type which
recalls the New York 'ziggurats' of the latter part of the second decade of this
century, but more particularly Saarinen's design for the Chicago Tribune
tower of 1922. Comparing Bragdon's drawing with the charcoal sketch 'Glass'
from Hugh Ferriss's Metropolis of Tomorrow, dating from 1926 (the book is
from 1929), small details such as the globe in the foreground, the three-
dimensional moon and the pointed bastion confirm Bragdon's dependence on
Ferriss's work (Fig. 13).[90] The figure of Sinbad performs the same mediating
function – think of Caspar David Friedrich's 'Voyager amidst the sea of
clouds' (1818 – Hamburg, Kunsthalle) or the 'Two men contemplating the
Moon' (1819 – Dresden, Staatliche Kunstsammlungen, Gemäldegalerie Neue
Meister) – as the draughtsman-Ferriss silhouette, his back turned to the
viewer, taking in the fairy-tale landscape of congealed geysers of glass.

The two artists were working from various, though not very different, angles,
yet their manifold sources of inspiration were similar – 'commercial gothic',
the New York set-back mode, European natural expressionism and Eliel
Saarinen – all of which briefly converged in 1922, the year of the Chicago
Tribune Competition.

*Fig. 12. 'Sinbad, from the roof of the megopolis [= megalopolis], views the city of frozen fountains' (from Claude Bragdon,* The Frozen Fountain, *New York, 1932). Bragdon's drawing has been inspired by Hugh Ferriss's vision of the Crystal City (Fig. 13).*

*Fig. 13. 'Glass', Hugh Ferriss's interpretation of skyscrapers as the congelation of a mineral geyser (from Hugh Ferriss,* The Metropolis of Tomorrow, *New York, 1929).*

*Living Architecture; A Discussion of Present Day Problems,* etc., Arthur Woltersdorf, ed., Chicago, 1930, pp. 161–171 (on p. 168 Pond mentions his 'Set-Back Building Design', ... 'from "The Brickbuilder" of 1898', which was not unlike Sullivan's proposal of 1891, to which Pond indeed made reference. It is interesting to note, as Donald Hoffmann did in his article 'The Setback Skyscraper City of 1891: An Unknown Essay by Louis H. Sullivan', *J.S.A.H.*, 20, 1970, pp. 181–187, that these essays in setback design were serious predecessors of the post-1916 New York Zoning Law-dictated buildings); 'How I Approach an Architectural Problem', *Pencil Points*, XIII, July 1932, pp. 459–465 (in which the setback proposal is repeated on p. 463); and *Big Top Rhythms; A Study in Life and Art*, Chicago, 1937.

88. Irving Pond, *The Meaning*, op. cit., p. 202. Pond's line of beauty, however different in origin, is not unlike William Hogarth's 'serpentine line', 'line of grace', or 'line of beauty' (*Analysis of Beauty*, London, 1974 (1753¹), pp. 55ff.).

89. Claude Bragdon, 'The Frozen Fountain', op. cit., p. 724. In the 1932 book Bragdon clarified this by contrasting the 'steel-framed building' and the 'true skyscraper'. 'In the steel-framed building,' Bragdon wrote, 'the height of which is less, or not too much greater than its breadth, it is all right to emphasize the horizontal dimension, ... , but in a true skyscraper it seems to me that the lines should sweep unbrokenly upward,' etc. (p. 16). Note the difference in interpretation of the qualification 'true' with Bragdon on the one hand and with American positivism and European modernism on the other hand. See: 'The Skyward Trend of Thought', p. 26.

90. Bragdon admired Ferriss for 'his architectural sense and his artistic sensitiveness.' 'Ferriss,' he wrote, 'served his masters so well that he himself enslaved some of them, .... His book, *The Metropolis of Tomorrow*, appears to be exerting an influence on skyscraper design analogous to that which Piranesi's prison etchings exercised upon George Dance's design for Old Newgate' (*The Frozen Fountain*, op. cit., p. 32).

91. *The Western Architect*, 31, January 1922, pp. 3–11.

92. *The International Competition for a New Administration Building for The Chicago Tribune MCMXXII*, Chicago, 1923, p. 10.

93. *The Linebook, 1925*, published by The Chicago Tribune, Chicago, 1925, p. 5, signed: Le Mousquetaire. Interesting, contemporary, information on the *Chicago Tribune* is to be found in: . . . *Pictured Encyclopedia of the World's Greatest Newspaper, A Handbook, etc.*, Chicago Tribune, Chicago, 1928.

94. The first post-war super-tall skyscrapers, built according to the box-shape formula, began to be built in the late 1960s, as for example S.O.M.'s John Hancock Center in Chicago, 1959, and Roth & Yamasaki's World Trade Center of New York, finished in 1976.

95. Judging the plans for the prospective building, the *Improvement Bulletin* of December 10, 1910, wrote: 'We believe that Gilbert was the first to make a serious attempt to relieve the rectangular bareness of the steel building skyscraper with beauty of form and color' (Cass Gilbert Scrapbook, New York Historical Society, New York, N.Y.). The Woolworth Building was awarded the medal of honour for being the 'highest and finest office building in the world' at the 1915 Panama Pacific International Exposition in San Francisco (*The Cathedral of Commerce*, New York, 1921, n.p.). Foreign interest was shown when members of the Münchener Studienkommission ordered a large model of the Woolworth Building for the Münchener Kunstschule in 1912: '. . . und darin darf man ohne Übertreibung die höchste Anerkennung erblicken' (Heinrich Reinhold Hirsch, 'Der moderne Thurm zu Babel', *New York Staatszeitung – Sonntagsblatt*, June 23, 1912). Talbot Hamlin, *The American Spirit in Architecture*, New Haven, 1926, wrote: 'To many people this building will always be the skyscraper par excellence' (p. 197). Because of its references to 'styles from the past', the Woolworth Building was held in low regard by modernist critics, whereas the abovementioned 'rectangular bareness' of the Chicago tall building was admired by Giedion c.s., the style of the Woolworth Building was seen as a pestilent influence that nullified the Chicago tradition. 'The [Chicago] school might just as well never have existed; its principles were crowded out by the vogue of "Woolworth Gothic"' (Sigfried Giedion, *Space, Time and Architecture*, op. cit., p. 314 + note). Other depreciatory comments are to be found in Sheldon Cheney, *The New World Architecture*, New York, 1935 (1930[1]), p. 70: 'Here is the final reach of the apostles of the past in their effort to hold the machine building of the present to architectural forms. And this is all summed up in the Woolworth Building.' Cheney followed a train of thought, popular among modernists, that a product made by a machine should also look like a machine, which is an interesting parallel to the attitude which teaches that whatever man creates should be endowed with his qualities and thus must look like man.

## Stabat Mater

Some of the events of 1922 are too well known to describe here in full. Sullivan's 'Tall Office Building Artistically Considered' was reprinted in the January issue of *The Western Architect* as a subconscious up-beat for the great Chicago Tribune Competition which took place later in the year.[91] This competition is perhaps justly regarded as one of the most important events in the history of the American skyscraper. It should be noted that it was instigated by a newspaper which, by a coincidence, was also called the *Tribune*. It should also be noted that the growth rings of the empire (see Fig. 2) had by this time encompassed the Midwest, and it was thought that a new cosmic centre should be founded away from the old East.

Among the mythical qualities Chicago had by then acquired, beauty was the only one lacking, and the Chicago Tribune announced that not height but beauty was required. 'To erect the most beautiful and distinctive office building in the world is the desire of *The Tribune*, and in order to obtain her design for such an edifice, this competition has been instituted.'[92]

This cry for beauty and distinction was in fact an incentive to deliver the long-awaited solution to 'the skyscraper problem'. Tallness had lost its appeal. That is to say, the desire to build high was still as powerful as ever – some lines from 'The Tribune Tower', a 'poem' of 1925 composed in praise of the finished building gives an indication of its lasting symbolic value: 'Towering, watching, guarding, commanding, / A banner in stone, a symbol of might'[93] – but the enterprise had to be temporarily abandoned for lack of the means to clothe this upward aspiration. The boxy shape proposed by Sullivan and his Chicago colleagues was no more effective than a London taxi is for expressing speed.[94] The best solution thus had been the 'commercial Gothic' of Cass Gilbert. His widely acclaimed masterpiece of 1913, the Woolworth Building, the tallest building in the world, was generally acknowledged, before the advent in the 1930s of the Chrysler and Empire State Buildings, as having most successfully wedded connotations of commercial pride with superbly beautiful architecture.[95] 'The Woolworth Building,' Ethel Fleming wrote in 1929, 'is indeed frozen music, it is poetry made visible.'[96] And, to remain in the domain of musical analogies, Gilbert himself was said to have remarked: 'To me a Gothic skyscraper is like a musical harmony, like *Stabat Mater*, whose final notes give us the highest pitch of emotion before they are lost in silence.'[97] It was indeed this quality of infinity, the subtle transition of the vertical lines into the sky, that was gradually recognized as the perfect expression of the skyscraper's ambition. Irving Pond, in his important, but for some reason forgotten, book *The Meaning of Architecture* (1918), joined the artistic consensus by suggesting a transitional technique for dissolving horizontal lines into verticals by means of a 'sfumato' effect based on an organic analogy. The horizontal skyline should be dissolved in the way that 'the flowing life in the stem may break into leaf and flower.'[98] Louis Sullivan had already put this theory into practice, quite literally, in his decoration, in 1899, of the most northern of the Holabird & Roche *Gage* Group façades (Fig. 14). The two central, slender, stem-like piers do indeed break into flowers, but they are kept down by the cornice in a similar fashion to acanthus leaves on the Corinthian capital, which break out and curl downwards the moment they hit the abacus (Fig. 15).

96. Ethel Fleming and Herbert S. Kates, *New York*, London, 1929, p. 7: '... one cannot fail to notice the edifice that has caught to itself all the poetry, all the soaring, swinging grace that man can achieve out of stone − the Woolworth Building. ... The Woolworth Building is indeed frozen music, it's poetry made visible.'

97. Francisco Mujica, *History of the Skyscraper*, New York, 1929, p. 34.

98. Irving K. Pond, *Meaning of Architecture*, op. cit., p. 203.

*Fig 14 (right). Irving Pond proposed to dissolve the horizontal skyline, similar to the way 'the flowing life in the stem may break into leaf and flower.' A literal application of this theory had already been practised by Louis Sullivan in Holabird & Roche's* Gage *Group, Chicago, 1899, decoration. A free flowering of the stem was obstructed, however, by the heavy cornice.*

*Fig. 15 (below). Sullivan's decorative treatment followed the model of the Corinthean capital in which the Acanthus leaves, in their climbing upward, are deflected by the abacus and made to curl downward (from Claude Bragdon,* The Frozen Fountain, *New York, 1932).*

99. Claude Bragdon, *The Frozen Fountain*, op. cit., p. 30.

100. Frank Lloyd Wright, *Ausgeführte Bauten*, Berlin, 1910, Introduction, n.p.

101. David Van Zanten, 'Twenties Gothic', *New Mexico Studies in the Fine Arts*, VII, 1982, pp. 21–23.

102. Montgomery Schuyler, 'Modern Architecture', *The Architectural Record*, IV, July–September 1894, pp. 1–13, in: Jordy and Coe, *American Architecture*, op. cit., I, p. 115.

103. James Early, *Romanticism and American Architecture*, New York/London, 1965, pp. 88/89, 92. Basic studies on the Gothic principles and Nature are the two essays 'The First Gothic Revival and the Return to Nature', and '"Nature" as Aesthetic Norm' by Arthur D. Lovejoy, *Essays in the History of Ideas*, Baltimore, 1948, pp. 136–165; 69–77. The relationship between Gothic architecture and organic architecture was noted and extended by a number of American theorists. Bragdon's essay 'Organic Architecture' (in: *Six Lectures on Architecture*, Chicago, 1915, pp. 123–145) is, in this context, the logical choice. Classical/Renaissance architecture is categorized as being 'arranged', whereas Gothic architecture is 'organic'. More of a curiosity is: C. Matlack Price, *The Practical Book of Architecture*, Philadelphia/London, 1916, p. 114: 'The explanation of the failure of the greater proportion of our Gothic churches lies in the circumstance that their architects have failed to consider the *organic* nature of gothic architecture, have failed to recognise its similarity to a tree. A tree grows out of a seed, putting forth branches as it comes into its growth and these put forth leaves.' The notion was, of course, analogous to Sullivan's ideas, as for example in *A System of Architectural Ornament*, 1924, n.p., in the chapter entitled 'The Inorganic and the Organic' – following closely Schelling's 'Das Anorganische und das Organische', *Philosophie der Kunst* (1859), p. 216: 'Hence, for the germ of the typical plantseed with its resident powers', etc., and 'Emotional Architecture as Compared with Intellectual', in: *Kindergarten Chats*, op. cit., p. 200, 'That the Gothic architecture . . . sympathizing deeply with Nature's visible forms . . .' and many other places.
Obviously, Gothic architecture and the natural growth of plants, trees, etc., were often related in the 18th and 19th centuries. See Joseph Rykwert, *On Adam's House in Paradise*, New York, 1972, pp. 75–103.
For other interpretations of the application of the Gothic style to the skyscraper, in particular pertaining to the Gothic entries in the Chicago Tribune Competition, see: Diana Agrest, 'Architectural Anagrams: The Symbolic Performance of Skyscrapers', *Oppositions*, 11, Winter 1977, p. 35: '. . . the winning entry by Howells and Hood, like its predecessor, the Woolworth Building by Cass Gilbert, is typically connotative of the Gothic now endowed with associations of splendor and wealth.' And: David Van Zanten, 'Twenties Gothic', *New Mexico Studies in the Fine Arts*, VII, 1982, pp. 19–24. See also Narciso Menocal, *Architecture as Nature*, op. cit., pp. 190/191, n. 64.

104. James Early, *Romanticism*, op. cit., p. 93.

105. Ibid., p. 99.

*Fig. 16. 'The real American spirit . . . lies in the Middle West . . . . It is alone in an atmosphere of this nature that the Gothic spirit in building can be revived' (Frank Lloyd Wright) (Grant Wood,* American Gothic, *1930. Chicago, Art Institute of Chicago).*

Bragdon also favoured the idea of the skyscraper following in the footsteps of the Gothic cathedral, and it is significant that he, the alleged 'disciple' of Sullivan, in order to make clear his disapproval of the termination of the Wainwright-Guaranty type, went so far as to use the master's famous dictum in his praise of the Woolworth Building, which, as he said, 'is certainly "a proud and soaring thing" and [which] remains today in many respects the finest embodiment of the skyscraper idea.' [99]

It was therefore predictable that most of the Americans entering the competition felt obliged to follow the magic Gothic formula. The Gothic spirit was even thought to be native to Western culture. Frank Lloyd Wright had declared in 1910 that 'the real American spirit . . . lies in the West and the Middle West . . . . It is alone in an atmosphere of this nature that the Gothic spirit in building can be revived' (Fig. 16). [100]

But to revive this spirit in a literal imitation of the Gothic *style* was not exactly what McCormick, or the Midwest, wanted. [101] To the rationalist and mystic alike, the imitation of Gothic forms was just as unacceptable as the imitation of natural forms in organic architecture: 'It is an imitation not of the forms of nature,' Montgomery Schuyler justly wrote, 'but of the process of nature.' [102]

James Early, in his seminal essay 'Nature, the Gothic and Functionalism,' described the conditions which led to the adoption, in America, of the Gothic, tracing them back to Goethe's interpretation of Strasbourg Cathedal, Schlegel's *Principles of Gothic architecture* and, of course, Wordsworth's conception of Nature as the moral teacher of man. [103] But, as Early observed, it was John Ruskin who, being far more popular in America than he ever was in his own country, laid the ground for the American vision of Gothic as a manifestation of Nature in the constructions of man. The Gothic was, according to him, not so much an architectural style which by its naturalistic character could be seen as *analogous* to nature, but a creative principle *identical* with Nature. American writers such as James Freeman Clarke and Horace B. Wallace identified Gothic architecture with organic growth. Wallace, for example, wrote in 1855: 'Chartres or Ely is a tree, growing freely and boldly, encountering obstacles and surmounting or working them in with what makes deviation a new and a higher illustration of principle, exhibiting a thousand beauties of light and shade by its interlacing branches and its flowering foliage, glittering with dewy freshness, and full of the song of birds.' [104] Emerson demanded from the artist that he stay as close as possible to the will of Nature, to be directed by Nature, rather than to correct it: 'We in seeing a noble building, which rhymes well, as we do in hearing a perfect song, that it is spiritually organic, that is, had a necessity in nature, for being, was one of the possible forms in the Divine mind, and is now discovered, and executed by the artist, not arbitrarily composed by him.' [105]

The Gothic cathedral, Emerson believed, was 'a blossoming in stone, subdued by the insatiable demand of harmony in man. The mountain of granite blooms into an eternal flower with the areal proportions and perspective of vegetable beauty.' [106]

### Energy

Magic growth and the Midwest have always been held to be synonymous. Picture postcards were expressly made to communicate these wonders in unmistakable terms to people in less privileged places (Figs. 17, 18, 19). [107]

Fig. 17. 'Humoristische Postkarten aus dem Westen' (from Arthur Holitscher, Amerika, Heute und Morgen, *Berlin, 1923). The alarmingly inflated cabbages and corn cobs were to communicate the western paradise to foreigners in terms of easily understandable quantity.*

Fig. 18. Several Tall Buildings on Madison Street, Chicago. *In the foreground the Union Trust Building, the former headquarters of the* Chicago Tribune. *The white building in the distance is Louis Sullivan's Carson, Pirie, Scott Store (postcard).*

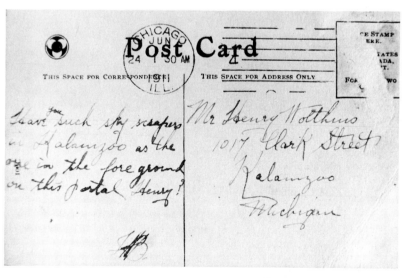

Fig. 19. The same postcard, verso. One Dutch immigrant writes to the other: 'Have you such sky scrapers in Kalamzoo [sic!] as the one in the foreground on this postal Henry?' *Whether they are inflated cabbages or buildings is immaterial; it is important to communicate the presence of plenty and the consequent well-being (postcard).*

*Fig. 20. 'All Gone But Wife & Children. "Energy".'*
*William D. Kerfoot, the legendary prophet of the*
*essential post-1871 gospel: 'ENERGY' (from Rev.*
*E.J. Goodspeed,* History of the Great Fires in
Chicago and the West, *New York, etc. 1871).*

106. Ralph Waldo Emerson, *Essays*, 1st and 2nd
series, 'History', London/New York, 1906, p. 18.

107. The 'Humoristische Postkarten aus dem
Westen' were reproduced in Arthur Holitscher,
*Amerika, Heute und Morgen; Reiseerlebnisse*, Berlin, 1923, plate between pp. 176–177.

108. The magic of American city fires is best captured by the Reverend E.J. Goodspeed, *History of
the Great Fires in Chicago and the West, A Proud
Career Arrested by Sudden and Awful Calamity;
Towns and Counties Laid Waste by the Devastating
Element. ... To which is appended a Record of the
Great Fires in the Past*, New York, etc., 1871. The
speed with which the book was published is amazing: less than three months for 676 pages and several
dozen engravings. The famous scene of Kerfoot's
shack in the burnt district is on p. 501. 'Chicago will
rise again' is on p. 339. The popularity of books like
Goodspeed's must have been considerable and comparable to present-day disaster movies. Quite inspiring a publication and similar in its cinematic subtitling was: *San Francisco's Great Disaster, A Full
Account of the Recent Terrible Destruction of Life
and Property by Earthquake, Fire and Volcano in
California and at Vesuvius and A Brief Account of
Ancient and Modern Earthquakes and Volcanic
Eruptions in All Parts of the World*, by Sidney
Tyler and Ralph Stockman Tarr, Philadelphia,
1906.

109. E.V. Goodspeed, *History of the Great Fires*,
op. cit., p. 514.

*Fig. 21. 'Chicago Will Rise Again' (from Rev. E.J.
Goodspeed,* History of the Great Fires in Chicago
and the West, *New York, etc. 1871). Whereas Manhattan's spires were compared with rich vegetative
growth, Chicago's steel-framed buildings seemed to
have been made in the cavernous forges of Vulcan
and been flung in a single eruption to the still
smouldering surface.*

The leading name was 'energy'. A few days after the Chicago fire of October
9, 1871, William D. Kerfoot performed an act of cosmogony on the ashes of
the burnt business district when he erected a shed to which he nailed his emblematic message: 'Wm. D. Kerfoot – All Gone But Wife & Children.
"ENERGY"' (Fig. 20). [108]
A new generation of tall, dark steel and terracotta buildings followed, as the
phoenix Chicago rose elegantly on the skyline (Fig. 21). John G. Whittier
jingled for the occasion:

Then lift once more thy towers on high,
And fret with spires the western sky,
To tell that God is yet with us,
And love is still miraculous! [109]

Whereas Manhattan's spires were compared with the luxurious growth of a
forest, Chicago's steel frames seemed to have been forged in Vulcan's cave

110. Thomas E. Tallmadge, 'A Critique of the Chicago Tribune Building Competition', *The Western Architect*, XXXII, 1, January 1923, p. 7. Tallmadge's evocative language was again used by Charles Henry Whitaker, *Rameses to Rockefeller; The Study of Architecture*, New York, 1934, pp. 295/296. See also: Ciucci, Dalco, Manieri-Elia, Tafuri, *The American City etc.*, p. 510, n. 50.

111. Louis H. Sullivan, 'The Chicago Tribune Competition', *The Architectural Record*, LIII, 1 January 1923, p. 153.

112. Thomas E. Tallmadge, 'A Critique', op. cit., p. 7.

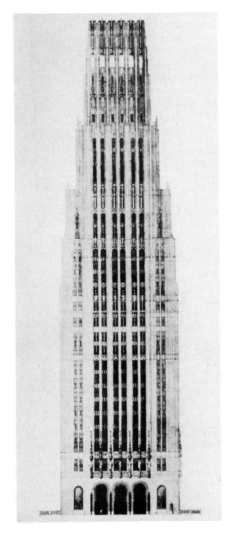

*Fig. 22. Eliel Saarinen; competition entry for the Chicago Tribune, 1922. 'It ascends and ascends until its lovely crest seems at one with the sky' (Louis Sullivan). This was the solution to the problem of the skyscraper which had remained unsolved for about a quarter of a century. (from* The International Competition for a New Administration Building for The Chicago Tribune MCMXXII, *Chicago, 1923).*

and sent, in a single eruption, to the still smouldering surface. As in New York, the beginning of Chicago's architectural evolution was wild and uncontrolled. Pride in the growth and prosperity of the city had never, with the exception of the White City of 1893, found a proper expression in architecture; there was, instead, an accretion of more buildings of an existing kind, repeated ad nauseam. The 1920s marked the beginning of a large-scale clean-up, with strict attention to the requirements of beauty and, of course, energy. When Eliel Saarinen (1873–1950) presented his highly personal solution to *The Tribune*'s challenge, everybody, and that means everybody, including the uncooperative jury and the eventual winners, Hood and Howells, instantly recognized that this was what they had all been looking for.

Thomas Eddy Tallmadge jubilated in *The Western Architect* (the magazine which for years after proudly carried Saarinen's design in its vignette) (see: 'Skyward Trend', Fig. 23, p. 29), that 'the second prize was a work of unquestioned genius,' and he went so far as to express his admiration in Sullivanian terms: 'It is as though some Titanic seed, planted deep in the earth, had suddenly sprung from the mould into the light in a shimmering bloom of stone and steel.'[110] And Sullivan himself wrote:

In its single solidarity of concentrated intention, there is revealed a logic of a new order, the logic of living things; and this inexorable logic of life is most graciously accepted and set forth in fluency of form. Rising from the earth in suspiration of the earth and as of the universal genius of man, it ascends and ascends ... until its lovely crest seems at one with the sky. (Fig. 22).[111]

The thoughts and strategies which enabled Saarinen to achieve this legendary victory as a loser can only be conjectured. The general opinion is that he was 'a genius', highly susceptible to the mythical sensitivity of the West. According to Tallmadge, he was supported by 'superhuman assistance'.[112] Still more conjectures could be added. The first indication of the direction of Saarinen's architectural thinking is his contribution 'A New Architectural Language for America' of February 2, 1923 for *The Western Architect*. It appears that his prime inspiration – most appropriate to our subject – was 'the forest' of Manhattan's skyscrapers. He wrote:

While working at the skyscraper design it occurred to me to find out how a whole city picture would appear under the vertical system throughout, and eliminating the horizontal element. I procured a photograph of New York City, showing a forest of skyscrapers with the greatest imaginable variation in height and width, placed a sheet of tracing paper over it and drew faithfully the same conglomeration of buildings, using, however, an exclusively vertical style of architecture.[113]

Saarinen was a great tower builder. His very first designs, for his own house and studio (1902), the Helsinki National Museum (1902), the Railway Station (1904), the competitive designs for the Peace Palace at The Hague (1906) and the Finnish Parliament House (1908), all have monumental towers.[114] 'The skyward trend of thought' came naturally to him. The Chicago type of building, on the other hand, made him feel uncomfortable – 'There was something blocklike and hard in the whole, which shocked me.'[115] – and he was glad to notice that the vertical was taking over:

More and more it is noticed that the horizontal featuring, borrowed from the antique and Renaissance, is giving room for the vertical in the Gothic, and this is very natural. The vertical emphasis is more logical and purposeful for an architecture which, like the Gothic, reaches up to the heights.[116]

Although the features of Saarinen's Chicago Tribune Tower are not in the Gothic style, he did design it according to the Gothic principles of tapering the

*Fig. 23. Hugh Ferriss, 'Buildings Like Crystals –
Night in the Science Zone' (from Hugh Ferriss,* The
Metropolis of Tomorrow, *New York, 1929).*

113. Eliel Saarinen, 'A New Architectural Language
for America', *The Western Architect*, XXXII, 2,
February 1923, p. 13.

114. See Albert Christ-Janer, *Eliel Saarinen,
Finnish-American Architect and Educator*, Chica-
go/London, 1979 (1948 [1]); *Saarinen in Finland*, Museum of Finnish Architecture, exhibition catalogue
15 VIII – 14 X 1984, and *Design in America; The
Cranbrook Vision 1925–1950*, Detroit/New York,
1983. Specially relevant is the contribution by David
G. De Long, 'Eliel Saarinen and the Cranbrook
Tradition in Architecture and Urban Design',
pp. 47–89.

115. Eliel Saarinen, 'A New Architectural Language', op. cit., p. 13.

116. Loc. cit.

117. Loc. cit.

mass towards the top and of forming the top in such a way 'that the logical
construction can be followed by the eye in all the different parts of the
building clear up to the highest pinnacle.'[117] In fact, Saarinen's style was not
unlike the less successful one by Bertram Grosvenor Goodhue. About six
months earlier Goodhue surprised the Chicago Architectural League at their
annual exhibition, April 22, 1922, with his breathtaking design for a skyscraper church of unprecedented height, the Convocation Tower, planned for

*Fig. 24. Whether Ferriss was influenced by European natural expressionism is hard to prove. In any case this picture of a crystal, expressly meant to be a model for architectural design, appeared in the Dutch magazine* Wendingen, *VI, 1924.*

118. *The Western Architect*, XXXI, April 1922, p. 50 (see 'Sacred Skyscrapers and Profane Cathedrals', p. 72).

119. Hugh Ferriss, *The Metropolis of Tomorrow*, New York, 1929, p. 125.

120. W. Steenhof, 'Kristallen; Wondervormen der natuur', *Wendingen*, VI, 11/12, 1924, fig. 21.

121. See for the European connection: Cervin Robinson & Rosemarie Haag Bletter, *Skyscraper Style; Art Deco New York*, New York, 1975, pp. 52ff.

122. Claude Bragdon, *The Frozen Fountain*, op. cit., p. 31.

*Fig. 25. The European way to handle the frozen fountain in architecture; Hans Poelzig's famous sketch for the Grosses Schauspielhaus, Berlin, 1918–1919 (from Wolfgang Pehnt,* Die Architektur des Expressionismus, *Stuttgart, 1973).*

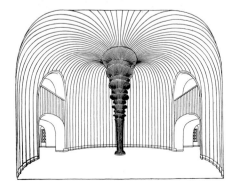

Madison Square, New York, and drawn by Hugh Ferriss in 1921 (see 'Sacred Skyscrapers and Profane Cathedrals', Fig. 19). In this design the most significant elements of skyscraper expression were so cleverly blended that it was spoken of as '*the* wonderful drawing of the exhibition.'[118]

Of course Ferriss's contribution to the scheme was conspicuously present: the dramatic set-back, for which Ferriss held the undisputed patent, and a crystalline faceting, which he later brought to perfection in studies like 'Buildings Like Crystals − Night in the Science Zone', from *The Metropolis of Tomorrow* (Fig. 23).[119] Whether Ferriss was influenced by European expressionism is hard to prove, although a picture of a crystal, favourite topic of Hendrik P. Berlage and his ideological offspring, in the Dutch magazine *Wendingen*, 11/12, 1924, comes amazingly close (Fig. 24).[120]

Other analogies with nature, such as the frozen fountain, were the subject of experiments in Europe, as may be seen in Hans Poelzig's famous sketches for the foyer of the Grosses Schauspielhaus, Berlin 1918–19 (Fig. 25). But as compared to the 'fountains' lending their form to the more naturally inclined action of the skyscraper, Poelzig's visualized dynamics remained an isolated case.[121]

Goodhue, Bragdon recalled, was full of praise for Saarinen's design, which he said was in 'a class by itself and superior to all the others', including his own.[122]

## An artistic coup d'état

Bragdon, more than anyone, was immensely pleased with Saarinen's ascent; not only did it fuel his emerging theory of the fountain, but it turned the theory of skyscraper design right around to where he thought it should be. It was an artistic coup d'état of enormous consequence. Sheldon Cheney, author of *The New World Architecture* (1930), wrote that it was 'like the beginning of a deluge. It was as if a dam had broken' and that of the thousand skyscrapers built since, at least three-quarters have followed Saarinen's example. [123] That Raymond Hood and John Mead Howells succumbed to its irresistible charm was due, Bragdon thought, to

the workings of poetic justice: though the victory was theirs, and the spoils of victory in good American dollars, the winners themselves were convicted of sin and suffered conversion. For what other inference can be drawn from the appearance of the New York Evening News Building, by these same architects, which is quite in the spirit of Saarinen's design and as unlike their own previous effort as can well be imagined. [124]

Fig. 26 (above). In his search for the ideal termination of the skyscraper, Claude Bragdon had sought to reconcile modern with Gothic architecture. He had judged that Senlis Cathedral and John Mead Howell's Panhellenic Building were two equally worthy representatives of the technique of tapering a tower in such a way that it seems to dissolve, as the expiring jet of a fountain, into the sky (from Claude Bragdon, The Frozen Fountain, *New York, 1932).*

Fig. 27 (right). John Mead Howells, Panhellenic Building, New York, 1928. Howells, together with Raymond Hood, winner of the Chicago Tribune competition, was, like all others, so impressed by Saarinen's solution that he could hardly wait to apply the same principles to the first large skyscraper commission he got (from Marcel Chappey, Architecture internationale, *Paris, 193?).* Evidently, Bragdon had used the photograph to base his own sketch upon.

123. Sheldon Cheney, *The New World Architecture*, op. cit., pp. 151/152.

Stronger even was the impact on Howells's extremely elegant Panhellenic Tower of 1928, a sketch of which Bragdon used as an illustration to his theory, sketched after the photograph (Figs. 26 & 27).[125] Hood, as we have seen, combined the same elements in his R.C.A. Tower, to which he added the unmistakable emblem of the fountain, as it is usually frozen and used as a skating rink (the Energy Bringing Prometheus riding on its crest makes it into a classic case of symbolism redundant) (Fig. 28).

Fig. 28. Raymond Hood & Associates, R.C.A. Building and Fountain, New York, 1931–1934. A case of redundant symbolism. The eastern half of the slab is cascading downwards, and like the waters of a fountain, is ending its voyage in the basin at the foot of the tower. Then the waters are sent up again in little jets in order to demonstrate in detail the principles of the largest frozen fountain ever built. Prometheus is riding over the little fountain to emphasize the message of which this whole gigantic complex is the carrier, namely that of the massive eruption of energy, drained from the subterranean powers and brought to the surface as a gigantic congealed geyser. That the little fountain is frozen part of the year is a superfluous attempt to explain over and over again that the R.C.A. Building is indeed a colossal frozen fountain (postcard).

124. Claude Bragdon, The Frozen Fountain, op. cit., pp. 31/32. Meant is: Daily News Building.

125. Ibid., p. 16, fig. 3. The photo was taken from Marcel Chappey, Architecture internationale, Paris, 193?, p. 48.

A similar example is the decoration by the Midwestern architects Keck & Keck of the Miralago Ballroom, Cook County, Illinois, 1929, in which two fountains are turned into reflections of each other (Fig. 29). [126]

The 1920s produced a host of Saarinen-inspired, set-back 'fountains', generally called 'Art-Deco' skyscrapers, showing the atavistic origin of their design in badges over doors, in grills and on their crests (Fig. 30). [127] The idea of adorning these buildings with the symbols of creation was, it seems, in order to communicate to later generations the by then forgotten knowledge that the skyscraper itself had been the model for this iconic representation of subterranean eruptions, congealed geysers and frozen fountains.

*Fig. 29. Two fountains reflecting each other in the Miralago Ballroom, Cook County, Illinois, Keck & Keck, architects, 1929. It is hard to imagine this frozen fountain not representing a skyscraper (from Narciso Menocal,* Keck & Keck, Architects, *Madison, Wis., 1980).*

*Fig. 30. So-called 'art deco' skyscrapers are showing the atavistic origin of their design as badges over doors and as memorial tablets in façades. A frozen fountain in the façade of 181 Madison Avenue, New York (from Don Vlack,* Art Deco Architecture in New York, 1920–1940, *New York, 1974).*

126. *Keck & Keck, Architects*, Elvehjem Museum of Art, University of Wisconsin, Madison, exhibition catalogue with an introduction by Narciso Menocal, Madison, Wis., 1980, p. 13, fig. 4.

127. Don Vlack, *Art Deco Architecture in New York, 1920–1940*, New York, etc., 1974, p. 37, fig. 33: '181 Madison Avenue.' A building which is literally covered with fountains and symbols of varying meanings is the former Cities Services Building, now 60 Wall Tower by Clinton & Russell, architects, 1932. Employing light-coloured stone to accentuate its crest, the building performs impressively as a foam-topped fountain. It is hard to believe that the ornaments profusely applied to inter-war skyscrapers were intended as merely ornamental – 'art deco' – and are not, as the above-quoted studies imply, to communicate on a higher symbolic level. Art historians, trained to read and interpret the sculpted façades of medieval cathedrals, seem to have a blind spot the moment the building is not situated in the far past. See also *American Art Deco Architecture*, Finch College Museum of Art, New York, exhibition catalogue with a text by Elayne H. Varian; November 6, 1974–January 5, 1975.

*Fig. 31 (right). Eliel Saarinen, Kingswood School, Cranbrook Academy of Art, Bloomfield Hills, Michigan, 1929–1931. Saarinen got the opportunity to build himself a laboratory in which he could freely experiment with organic and growth-expressive forms.*

*Fig. 32. Eliel Saarinen, Gatepost, Cranbrook Academy of Art, Bloomfield Hills, Michigan. Two frozen fountains placed over the entrance to the compound provide the key to reading the architecture properly.*

128. Egerton Swartwout, 'Review of Recent Architectural Magazines', *American Architect and Architectural Review*, 123, June 20, 1923, p. 575.

129. David G. De Long, 'Eliel Saarinen and the Cranbrook Tradition', op. cit., pp. 50–55. See also Alfred McClung Lee, *The Daily Newspaper in America; The Evolution of a Social Instrument*, New York, 1937, p. 197: 'George G. Booth, then chairman of the board of the Booth Newspapers and president of the *Detroit News*, gave $6,500,000 to the Cranbrook Foundation, organized in 1927 by himself and his wife Ellen Scripps Booth [Scripps was another newspaper imperium] for the completion and maintenance of an educational and cultural project they had launched at "Cranbrook", their country estate.'

130. I am grateful to Prof. Leonard Eaton who gave me the opportunity to visit Cranbrook under his professional guidance.

## An idyllic garden

The *Tribune* Building by Saarinen was said to be 'a splendid interpretation of the spirit of the American people.'[128] But did the American people interpret the spirit of its designer equally well? Did they appreciate his work enough to invite him to build one of his splendid towers? Or was he to be satisfied and honoured by the mere knowledge that 'three-quarters of the thousand newly built skyscrapers' represented an infraction of his copyright? What might have become the classic tale of the inventor laureate whose invention was praised but never applied was abruptly changed by George G. Booth, owner, again, of a newspaper, *The Detroit News*. Although Booth did not envisage a tower for his paper (which seems to have been a good idea), he nevertheless financed a design for the Detroit Riverfront, and, a little later, in 1924, he commissioned Saarinen to design the Cranbook Academy of Art at Bloomfield Hills, Michigan.[129]

Here, and more particularly in the Kingswood School of Cranbrook, 1929–1931, Saarinen had the opportunity to build himself a laboratory in which he could experiment with organic and growth-expressive forms (Fig. 31).[130] On the gate-posts leading to the school, two frozen fountains were placed announcing the character of the compound and providing the key to its principles (Fig. 32). In order to secure the attention of anyone who might have missed the impact of the superstructure, a seven-armed fountain,

*Fig. 33. Eliel Saarinen, Gatepost (detail), Cranbrook Academy of Art, Bloomfield Hills, Michigan. A small frozen fountain in the shape of a Jewish menorah, offering a stylized, head-on view of the inside of the higher-placed fountains, is carved into the left-hand pedestal.*

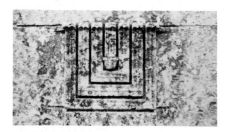

*Fig. 34 (below). Once the two gateposts are brought together they will form a series of Gothic arches, not unlike 'the Corridor of Frozen Fountains' of Fig. 35.*

*Fig. 35 (right). 'Sinbad in the Corridor of Frozen Fountains', another way of describing a groin-vaulted gallery (from Claude Bragdon, The Frozen Fountain, New York, 1932).*

its crests bending outwards, was carved into the left-hand post (Fig. 33). Resembling the Hebrew menorah, it offers a view of the inside of the two stone fountains, whose seven ribs seem to reach over the entrance-way. It is clear that the two fountains, if fitted together, would make several series of Gothic arches, diminishing in number (seven, six, five) on their way upwards, and all that would produce a Gothic vaulted corridor such as the one Sinbad encountered in the 'corridor of frozen fountains' (Figs. 34 & 35). Inside, fountains are seen at work supporting porticos, carrying entablatures and even being themselves fountains (Fig. 36). The chimney-stacks positioned at the extremities of the pavilions rise up unnecessarily tall, so that they resemble miniature skyscrapers: big-city elements scaled down to garden conditions (Fig. 31). The alleged affinity between Saarinen and Wright is, in such cases, eloquently contradicted: whereas Wright was always dominated by the horizontal, Saarinen, always and in all circumstances, cultivated his predilection for the vertical.[132] If there was anyone who got carried away by the 'deluge' Saarinen's skyscraper caused, it was Saarinen himself. Everywhere, outside and inside, in the decoration of the interior, in the tapestries, in the rugs and in the leaded glass, the motif of the fountain/skyscraper was incorporated (Fig. 37). Pipsan Saarinen, Eliel's daughter, went so far as to weave a silk dress decorated with four large skyscrapers.[133]

SINBAD IN THE CORRIDOR          OF FROZEN FOUNTAINS

Fig. 36. Eliel Saarinen, Kingswood School, Cranbrook Academy of Art, Bloomfield Hills, Michigan,
1929–1931. Courtyard with a fountain which is, indeed, a fountain. The smokestacks are shaped as
stepped-back skyscrapers, reminiscent of Saarinen's
own Chicago Tribune design, which became noted
for its telescopic action.

131. Claude Bragdon, *The Frozen Fountain*, op.
cit., p. 18. The little Arabian Nights Sinbad figure is
the literary 'Leitmotiv' of *The Frozen Fountain*.

132. Eliel Saarinen, 'A New Architectural Language', op. cit., p. 13; Eliel Saarinen, *The Search
for Form in Architecture*, New York, 1985 (1948 [1]),
pp. 133–135; 166–168; Saarinen's thoughts on organic form are usually expressed in phytoid analogies such as were used by Sullivan to indicate the
process of growth. The gradual growth of plants
and trees from the seed is the dominant simile.

133. *Design in America*, op. cit., p. 189, fig. 153:
'Pipsan Saarinen Swanson. (Designer). Dress c.
1933–35. Silk; plain weave with applied panels of
silk, satin weave with leather, gold paint, 45¾ ×
approx. 35″ (at hip). Collection Ronald Saarinen
Swanson').

Fig. 37. The same skyscraper-shaped figures, incor-
porated in the leaded glass panels of the Kingswood
School, Cranbrook Academy of Art, Bloomfield
Hills, Michigan.

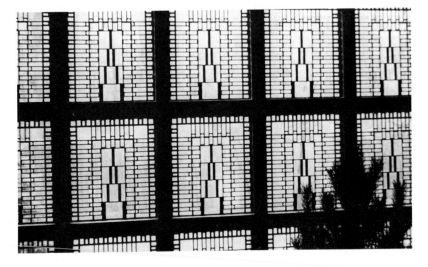

134. Ibid., p. 191, fig. colourplate 40: 'Lillian Holm (Designer and weaver). 'First Sight of New York'. 1930's. Linen, wool, and cotton; plain weave with discontinuous wefts (initaled LH). 82 × 64 1/8″. Flint Institute of Arts, Gift of Lillian Holm in memory of Ralph T. Sayles.'

135. By courtesy of Mr. Leendert De Jong, Amsterdam.

136. Eliel Saarinen, *The City; Its Growth, Its Decay, Its Future*, New York, 1943 (above, note 132). In *The City* Saarinen was most explicit in his thoughts on the skyscraper (pp. 185–99): 'Vertical Concentration'. Again the natural analogy is evident in a phrasing like: '. . . it is for the civic organization to determine where and how skyscrapers should be allowed to *grow*' (my italics) (p. 195).

*Fig. 38 (below). Lillian Holm, 'First Sight of New York', tapestry. Lillian Holm was a designer and weaving instructor at the Cranbrook Academy of Art during the 1920s and 1930s. This tapestry, representing an agglomeration of skyscrapers submitted to the law of the centripetal force, was in fact not so much a 'first', but rather a 'second' view of New York, since it was clearly dependent on the 1937 Christmas issue cover of* Fortune *magazine (see Fig. 39) (from* Design in America; The Cranbrook Vision, 1925–1950, *Detroit/New York, 1983).*

*Fig. 39 (right). Cover of* Fortune, December 1937, *Christmas issue.*

The school's obsession with the skyscraper reached its zenith with an undated tapestry made by one of its instructors, Lilian Holm, entitled: 'First Sight of New York' (Fig. 38). [134] It shows a bouquet of artfully arranged skyscrapers, windows alight against a dark background, sketching, in their collective centripetal action, the familiar outline of a Manhattan-style steel and stone Christmas tree. Which, in fact, it was. Never had hard-core capitalism and sweetly naive arts-and-craftsmanship been more harmoniously blended than in this, what Sullivan would have called the 'high romance' of the commercial tower, since what Holm designed was not in fact a 'first' sight of New York, but a 'second' one, being a copy of the festive cover of the 1937 *Fortune* Christmas issue (Fig. 39). [135] This, incidentally, gives us a reasonably accurate post quem date for the rug.

If New York was a forest, Cranbrook could be only a modest, idyllic, botanic garden in which Saarinen was cross-breeding the ideal skyscraper with its natural ideologies. His staff, family and pupils visualized his experiments in end-

*Fig. 40. The Bank of Manhattan Building, New York, 1929/1930, H. Craig Severance, architect. Drawing by Hugh Ferriss, showing the building in its last phase of completion (from Hugh Ferriss, The Metropolis of Tomorrow, New York, 1929).*

less reworkings of the theme until they had reached their harmless decorative quality. On his researches into form at Cranbrook Saarinen wrote two books: *The City, Its Growth, Its Decay, Its Future* (1943) and *The Search for Form in Art and Architecture* (1947). [136]

The latter in particular is remarkable for its similarity to the writings of Sullivan and Bragdon. Both style and content seem to derive from the same sources. Bergson's *Évolution créatrice* served Bragdon, Sullivan and Saarinen equally well. [137] The simile of 'the growth of the seed into a tree' is often used by Saarinen, and his esoteric ideas on creation and the universe, as well as the organic principle, were identical to those of the other two. [138] Saarinen appeared to be so much at ease with the teachings of Emerson and of American naturalism that Sullivan was convinced that this 'foreigner' possessed 'the insight required to penetrate to the depths of the sound, strong, kindly and aspiring idealism which lies at the core of the American people.' [139]

That this foreigner had successfully and definitively mastered the problem of the skyscraper was therefore no great mystery, since he had arrived at it by 'intuition' – the natural way.

## Epilogue

As Bragdon wrote in 1931, just after the Chrysler Building was completed, that its 'silver pinnacle catches the sunlight like a fountain's highest expiring jet,' he did not mean to say, of course, that there was an actual fountain to be seen at work, surging, ascending, and finally expiring in a single jet. The movement of the rising waters was cleverly suggested by its shape and material (steel, glass and a nickel-compound called 'Monel'), but it was a suggestion nevertheless. Although it is true indeed that a building is in perpetual motion, the movement of the fountain of energy was never meant to exceed the status of an illusion or a principle of design. The fountain was to suggest arrested motion, as a frozen fountain, embodying the creative powers caught in the act.

With the Chrysler Building it all went differently. It did live. Its 'highest expiring jet' was not just an illusionary vision, caused by the play of light upon polished steel, but a real, palpable, moving device. The story is well known and can be summarized briefly. In 1929/1930 the mid-town situated Chrysler Building, originally built as his private undertaking by the architect William van Alen, got involved in a race for the tallest building in the world with the down-town based Bank of Manhattan Building, now known under its address '40 Wall Street', by H. Craig Severance, architect (Fig. 40). The Bank of Manhattan finished first and reached a total height of 927 feet (about 280 metres). The Chrysler Building's originally announced height was beaten by a mere two feet. But then the miraculous happened: from out of its pointed Monel-plated crest a steel mast was raised to a new total height of 1048 feet (about 315 metres), beating not only its opponent by a liberal margin but also the Eiffel Tower's long-standing record of 1000 feet (Fig. 41).

137. Bergson's influence on Sullivan has not been noted by the abovementioned writers (Menocal, Morrison), nor by Sherman Paul, *Louis Sullivan; An Architect in American Thought*, Englewood Cliffs, N.J., 1962. It seems unlikely, though, that Sullivan would have remained ignorant of such an important source to which Claude Bragdon made regular references (*Four Dimensional Vistas*, op. cit., pp. 62, 143). Saarinen in any case shows himself a staunch admirer by quoting him emphatically, in 'The Search of Form', op. cit., chapter VI, 'Form and Vitality', pp. 144ff.; and, of course, the paragraph on 'Creative Vitality', pp. 147–151; Ch. IV, 'The Creative Instinct', pp. 109ff. and so on.

138. See above, notes 132, 136, 137.

139. Louis H. Sullivan, 'The Chicago Tribune', op. cit., p. 156.

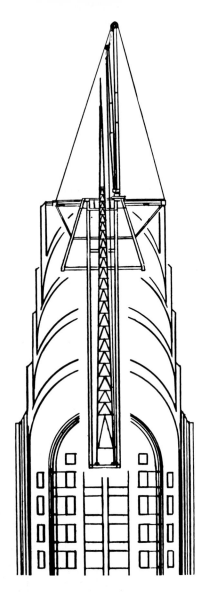

This amazing occurrence is usually cited to illustrate the picturesque predelic-tion of American skyscraper-builders for records, the breaking of records and for record-breaking tallness. But there is more to it. Predominant in this per-formance is its ritualistic aspect. Investing buildings with life was, as we have seen, not an unusual obsession. Inverse architectural anthropomorphism was also practised by the Chrysler Building's architect who had appeared at the 1933 New York Beaux-Arts Ball as the well-documented travesty of his own creation (Fig. 42).[140]

*Fig. 41 (above). A cut-away view of the top of the Chrysler Building, showing the secret device which was hoisted into place the moment after its nearest competitor, The Bank of Manhattan Building, had reached its ultimate height. This steel spire added enough extra height to the Chrysler Building for it to become the tallest building in the world. During this procedure the building did what otherwise could only have happened in the imagination of the be-holder: it grew visibly (from Thomas Walton, 'The Sky Was No Limit', Portfolio, April/May 1979).*

140. William Van Alen's architectural travesty was given most notoriety by Rem Koolhaas, *Delirious New York*, New York, 1978, p. 107. The so-called 'Architects Ball' was first mentioned in *Pencil Points*, XII, 2, February 1931, p. 145. The ball was held at the Hotel Astor, New York, on January 23, 1931.
The picture was also published in *Architecture Plus*, September/October 1974, p. 12. The École des Beaux-Arts had a long tradition of costume-balls and the one of 1931 was no exception.

141. For cosmic symbolism and the tree, see Mircea Eliade, *The Sacred and the Profane*, New York, 1961, pp. 45/46, and above, 'The Myth of Natural Growth, I', notes 134, 135, 136.

*Fig. 42. William Van Alen, the Chrysler Building's architect, in his act of inverse anthropomorphic travesty (from* Pencil Points, *XII, 2, February 1931, p. 145).*

For those who had had the privilege of being able to watch the raising of the spire it must have been an unforgettable spectacle. They had witnessed the slow progress of its construction year by year, and then, one day, this whole process was to come to completion. But what made this occasion into an atavistic ritual was the erection of the spire. It could clearly be observed that the building was growing, that this thoroughly anthropomorphic structure was stretching itself. The whole process of building was condensed into this single performance. In fact, the act of building was ceremoniously imitated and executed in a swift acceleration, i.e. relative to the real time of construction. Real time, in other words, was transformed for the occasion into ceremonial time. The act of architectural creation was imitated, re-enacted, high on top of the man-made mountain. The raising of the spire was in no way different from other acts of cosmogony, such as the raising of the pine-tree when the highest point of the house under construction is reached. Again, the cosmic symbolism is made redundant: the skyscraper itself is, as a man-made mountain, the image of the centre of the world − an axis mundi − just as the tree is, superimposed on its summit. [141]

Whatever the popular reception might have been, regarding it either as an obscenity or as a smartly played, if slightly below-the-belt, trick on the opponent (Fig. 43), the majesty of this pure act of cosmogony must have transcended it all.

*Fig. 43. This act of architectural cosmogony was not rightly valued by everybody. A contemporary cartoon is accompanied by the following text: 'Enthusiastic Architect: "You see, this spike runs down the entire length of the building and if anyone builds a taller building we can jack up the spike and still be the tallest!"' (from Pencil Points, XII, 1, January 1931). The apparent sarcasm was not spent on Van Alen who claimed the 'spike' to be an integral part of the building's structure.*

SELECTED
GENERAL
BIBLIOGRAPHY

James Truslow Adams    *The Epic of America*, Garden City, New York, 1941. (1931 [1]).

Thomas Adams & Harold M. Lewis, Lawrence M. Orton    *Regional Plan of New York and Its Environs*, Volume 1: *The Graphic Regional Plan*, New York, 1929; Volume 2: *The Building of the City*, New York, 1931.

Walter Raymond Agard    *The New Architectural Sculpture*, New York, 1935.

Diana Agrest, ed.    *A Romance with the City – Irwin S. Chanin*, New York, 1982.

—    'Architectural Anagrams: The Symbolic Performance of Skyscrapers', *Oppositions*, Winter 1977: 11, pp. 26–51.

Jean-Jacques Ampère    *Promenade en Amérique*, Paris, 1887.

Stanley Peter Anderson    *American Ikon: Response to the Skyscraper 1875–1934*, unpublished Ph.D. thesis, University of Minnesota, 1975.

Wayne Andrews    *Architecture, Ambition and Americans; A Social History of American Architecture*, New York/London, 1964 (1947 [1]).

Roger Ward Babson    *Religion and Business*, New York, 1922.

Gaston Bachelard    *L'Air et les songes*, Paris, 1947.

Vernon Howe Bailey    *Magical City, Intimate Sketches of New York*, New York/London, 1935.

Paul R. Baker    *Richard Morris Hunt*, Cambridge, Mass., 1980.

Alan Balfour    *Rockefeller Center, Architecture as Theatre*, New York, 1978.

Günther Bandmann    *Mittelalterliche Architektur als Bedeutungsträger*, Berlin, 1951.

—    *Ikonologie der Architektur*, Darmstadt, 1969.

Daniele Baroni    *Grattacieli, Architettura Americana tra Mito e Realtà 1910–1939*, Milano, 1979.

Roland Barthes    *La Tour Eiffel*, Paris, 1964.

Alice Hunt Bartlett, ed.    *The Anthology of Cities*, London, 1927.

Jerome Paine Bates, A.M.    *The Imperial Highway, or The Road To Fortune and Happiness with Biographies of Self-Made Men, Their Business Traits, Qualities and Habits*, Chicago, 1888 (1881 [1]).

Eugenio Battisti    'Claude Bragdon: Teosofia e Architettura', *Psicon*, 2/3, Gennaio/Giugnio 1975, pp. 147–151.

Charles A. Beard, ed.    *A Century of Progress*, New York/London, 1933.

Thomas Beer    *The Mauve Decade; American Life at the End of the Nineteenth Century*, New York, 1926 [1].

Walter Curt Behrendt    *Der Sieg des neuen Baustils*, Stuttgart, 1927.

—    *Modern Building, its Nature, Problems and Forms*, New York, 1937 [1].

Edward Bellamy    *Looking Backward, 2000–1887*, New York, 1960 (1888 [1]).

Henri Bergson    *Les deux sources de la morale et de la religion*, France, 1946 (1932 [1]).

—    *L'Évolution créatrice*, Paris, 1911 (1907 [1]).

| | |
|---|---|
| Edwyn Bevan | *Symbolism and Belief*, Boston, 1957. |
| George L. Bird and Frederic E. Merwin, eds. | *The Press and Society*, New York, 1951. |
| William Harvey Birkmire | *Skeleton Construction in Buildings*, New York/London, 1900 (1893 [1]). |
| Rosemarie Bletter | 'Metropolis réduite', *Archithese*, (*Metropolis 2*), 18, 1976, pp. 22–28. |
| Sir Reginald Blomfield | *The Touchstone of Architecture*, Oxford, 1925. |
| Edward Bok | *The Americanization of Edward Bok, the Autobiography of a Dutch Boy, Fifty Years After*, New York, 1920. |
| — | *Dollars Only*, New York/London, 1926. |
| William Bonner | *New York; The World's Metropolis*, New York, 1929. |
| Juan Pablo Bonta | *Architecture and its Interpretation, A Study of Expressive Systems in Architecture*, New York, 1979. |
| Alfred C. Bossom | *Building to the Skies, The Romance of the Skyscraper*, London, 1934. |
| | *Alfred C. Bossom's American Architecture 1903–1926*, Dennis Sharp, ed., London, 1984. |
| Paul Bourget | *Outre-Mer, Notes sur l'Amérique*, Paris, 1895. |
| Mouzon William Brabham | *Planning Modern Church Buildings*, Nashville, 1928. |
| Claude Bragdon* | 'Architecture in The United States', I, 'The Birth of Taste', *The Architectural Record*, XXV, July–August 1909, pp. 426–433; II, 'The Growth of Taste', XXVI, June–August 1909, pp. 38–45; II, 'The Skyscraper', XXVI, June–August 1909, pp. 85–96. |
| — | *The Beautiful Necessity*, Seven Essays on Theosophy and Architecture, London, 1922 (?) (1910 [1]). |
| — | *Man the Square, A Higher Space Parable*, Rochester, 1912. |
| — | *A Primer of Higher Space the Fourth Dimension*, New York, 1929 [2] (1913 [1] en 1923 [1]). |
| —, Ralph Adams Cram, Thomas Hastings | *Six Lectures on Architecture*, The Scammon Lectures for 1915, published for the Art Institute of Chicago by the University of Chicago Press. |
| Claude Bragdon | *Projective Ornament*, Rochester, 1915. |
| — | *Four-Dimensional Vistas*, London, 1916. |
| — | *The Secret Springs*, An Autobiography, London, 1917. |
| — | *Architecture and Democracy*, New York, 1918. |
| — & Peter D. Ouspensky | *Tertium Organum, the Third Canon of Thought, A Key to the Enigmas of the World*, translated from the Russian by Nicholas Bessaraboff and Claude Bragdon – with an introduction by Claude Bragdon, New York, 1929 (1920 [1]). |
| — (alias Tesseract) | 'Space and Hyperspace', in Henry P. Manning, *The Fourth Dimension Simply Explained, A Collection of Essays Selected from Those Submitted in the Scientific American's Prize Competition*, London, 1921, pp. 91–99. |
| — | 'Louis H. Sullivan', *Journal of the American Institute of Architects*, 12, May 1924, p. 241. |
| — | *The New Image*, New York, 1928. |
| — | *Merely Players*, New York, 1929. |
| — | 'The Frozen Fountain', *Pencil Points*, XII, October 1931, 10, pp. 721–724. |
| — | *The Frozen Fountain, Being Essays on Architecture and the Art of Design in Space*, New York, 1932. |

* See for a more detailed bibliography, 'The Myth of Natural Growth II', note 69.

| Fernand Braudel | *Civilisation matérielle, économie et capitalisme, XVe-XVIIIe siècle, I-III: Les structures du quotidien; Le possible et l'impossible; Les jeux de l'échange; Le temps du monde*, Paris, 1979. |
| Elie Brault | *Les Architectes par leurs Oeuvres*, 4 Vols., Paris 18?. |
| Horst Bredekamp | 'Die Erde als Lebewesen', *Kritische Berichte*, Jahrgang 9, Heft 4/5, 1981, p. 5–38. |
| H. Addington Bruce | *Above the Clouds & Old New York, An Historical Sketch of the Site and a Description of the Many Wonders of the Woolworth Building*, New York, 1913. |
| Raymond Bruchberger, Dominican | *One Sky to Share, The French and American Journal of*, New York, 1952. |
| Ursula Brumm | *Die religiöse Typologie im Amerikanischen Denken*, Leiden, 1963. |
| James Bryce | *The American Commonwealth*, 2 Vols., New York, 1911 (1888 [1]). |
| Maria Brzóska | *Anthropomorphe Auffassung des Gebäudes und seine Teile*, Jena, 1931. |
| Building Trades | *History of Architecture and the Building Trades of Greater New York*, Vol. I and II, New York, 1899. |
| Peter Buitenhuis | 'Aesthetics of the Skyscraper: The Views of Sullivan, James and Wright', *American Quarterly*, IX, 1957, pp. 316–324. |
| John Burchard and Albert Bush-Brown | *The Architecture of America, a Social and Cultural History*, Boston, 1961. |
| Hezekiah Butterworth | *ZIG-ZAG Journeys in the White City with Visits to the Neighbouring Metropolis*, Boston, 1894. |
| M.A. Caparu | 'The Riddle of the Tall Building: Has the Skyscraper a Place in American Architecture?', *The Craftsman*, X, July 1906, 4, pp. 477–488. |
| Andrew Carnegie | *The Empire of Business*, London/New York, 1902 [1]. |
| | *The Cathedral of Commerce, The Highest Building in the World, Woolworth Building, New York*, with contributions by S. Parker Cadman and Edwin A. Cochran, New York, 1917. |
| Sheldon Cheney | *The New World Architecture*, New York, 1935, 2nd ed., 389 ills. |
| — & Martha Cheney | *Art And The Machine, An Account of Industrial Design in 20th Century America*, New York, 1936. |
| | *Chicago 150 Ans d'Architecture 1833–1983*, eds. Ante Glibota & Frédéric Edelman, Paris, 1984. |
| | *Chicago, + 100 Jahre Architektur in Kontinuität von Struktur und Form*, with contributions by Carl W. Condit, Oswald W. Grube et al., die Neue Sammlung-Staaliches Museum für Angewandte Kunst, München, 1973. |
| | *Chicago, The World's Youngest Great City*, Chicago, 1919. 'The Chicago Civil Geria and Its New Home' by Herbert M. Johnson, p. 67. |
| Chicago Tribune | *The International Competition for a New Administration Building for the Chicago Tribune, MCMXXII*, Chicago, 1923. |
| Albert Christ-Janer | *Eliel Saarinen*, Finnish-American Architect and Educator, Chicago and London, 1979 rev. ed. |
| Giorgio Ciucci, Francesco Dal Co, Mario Manieri-Elia, Manfredo Tafuri | *The American City from the Civil War to the New Deal*, London/Toronto/ Sydney/New York, 1980 (1973 [1]). |
| Allen Churchill | *Park Row*, New York, 1958. |
| William Gilford Clark & J.L. Kingston | *The Skyscraper; A Study in the Economic Height of Modern Office Buildings*, New York, Cleveland, 1930. |
| Eugene Clute | 'Dr. John Wesley Kelchner's Restoration of King Solomon's Temple and Citadel by Helme and Corbett, Architects', *Pencil Points*, Vol. VI, 11, 1925, pp. 69–86. |
| Peter Collins | *Changing Ideals in Modern Architecture, 1750–1950*, Montreal, 1975. |
| John P. Comer | *New York City Building Control, 1800–1941*, New York, 1942. |

| | |
|---|---|
| Henry Steele Commager | *The American Mind, an Interpretation of American Thought and Character, since the 1880's*, New Haven, 1950. |
| Carl W. Condit | *American Building Art, The Nineteenth Century*, New York, 1960. Id., *The Twentieth Century*, New York, 1961. |
| — | *The Chicago School of Architecture. A History of Commercial and Public Building in the Chicago Area, 1875–1925*. Chicago etc., 1966. Originally: *The Rise of the Skyscraper*. |
| — | *Chicago 1910–1929, Building, Planning and Urban Technology*, Chicago, 1973. |
| Harvey Wiley Corbett | 'America Builds Skyward' in: *America as Americans See It*, ed. Fred. J. Ringel. The Literary Guild – New York, 1932. |
| Le Corbusier | *Quand les cathédrales étaient blanches*, Paris, 1937. |
| Ralph Adams Cram | *Convictions and Controversies*, Boston, 1934. |
| — | *The Substance of Gothic, Six Lectures on the Development of Architecture from Charlemagne to Henry VIII, Given at the Lowell Institute, Boston, in November en December, 1916*, Boston, 1917. |
| Walter L. Creese | *American Achitecture from 1918 to 1923, With Special Emphasis on European Influence*, unpublished doctoral thesis, Harvard, 1949. |
| Herbert D. Croly | 'The Skyscraper in the Service of Religion', *The Architectural Record*, 55, February 1924, 2, pp. 203/204. |
| Merle Curti | *The Growth of American Thought*, New York/London, 1943. |
| Charles Darwin | *The Expression of the Emotions in Man and Animals*, London, 1904 (1872[1]). |
| Samuel Philips Day | *Life and Society in America*, London, 1880. |
| Charles Dickens | *American Notes and Pictures from Italy*, London, 1868 (1842[1]). |
| S.H. Ditchett | *Marshall Field and Company, Die Lebensgeschichte eines großen Amerikanischen Warenhaus-Konzerns*, Berlin, 1925. |
| John Dos Passos | *The 42nd Parallel*, London, 1938. |
| — | *Manhattan Transfer*, Leipzig, 1932 (1925[1]). |
| Joan E. Draper | *Edward H. Bennett – Architect and City Planner, 1874–1954*, Chicago, 1982. |
| Theodore Dreiser | *Newspaper Days*, New York, 1922. |
| Henry Drummond | *The Ascent of Man*, London, 1896. |
| R.L. Duffus | *Mastering a Metropolis, Planning the Future of the New York Region*, New York/London, 1930. |
| James Early | *Romanticism and American Architecture*, New York/London, 1965. |
| Leonard K. Eaton | *American Architecture Comes of Age: European Reaction to H.H. Richardson and Louis Sullivan*, Cambridge, Mass., London, 1972. |
| G.H. Edgell | *The American Architecture of To-Day*, New York/London, 1928. |
| Donald Drew Egbert | 'The Idea of Organic Expression and American Architecture', *Evolutionary Thought in America*, Stow Persons, ed., New Haven, Conn., 1950, pp. 344–366. |
| Leopold Eidlitz | *Nature and the Function of Art, More Especially of Architecture*, New York, 1881. |
| Mircea Eliade | *Images et symboles, essais sur le symbolisme magico-religieux*, Paris, 1952. |
| — | *Le Mythe de l'éternel retour, archetypes et répétition*, Paris, 1961. |
| — | *Mythes, rêves et mystères*, Paris, 1957. |
| — | *The Sacred and the Profane, the Nature of Religion*, New York, 1961. |
| — | *Traité d'histoire des religions*, Paris, 1964. |

| Ralph Waldo Emerson | *First and Second Series of Essays*, London/New York, 1906. |
| — | *The Works*, 5 vols., London, 1913/1914. |
| | *Exhibitive of the Features and Attractions of the Masonic Temple*, New York, 1892. |
| Henri-Paul Eydoux | *Monuments curieux et sites étranges*, Paris, 1974. |
| James Fergusson | *An Historical Inquiry into the Principles of Beauty in Art more Especially with Reference to Architecture*, London, 1849. |
| — | *History of the Modern Styles of Architecture, being a sequel to the Handbook of Architecture*, III, London, 1862. |
| — | *History of Indian and Eastern Architecture*, 2 Vols., London, 1910. |
| James Barr Ferree | *The Modern Office Building*, New York, 1896. |
| — | 'An American Style of Architecture', *The Architectural Record*, Vol. I, July–Sept. 1891, pp. 39–45. |
| — | 'The High Building and Its Art', *Scribner's Magazine*, XV, March 1894, pp. 297–318. |
| Hugh Ferriss | *The Metropolis of Tomorrow*, New York, 1929. |
| — | *Power in Building, An Artist's View of Contemporary Architecture*, New York, 1953. |
| Johann Bernhard Fischer von Erlach | *Entwurff einer historischen Architectur*, Wien, 1721 (Reprint Dortmund, 1978). |
| James Marston Fitch | *American Building, I; The Historical Forces that Shaped It*, New York, 1973 (1947[1]). |
| — | *American Building, II; The Environmental Forces that Shape It*, Boston, 1972 (1948[1]). |
| — | *Architecture and the Esthetics of Plenty*, New York/London, 1961. |
| Ethel Fleming | *New York*, with illustrations by Herbert S. Kates, London, 1929. |
| Robins Flemming | 'A Half Century of the Skyscraper; Tracing the Expansion and Refinement of a Brilliant American Achievement', *Civil Engineering*, 1934, Vol. 4, 12, pp. 634–638. |
| Ford Madox Ford | *New York Is Not America, Being a Mirror to the States*, New York, 1927. |
| — | *Great Trade Route*, London, 1937. |
| Pierre Francastel | *Art et technique aux XIXe et XXe siècles*, Paris 1962. |
| Paul Frankl | *New Dimensions*, The Decorative Arts of Today in Words & Pictures, New York, 1928. |
| John Foster Fraser | *America at Work*, London, 1904. |
| James G. Frazer | *The Golden Bough*, The Roots of Religion and Folklore, London, 1890. |
| Frank Friedel | 'Boosters, Intellectuals and the American City', *The Historian and the City*, Oscar Handlin, ed., Cambridge, Mass., 1966, pp. 115–120. |
| Kenneth Turney Gibbs | *Business Architectural Imagery: The Impact of Economic and Social Changes on Tall Office Buildings 1870–1930*, Unpublished Ph. D. Thesis, Cornell University, 1976. |
| Sigfried Giedion | *Space, Time and Architecture, The Growth of a New Tradition*, Cambridge, 1946 (1941[1]). |
| Cass Gilbert | *Reminiscences and Addresses*, New York, 1935. |
| Albert Gobat | *Croquis et impressions d'Amérique*, Berne, 1905 (?). |
| Jocelyn Godwin | *Robert Fludd*, Hermetic Philosopher and Surveyor of Two Worlds, Boulder, Co., 1979. |
| Paul Goldberger | *The Skyscraper*, New York, 1981. |
| Richard A. Goldthwaite | *The Building of Renaissance Florence, an Economic and Social History*, Baltimore/London, 1980. |
| Rev. E.J. Goodspeed, D.D. | *History of the Great Fires in Chicago and the West*, Chicago, 1871. |
| Geoffrey Gorer | *The Americans; A Study in National Character*, London, 1948. |
| Dean Gottman | 'Why the Skyscraper ?', *Geographical Review*, Vol. LVI, 2, April, 1966, pp. 190–212. |

Jacques Gréber — *l'Architecture aux États-Unis*, preuve de la force d'expansion du génie français, Paris, 1920.

Horatio Greenough — *Form and Function*, Berkeley/Los Angeles, 1957.

Angelo de Gubernatis — *La mythologie des plantes ou les légendes du règne végétal*, 2 Vols, Paris, 1882.

Alfred C. Haddon — *Evolution in Art: As Illustrated by the Life-Histories of Designs*, London, 1895.

Talbot Faulkner Hamlin — *The American Spirit in Architecture*, in:, *The Pageant of America*, XIII, New Haven, 1926.

Neil Harris — *The Artist in American Society*, New York, 1982 (1966 [1]).

Dolores Hayden — 'Skyscraper Seduction — Skyscraper Rape', *Heresies*, 2 (1977), pp. 108—115.

John L. Heaton — *The Story of a Page*, New York/London, 1923.

Georg Wilhelm Friedrich Hegel — *Ästhetik*, 2 Vols., Berlin/Weimar, 1984 (1842 [1]).

Linda Dalrymple Henderson — *The Fourth Dimension and Non-Euclidian Geometry in Modern Art*, Princeton, NJ, 1983.

Ernst von Hesse Wartegg — *Nord-Amerika, seine Städte und Naturwunder, sein Land und seine Leute*, Leipzig, 1880.

Georg Hill — 'Some Practical Limiting Considerations in the Design of the Modern Office Building', *The Architectural Record*, II, 4, April-June 1893, pp. 443—468.

Karl Hinckeldeyn — 'Hochbau-Constructionen und innerer Ausbau in den Vereinigten Staaten', *Centralblatt der Bauverwaltung*, VII, (12,19 März 1887), pp. 102—103, 116—118.

Henry-Russell Hitchcock — *Modern Architecture — Romanticism and Reintegration*, New York, 1970 (1929 [1]).

— 'Frank Lloyd Wright and the Academic Tradition of the Early Eighteen-Nineties', *Journal of the Warburg and Courtauld Institutes*, 7, 1944, pp. 46—63.

— 'Sullivan and the Skyscraper', *R.I.B.A. Journal*, 60, 1953, pp. 353—360.

Donald Hoffmann — *The Architecture of John Wellborn Root*, Baltimore/London, 1973.

— 'The Setback Skyscraper City of 1891: an Unknown Essay by Louis H. Sullivan', *Journal of the Society of Architectural Historians*, XX, 1970, pp. 181—187.

Richard Hofstadter — *Anti-intellectualism in American Life*, New York, 1974.

— *Social Darwinism in American Thought*, Boston, 1971 (1944 [1]).

Arthur Holitscher — *Amerika, Heute und Morgen; Reiseerlebnisse*, Berlin, 1923.

Vivian C. Hopkins — *Spires of Form: A Study of Emerson's Aesthetic Theory*, Cambridge, 1951.

Louis Jay Horowitz and Boyden Sparkes — *The Towers of New York; The Memoirs of a Master Builder*, New York, 1937.

Le Baron de Hübner — *Promenade autour du monde*, 2 Vols. Paris, 1881.

J. Huizinga — *Amerika, levend en denkend, Losse opmerkingen*, Haarlem, 1926.

— *Mensch en menigte in Amerika, Vier essays over moderne beschavingsgeschiedenis*, Haarlem, 1918.

Jules Huret — *L'Amérique moderne*, Paris, 1911.

Ada Louise Huxtable — 'The Tall Building Artistically Reconsidered; The Search for the Skyscraper Style', *The Architectural Record*, January, 1984, pp. 63—75.

*Immovable Objects Exhibition, An outdoor exhibition about the city design on view throughout lower Manhattan from Battery park to Brooklyn Bridge from June 18 to August 8, 1975*, Cooper Hewitt Museum of Design and, the Smithsonian Institution, Designed by *Works*. Text by Donald M. Reynolds, et al., 32 pp. fol.

*Industrial Chicago*, 2 Vols., Chicago, 1891.

Washington Irving — *A History of New York, from the Beginning of the World to the End of the Dutch Dynasty, by Diedrich Knickerbocker*, London, 1900 (1809 [1]).

| | |
|---|---|
| Jeter Allen Isely | *Horace Greeley And The Republican Party, A Study of the New York Tribune*, Princeton, 1947. |
| Henry James | *The American Scene*, London, 1907. |
| Theodore James Jr. | *The Empire State Building*, New York/Evanston/San Fransisco/London, 1975[1]. |
| William James | *The Varieties of Religious Experience*, ed. Martin E. Marty, Harmondsworth, 1985 (1902[1]). |
| James Jackson Jarves | *The Art-Idea: Sculpture, Painting and Architecture in America*, New York, 1866. |
| Robert Allen Jones | *Cass Gilbert, Midwestern Architect in New York*, unpublished Ph. D. Thesis, Case-Western Reserve University, 1976. |
| William H. Jordy | *American Buildings and their Architects*, III, *Progressive and Academic Ideals At the Turn of the Century*, Garden City, New York, 1976. |
| — | *American Buildings and their Architects*, IV, *The Impact of Modernism in the Mid-Twentieth Century*, Garden City, New York, 1976. |
| Michael Kammen | *People of Paradox, An Inquiry Concerning the Origins of American Civilization*, New York/Toronto, 1980 (1972). |
| Edgar Kaufmann, ed. | *The Rise of an American Architecture*, New York/Washington/London, 1970. |
| Gerard Keller | *Amerika in beeld en schrift, Tussen New York en de Meren*, Amsterdam, 18?. |
| Robert Kerr | 'The Problem of National American Architecture, The Question Stated', *The Architectural Record*, Vol. III, October-December 1893, 2, pp. 121–132. |
| Walter C. Kidney | *The Architecture of Choice; Eclecticism in America 1880–1930*, New York, 1974. |
| Walter H. Kilham | *Raymond Hood, Architect, Form Through Function in the American Skyscraper*, New York, 1973. |
| S. Fiske Kimball | *American Architecture*, Indianapolis, 1928. |
| Moses King, ed. | *New York; The American Cosmopolis, The Foremost City of the World*, Boston, 1894. |
| —, ed. | *King's Handbook of New York City, An Outline History and Description of the American Metropolis*, Boston, 1893 (1892[1]). |
| —, ed. | *King's Views of New York, 1906*, Boston, 1905. |
| —, ed. | *King's Views of New York 1896–1915 and Brooklyn 1905, An Extraordinary Photographic Survey Compiled by Moses King*, with a new introduction by A.E. Santaniello, New York, 1980. |
| Athanasius Kircher | *Mundus Subterraneus of De onderaardse wereld*, Amsterdam, 1682. |
| — | *Turris Babel, sive Archontologia*, Amsterdam, 1679. |
| Edward C. Kirkland | *Dream and Thought in the Business Community 1860–1900*, Ithaca, New York, 1956. |
| Rem Koolhaas | *Delirious New York, A Retroactive Manifesto for Manhattan*, New York, 1978. |
| John A. Kouwenhoven | *The Columbia Portrait of New York, An Essay in Graphic History*, New York/Evanston/San Francisco/London, 1972 (1953[1]). |
| Sarah Bradford Landau | 'The Tall Office Building Artistically Reconsidered: Arcaded Buildings in New York, c. 1850 to 1890', *In Search of Modern Architecture: A Tribute to Henry-Russell Hitchcock*, Cambridge, Mass., 1982. |
| Karl Lamprecht | *Americana; Reiseeindrücke, Betrachtungen, geschichtliche Gesamtansicht*, Freiburg i.B., 1906. |
| | *The Last Rivet, The Story of Rockefeller Center*, Merle Crowell, ed., New York, 1940 (?). |
| Alfred McClung Lee | *The Daily Newspaper in America; The Evolution of a Social Instrument*, New York, 1937. |
| Jean Ferriss Leich | *Architectural Visions; The Drawings of Hugh Ferriss*, with an essay by Paul Goldberger, New York, 1980. |

| | |
|---|---|
| Ann Tizia Leitich | *New York*, Bielefeld and Leipzig, 1932. |
| William R. Lethaby | *Architecture, Mysticism and Myth*, with illustrations by the author, New York, 1975 (1891[1]). |
| Claude Lévi-Strauss | *Structural Anthropology*, New York, 1963. |
| — | *The Raw and the Cooked, Introduction to a Science of Mythology*, Vol. 1, 1975 (1964[1]). |
| Dudley Arnold Lewis | *Evaluations of American Architecture by European Critics, 1875–1900*, unpublished Ph.D. Thesis, University of Wisconsin, 1962. |
| R.W.B. Lewis | *The American Adam, Innocence, Tragedy, and Tradition in the Nineteenth Century*, Chicago, 1955. |
| Sinclair Lewis | *Babbit*, London, 1973 (1922[1]). |
| Charles Lockwood | *Manhattan Moves Uptown*, Boston, 1976. |
| Arthur Lovejoy | *Essays in the History of Ideas*, New York, 1948. |
| Joseph Aug. Lux | *Ingenieur-Ästhetik*, München, 1910. |
| James D McCabe Jr. | *Lights and Shadows of New York Life, or Sights and Sensations of the Great City*, Philadelphia/Cincinnati/Chicago/St. Louis, 1872. |
| Henry P. Manning | *The Fourth Dimension Simply Explained, A Collection of Essays Selected from Those Submitted in the Scientific American's Prize Competition*, London, 1921. |
| Orison Swett Marden | *Success, A Book of Ideals, Helps, and Examples for All Desiring to Make the Most of Life*, Boston, 1897. |
| W.G. Marshall | *Through America, or Nine Months in the United States*, London, 1881. |
| Leo Marx | *The Machine in the Garden, Technology and the Pastoral Ideal in America*, London/Oxford/New York, 1979 (1964[1]). |
| Claude Massu | *L'architecture de l'école de Chicago, architecture fonctionnaliste et idéologie Américaine*, Paris, 1982. |
| | *The Master Builders, A Record of the Construction of the World's Highest Commercial Structure*, New York, 1913. |
| F.O. Mattiesen | *American Renaissance, Art and Expression in the Age of Emerson and Whitman*, New York, 1968 (1941[1]). |
| André Maurois | *Chantiers Américains*, Paris, 1933. |
| — | *États-Unis 39, journal d'un voyage en Amérique*, Paris, 1939. |
| Harold M. Mayer & Richard C. Wade | *Chicago, Growth of a Metropolis*, Chicago/London, 1973. |
| Narciso G. Menocal | *Architecture as Nature, the Transcendentalist Idea of Louis Sullivan*, Madison, Wisconsin, 1981. |
| Charles Merz | *The Great American Band Wagon, A Study of Exaggerations*, Decorations by Howard W. Willard, New York, 1928. |
| Michael A. Mikkelsen, et al. | *A History of Real Estate Building and Architecture in New York During the Last Quarter of the Century*, New York, 1898. |
| Percy Miller | *The Transcendentalists*, Cambridge, Mass., 1950. |
| Robert M. Miller | *History of American Methodism*, New York, 1964. |
| Helmut Minkowski | *Aus dem Nebel der Vergangenheit steigt der Turm zu Babel, Bilder aus 1000 Jahren*, Berlin, 1960. |
| Stanislaus von Moos | *Turm und Bollwerk, Beiträge zu einer politischen Ikonographie der italienischen Renaissancearchitektur*, Zürich 1974. |
| Alfred Morgan | *The Story of the Skyscrapers*, New York, 1934. |
| Hugh Morrison | *Louis Sullivan, Prophet of Modern Architecture*, New York, 1962 (1935[1]). |

| John Moser | 'American Architectural Form of the Future', *American Architect and Building News*, XIII, January–June 1883, pp. 303–305. |

Frank Moss — *The American Metropolis from Knickerbocker Days to the Present Time; New York City Life in All Its Various Phases*, 3 Vols., New York, 1897.

Frank Luther Mott — *American Journalism, A History: 1690–1960*, New York, 1962.

Hugo Münsterberg — *The Americans*, New York, 1905 (1904[1]).

James Fullarton Muirhead — *America The Land of Contrasts, A Briton's View of his American Kin*, London/New York, 1907 (1898[1]).

Francisco Mujica — *History of the Skyscraper*, New York, 1929.

Lewis Mumford — *The Brown Decades, A Study of the Arts in America 1865–1895*, New York, 1971 (1931[1]).

— *The Condition of Man*, London, 1944.

— *From the Ground Up*, New York, 1956.

— *Roots of Contemporary American Architecture*, New York, 1952.

— *Sticks and Stones; A Study of American Architecture and Civilization*, New York, 1924.

Roger Hale Newton — 'New Evidence on the Evolution of the Skyscraper', *Art Quarterly*, IV, Spring 1941, pp. 56–70.

*New York Life Insurance Company's Home Office Building, Madison Square, New York, Souvenir, Commemorating the Dedication of*, New York, 1929.

*The New York Sketch-Book of Architecture*, I-II, January–December 1874/ January–December 1875, Boston/New York, 1874–1876.

*Pictorial New York and Brooklyn, A Guide to the Same and Vicinity with Maps and Illustrations*, George F. Smith, ed., New York, 1959.

M.H. Nicholson — *Mountain Gloom and Mountain Glory: The Development of the Aesthetic of the Infinite*, Ithaca, New York, 1959.

Arthur Tappan North — *Raymond Hood*, New York, 1931.

Werner Oechslin — 'Apotheose einer monumentalen Architektur', *Archithese* (Metropolis 2), 18, 1976, pp. 13–22.

— 'Dinokrates – Legende und Mythos megalomaner Architekturstiftung', *Daidalos*, 15 Juni 1982, 4, pp. 7–27.

— 'Skyscraper und Amerikanismus. Mythos zwischen Europa und Amerika', *Archithese* (Metropolis 3), 20, 1976, pp. 4–12.

John O'Henry — *The Complete Works*, Garden City, New York, 1953.

*The Oldest Trust Company and Its Newest Home*, published by the City Bank and Farmers' Trust, New York, 1931.

Richard Oliver — *Bertram Grosvenor Goodhue*, New York/London, 1983.

Rudolf Otto — *Das Heilige*, 1918.

Sherman Paul — *Louis Sullivan – An Architect in American Thought*, Englewood Cliffs, N.J., 1962.

Robert Jan van Pelt — *Tempel van de Wereld, De kosmische symboliek van de Tempel van Salomo*, Utrecht, 1984.

Stow Persons — *American Minds, A History of Ideas*, New York, 1958.

*Pictured Encyclopedia of the World's Greatest Newspaper; A Handbook of the Newspaper as Exemplified by the Chicago Tribune*, Issued to Commemorate Its Eightieth Birthday, Chicago, 1928.

Deborah Frances Pokinski — *The Development of the American Modern Style, 1893–1933*, Ann Arbor, Mich., 1984.

| | |
|---|---|
| Irving Kane Pond | *The Meaning of Architecture, An Essay in Constructive Criticism*, Boston, 1918. |
| — | 'High Buildings and Beauty', Part I and II, *Architectural Forum*, 38, February 1923, pp. 42–77. |
| — | 'How I Approach an Architectural Problem', *Pencil Points*, Vol. XIII, July 1932, 7, pp. 459–465. |
| — | 'Toward an American Architecture, *Living Architecture*, Chicago, 1930. |
| Joseph Ponten | *Architektur die nicht gebaut wurde*, Stuttgart/Berlin/Leipzig, 1925, 2 Vols. |
| Robert Prestiano | *Robert Craick McLean and the Inland Architect*, Unpublished Ph.D. Thesis, 1973. |
| C. Matlack Price | *The Practical Book of Architecture*, Philadelphia/London, 1916. |
| Wolfram Prinz | *Schloss Chambord und die Villa Rotonda in Vicenza, Studien zur Ikonologie*, Berlin, 1980. |
| Frank Alfred Randall | *History of the Development of Building Construction in Chicago*, Berlin, 1980. |
| Otto Rappold | *Der Bau der Wolkenkratzer*, München/Berlin, 1913. |
| Richard L. Rapson | *Britons View America, Travel Commentary, 1860–1935*, Seattle/London, 1971. |
| | *Real Estate Record and Builders Guide*, Established March 21st 1868, New York City. |
| Adolf Reinle | *Zeichensprache der Architektur; Symbol, Darstellung und Brauch in der Baukunst des Mittelalters und der Neuzeit*, Zürich, 1976. |
| John W. Reps | *The Making of Urban America, A History of City Planning in the United States*, Princeton, 1965. |
| John B. Reynolds | *77 Stories – The Chrysler Building*, New York, 1930. |
| Paul Ricoeur | *History and Truth*, Evanston, Ill., 1965. |
| Fred J. Ringel, ed. | *America as Americans See it*, New York, 1932. |
| Cervin Robinson & Rosemarie Haag Bletter | *Skyscraper Style – Art Deco New York*, New York, 1975. |
| Heinz Ronner | 'Skyscraper: à propos Oekonomie', *Archithese* (Metropolis 2), 18, 1976, pp. 44–50. |
| John Wellborn Root | *The Meanings of Architecture*, New York, 1967. |
| Franco Rosso | *Alessandro Antonelli e la Mole di Torino*, Torino, 1977. |
| Paul de Rousiers | *La vie Américaine*, Paris, 1892. |
| G.S. Rousseau, ed. | *Organic Form, The Life of an Idea*, London/Boston, 1972. |
| Colin Rowe | 'Chicago Frame', *The Mathematics of the Ideal Villa*, Cambridge, Mass., 1976, pp. 89–119. |
| Leland M. Roth | *A Concise History of American Architecture*, New York, etc., 1980. |
| John Ruskin | *The Works*, Vol. XII, *Lectures on Architecture and Painting, etc.*, London, 1904. |
| Joseph Rykwert | *On Adam's House in Paradise – The Idea of the Primitive Hut in Architectural History*, New York, 1972. |
| — | 'Lodoli on Function and Representation', *Architectural Review*, CLX, 1976, 2, pp. 21–26. |
| Eliel Saarinen | *The City, Its Growth, Its Decay, Its Future*, New York, 1945 (1943[1]). |
| — | *The Search for Form in Art and Architecture*, New York, 1985 (1948[1]). |
| Andrew Saint | *The Image of the Architect*, New Haven/London, 1983. |
| George Santayana | *Santayana on America*, ed. Richard Colton Lyon, New York, 1968. |
| Montgomery Schuyler | *American Architecture and Other Writings*, edited by William H. Jordy and Ralph Coe, 2 Vols., Cambridge, Mass., 1961. |
| — | 'The "Sky-scraper" Up To Date', *The Architectural Record*, Vol. VIII, January–March 1899, no. 3, pp. 231-260 (not complete in Jordy & Coe). |

—     'The West Street Building', *Architectural Record*, XXII, 1907, pp. 102–109 (not in Jordy & Coe).

Vincent Scully     *American Architecture and Urbanism*, London, 1969.

*Sémiotique de l'espace, architecture, urbanisme, sortir de l'impasse*, contributions by Jean Zetoun, A.J. Greimas, et al., Paris, 1979.

O.F. Semsch, ed.     *A History of the Singer Building Construction, Its Progress from Foundation to Flagpole*, New York, 1908.

R.W. Sexton     *American Commercial Buildings of Today, Skyscraper Office Buildings − Banks − Private Business Buildings − Stores and Shops*, New York, 1928.

Ernest H. Short     *A History of Religious Architecture*, London, 1936. (Originally published as *The House of God*).

Earle Shultz and Walter Simmons     *Offices in the Sky*, Indianapolis/New York, 1959.

Alison Sky & Michelle Stone     *Unbuilt America, Forgotten Architecture in the United States from Thomas Jefferson to the Space Age*, New York etc., 1976.

Herbert Spencer     *A System of Synthetic Philosophy, The Principles of Biology*, 2 vols., London, 1894 (1867[1]).

Paul Starrett     *Changing the Skyline, An Autobiography*, with the collaboration of Webb Waldron, New York/London, 1938.

Col. William A. Starrett     *Skyscrapers and The Men Who Build Them*, New York/London, 1928.

Agnes Starrett Lynch     *Through One Hundred and Fifty Years: The University of Pittsburgh*, Pittsburgh, 1937.

Philip Steadman     *The Evolution of Designs, Biological Analogy in Architecture and the Applied Arts*, Cambridge/London/New York/Melbourne, 1979.

Roger B. Stein     *John Ruskin and Aesthetic Thought in America, 1840–1900*, (?), 1968.

I.N. Phelps Stokes     *The Iconography of Manhattan Island 1498–1909*, New York, 1928.

Russell Sturgis     *The Great American Architects Series, The Architectural Record*, nos. 1–6; May 1885–July 1899 (Reprint).

—, ed.     *A Dictionary of Architecture and Building*, New York/London, 1902.

Louis H. Sullivan     *The Autobiography of an Idea*, with an introduction by Claude Bragdon, New York, 1956 (1924[1]).

—     *Kindergarten Chats and Other Writings*, Isabella Athey, ed., New York, 1976 (1918[1]).

—     'The Chicago Tribune Competition', *The Architectural Record*, LIII, February 1923, 293, pp. 151–157.

Francis S. Swales     'The Architect and the Grand Plan', *Pencil Points*, Vol. XII, May, November 1931, issues 1–3, Vol. XIII, January, April, issues 4–5, pp. 166–177 (1), pp. 21–28 (4), pp. 229–235 (5).

Manfredo Tafuri     '"Neu-Babylon". Das New York der zwanziger Jahre und die Suche nach dem Amerikanismus', *Archithese* (Metropolis 3), 20, 1976, pp. 12–25.

Thomas E. Tallmadge     *Architecture in Old Chicago*, Chicago, 1975 (1941[1]).

—     *Committee Appointed by the Trustees of the Estate of Marshall Field for the Examination of the Structure of the Home Insurance Building*, Chicago, 1939.

—     *The Story of Architecture in America*, New York, 1936.

—     'A Critique of the Chicago Tribune Building Competition', *The Western Architect*, Vol. XXXII, January 1923, no. 1, p. 7–8.

Christopher Tunnard & Henry Hope Reed     *The American Skyline, The Growth and Form of Our Cities and Towns*, New York, 1956 (1953[1]).

Alexis de Toqueville — *De la démocratie en Amérique*, 3 Vols., Paris, 1864.

*Towers of Manhattan*, The New York Edison Company, New York, 1928.

Fanny Trollope — *Domestic Manners of the Americans*, Richard Mullen ed., New York, 1984 (1832[1]).

Theodore Turak — *William Le Baron Jenney: A Nineteenth Century Architect*, Unpublished Doctoral dissertation, University of Michigan, 1967.

Frederick Jackson Turner — *The Frontier in American History*, New York, 1921.

*Turris Babel*, special issue of *Rassegna*, V, 16, 4, dicembre 1983, with contributions by: Massimo Scolari, Helmut Minkowski, et al.

Ernest Lee Tuveson — *Millennium and Utopia, A Study in the Background of the Idea of Progress*, New York/Evanston/London, 1964 (1949[1]).

— *Redeemer Nation – The Idea of America's Millennial Role*, Chicago/London, 1986.

Thorstein Veblen — *The Theory of Business Enterprise*, New York, 1917 (1904[1]).

— *The Theory of the Leisure Class*, Harmondsworth, 1979 (1889[1]).

Cornelis Verhoeven — *Symboliek van de voet*, Assen, 1956.

Don Vlack — *Art Deco Architecture in New York 1920–1940*, New York/Evanston/ San Francisco/London, 1974.

George F. Warren, Frank A. Pearson — 'The Building Cycle', *Fortune*, XVI, August 1937, 2, pp. 84–88; 136, 138, 140.

J. Carson Webster — 'The Skyscraper: Logical and Historical Considerations', *Journal of the Society of Architectural Historians*, XVIII, December 1959, 4, pp. 126-139.

Winston Weisman — 'The Commercial Architecture of George B. Post', *Journal of the Society of Architectural Historians*, XXXI, March 1972, 1, pp. 176–203.

— 'Commercial Palaces of New York: 1845–1875', *The Art Bulletin*, 1954, 298.

— 'New York and the Problem of the First Skyscraper', *Journal of the Society of Architectural Historians*, XII, March 1953, 1, pp. 13–22.

Lloyd Wendt — *The Chicago Tribune: The Rise of a Great American Newspaper*, Chicago, 1979.

Charles Harris Whitaker — *The Story of Architecture: From Rameses to Rockefeller*, New York, 1934.

Raymond Williams — *The Country and the City*, New York, 1973.

Edmund Wilson — *Abbitte an die Irokesen;* mit einer Studie 'Die Mohawks im Stahlhochbau' von Joseph Mitchell, Frankfurt am Main/Berlin/Wien, 1977.

John Kennedy Winkler — *Five and Ten: The Fabulous Life of F.W. Woolworth*, New York, 1940.

Arthur Woltersdorf, ed. — *Living Architecture, A Discussion of Present-Day Problems in a Collection of Essays Written for and Sponsored by the Chicago Chapter of the American Institute of Architects*, with contributions by Irving Pond, George L. Rapp, Richard Schmidt, Thomas E. Tallmadge, Hubert Burnham, etc., Chicago, 1930.

Arthur Woltersdorff — 'The Father of the Steel Frame Building', *The Western Architect*, Vol. XXXIII, February 1924, no. 2, pp. 21/22.

*The World, its History and its New Home: The Pulitzer Building*, New York, 1899 (?).

Irvin G. Wyllie — *The Self-Made Man in America*, New Brunswick, New York, 1954.

Frances Yates — *Giordano Bruno and the Hermetic Tradition*, London, 1964.

— *The Art of Memory*, London/Chicago, 1966.

Roland Van Zandt — *The Metaphysical Foundations of American History*, The Hague, 1959.

E. Idell Zeisloft — *The New Metropolis*, New York, 1899.

Bruno Zevi — *Towards an Organic Architecture*, London, 1950.

Edward Robert de Zurko — *Origins of Functionalist Theory*, New York, 1957.